Contemporary Southern Politics

Contemporary Southern Politics

EDITED BY

JAMES F. LEA

Louisiana State
University Press

Baton Rouge and London

Copyright © 1988 by Louisiana State University Press
All rights reserved
Manufactured in the United States of America

10 9 8 7 6 5 4 3 2 1

Designer: *Laura R. Gleason*
Typeface: *Sabon*
Typesetter: *Focus Graphics*
Printer: *Thomson-Shore, Inc.*
Binder: *John H. Dekker & Sons, Inc.*

Library of Congress Cataloging-in-Publication Data

Contemporary southern politics.

    Includes bibliographies and index.
    1. Southern States—Politics and government—
1951–   . I. Lea, James F.
F216.2.C59   1988   320.975   87-29397
ISBN 0-8071-1386-7 (alk. paper)

This work is dedicated to the memory of two scholars who made seminal contributions to the study of southern politics

V. O. Key, Jr. (1908–1963)

and

James W. Prothro (1923–1986)

Contents

Contemporary Southern Politics

Introduction

In 1831 Vice-President John C. Calhoun of South Carolina—former secretary of war, future senator, and major theoretician for the South—declared that in the face of the country's expanding northern and western regions, the South was "a fixed and hopeless minority."[1] At approximately that point the southern region, which had been an integral part of the young nation and had provided such leaders as Thomas Jefferson, James Madison, and Andrew Jackson, embarked on a futile struggle to maintain a semifeudal, agrarian, and racially stratified society. This would eventually make residents of the "Confederate" states—Virginia, North and South Carolina, Tennessee, Florida, Georgia, Alabama, Mississippi, Louisiana, Texas, and Arkansas—the only Americans (until Vietnam and excepting, of course, native Americans) ever to lose a war. They would be the sole ones ever to be governed by a conquering military occupation force.

After Reconstruction the futile struggle resumed, and twentieth-century southern resistance to nationalizing, industrializing, and egalitarian trends was greatly to retard the region's economic, political, and social development. In 1938 President Franklin D. Roosevelt assembled a major "Conference on Economic Conditions in the South," stating that the "South presents right now the Nation's No. 1 economic problem." The foremost scholar of the region's politics, the late political scientist V. O. Key, Jr., wrote in 1949, "The cold hard fact is that the South as a whole has developed no system or practice of political organization and leadership adequate to cope with its problems."[2] And racially, the historic breach between white and black southerners often flared into violence during the civil rights movement—in the Montgomery bus boycott of 1956, the Little Rock school crisis in 1958, the University of Mississippi riots in 1962, Selma, Birmingham.

1. Quoted in Richard Hofstadter, *The American Political Tradition* (Rev. ed.; New York, 1974), 100.
2. V. O. Key, Jr., *Southern Politics in State and Nation* (New York, 1949), 4.

Given this heritage, it is well-nigh incredible that the American nation embarked on its third century with a Deep South son as president and over four million southern blacks registered to vote, and two thousand blacks holding office in a South where schools were more desegregated than in the rest of the country and the population was rapidly growing, the economy expanding, and a two-party system in place. Walker Percy, the foremost living writer from this region, sums up the change: "The South has entered the mainstream of American life for the first time in perhaps 150 years, that is, in a sense that has not been the case since the 1920s or '30s, and accordingly in a sense that has not yet dawned on most southerners."[3]

Politically, the emergence was signaled dramatically with George Wallace's startling successes in the primaries and general election of 1968 and his vote-leading Democratic primary totals in 1972—until Arthur Bremer shot and seriously wounded him during the Maryland campaign. Jimmy Carter's even more shocking success in 1976 verified that the South's role in national political life henceforth would be more akin to the pre-Calhoun era than to the century of political backwardness and stagnation ushered in by the bargain of 1876, when the planter elite negotiated an end to Reconstruction and moved to establish Jim Crow. And whatever one thinks of the deficiencies of Carter and his administration, he played a pivotal role in removing the last remnants of the old political constraints blocking a southern leader from national office. In a real sense the election of 1976 was, like that famous one a century earlier, one of redemption. But the latter was so in a way diametrically opposite to the former.

It wasn't solely or even primarily Carter's success that rejoined southern politics to national politics; nor was it the influence of an even more important southerner and American, Martin Luther King, Jr. Rather it was a certain critical "conjunction of circumstances," as Percy says—social, economic, and political ones—which occurred in the 1960s. The sixties were the watershed years ending the politics begun so long ago by Calhoun and his generation and carried on right down through the time of Carter's Georgia predecessor, Richard Russell, and his generation. Among the many things in that decade that changed the South, two were particularly important. First, some of the nation's prosperity began to reach the South, ameliorating the terrible poverty so many southerners had suffered for so long. Second, the civil rights movement freed blacks

3. Walker Percy, "Southern Comfort," *Harper's* (January, 1979), 79.

and enabled whites to begin cleansing themselves of their historical guilt. If the nagging "toothache" of racism, as Percy calls it, did not entirely disappear — and it did not — at least it came to be no more painful in Louisiana than in Illinois, in Tennessee than in Michigan. Southerners began to glimpse the possibility given in the famous phrase from the old slave spiritual which Dr. King's 1963 speech inscribed in the American consciousness and which graces his Atlanta tombstone: "Free at Last, free at Last, Thank God Almighty, I'm Free at Last."

Of course, many other events and circumstances in the 1960s helped finally to destroy the old style and substance of southern politics and to open up the possibilities this book explores. (And these can be linked to the tumultuous upheavals in the 1950s which cleared away much political underbrush and permitted new growth.) A two-party system — which had been eliminated in the late 1800s — reemerged with victories of the Goldwater forces in 1964, Republican gains in the off-year congressional elections of 1966, then Nixon's wins in 1968 and 1972. Because of the Civil Rights Bill of 1964 and the Voting Rights Act of 1965, in the states of Georgia, Mississippi, and South Carolina blacks now constitute approximately 25 percent of the electorate and are a force to be reckoned with throughout the South. The first black to hold a county office in the twentieth century, Sheriff Lucius Amerson of Macon County, Alabama, was elected in 1965. Seminal court cases, like *Baker* v. *Carr* in Tennessee in 1962, and the ongoing implementation of that judicial great divide of 1954, *Brown* v. *Board of Education*, had their impact. Perhaps of most importance in the long run, the enormous exodus which had seen more than 3 million whites and some 4.5 million blacks leave the South from 1940 to the late 1960s began to slow. By the first half of the seventies this would show up in the first net gain ever — by a few thousand — of blacks moving into the South versus blacks leaving. And the influx of whites, which became so visible in the 1970s, began. Education expanded, urbanization accelerated, and the South changed irrevocably in so many ways — some boring, as Percy points out, some spectacular, some good, some bad. The late T. Harry Williams suggested once that the key characteristic of southerners was that they were resolutely against change. But by 1976, Jack Bass and Walter DeVries would assert that "the only constant in Southern politics since World War Two has been change."[4] You do not, however, jettison the 150 years of experience Percy talks

4. See T. Harry Williams, *Romance and Realism in Southern Politics* (Baton Rouge, 1966), and Jack Bass and Walter DeVries, *The Transformation of Southern Politics: Social Change and Political Consequence Since 1945* (New York, 1976), 397.

about in a decade, or even two or three. Marx may have been guilty of overstatement on occasion, but there is much truth in his basic conception about men and their history: "Men make their own history, but they do not make it just as they please; they make it under circumstances directly encountered, given and transmitted from the past. The tradition of all the dead generations weighs like a nightmare on the brains of the living."[5] The South's historical nightmares are all too familiar—racism, violence, repression, mass exploitation, demagoguery. But better legacies from the South's strange history do exist. John Egerton—who worries about the "Americanization" of Dixie in much the same manner as Percy when he fears that the Sunbelt syndrome is overrunning us like kudzu—says the recent readmission to the Union would come at a terrible price if it meant giving up our "sense of history, grace and space, of soul."[6]

The intermingling and overlapping of the new and old, good and bad, in contemporary southern politics often baffles observers, particularly those from outside the region. What the South has been doing, politically speaking, with its new freedom in the two decades since the mid-sixties is the question addressed by the essays in this book. Primarily they try to give a contemporary political answer to the query in *Absalom, Absalom!*: "Tell me about the South. What is it like there? What do they do there?"[7] The authors endeavor to describe, clarify, and analyze what is going on in southern politics and government. Occasionally they judge a bit and assess whether there are glimmers of a creative synthesis between the best of the past and the brightest of the future that might come to constitute, in Percy's felicitous phrases, a "soupçon of difference," might "leaven the lump" of national politics.[8]

Key's preface—and his book remains the best by far ever written on southern politics—makes two critical points that bear restating. The first is a disclaimer that applies even more to this effort. "The South is changing rapidly. He who writes about it runs the risk that change will occur before the presses stop, no matter how he strives, as I have done, to identify and emphasize elements of continuity. There is no illusion that the whole story has been told or that solutions have been found." Key then stresses the significance of politics, a point that certainly needs reemphasizing in

5. Karl Marx, "The Eighteenth Brumaire of Louis Bonaparte," in Lewis S. Feuer (ed.), *Marx and Engels: Basic Writings on Politics and Philosophy* (Garden City, 1959), 320.

6. John Egerton, "Looks Like the Mason-Dixon Line Was Erased," New York *Times*, May 24, 1977, p. 35. See also his *The Americanization of Dixie: The Southernization of America* (New York, 1974).

7. William Faulkner, *Absalom, Absalom!* (New York, 1936), 174.

8. Percy, "Southern Comfort," 83.

view of our contemporary national life: "It is only hoped that some better understanding of the politics of the South is promoted, for the subject, though not without its rollicking aspects, is of the gravest importance."[9]

9. Key, *Southern Politics*, x.

The Setting of Southern PART ONE
Politics: The "Power Shift" and Public Attitudes

Two interrelated themes found in much analysis of contemporary American political life are that the nation is experiencing a historic shift in power to the Sunbelt and that it is undergoing a homogenization of national attitudes. The first trend is said to be thrusting the South and West into a position of economic and political leadership, and the latter is thought to doom any remnants of regional distinctiveness. As with all such broad generalizations about complex realities, much in them is true and much is false. The two essays below endeavor to shed light on these themes.

What is the real nature of the Sunbelt phenomenon? What are the facts concerning population and economic growth in the region? How are the various states of the Old South faring? What are the reasons for the economic and population growth of the region? Of particular importance, what role does government policy play in all of this? Given the weak economy of the times, is regional growth a zero-sum game, with the Sunbelt taking industries and jobs away from other regions? What are the implications of Sunbelt growth for public services, tax revenues, and public policies of various types? What are the implications for the distribution of political power in the southern states and for the South's role in national politics? Timothy O'Rourke considers these and many other provocative, important questions.

Earl Hawkey's essay is concerned with the nature of public opinion in the South today. Are the economic and population shifts, coupled with the new communications and transportation systems and the nationalization of politics, homogenizing attitudes and regional political cultures? Hawkey compares and contrasts the attitudes of southerners with those of their northern neighbors on general political orientations and some specific issues of economics and social welfare, plus race. Is the South the most conservative region of the nation as is often assumed, or is this pure myth with no basis in political reality? What about economic matters? Does the strain of populism still exist? To what extent has there been a deracialization of Dixie? And, a related question, has the North become more racist in recent years? If, as the power shift thesis holds, the South is destined to play an increasingly important role in the nation, then it behooves us to look carefully at how current public attitudes might shape that role.

The Demographic and Economic Setting of Southern Politics

TIMOTHY G. O'ROURKE

Fears mount that the 1980s could be an era of two Americas — one thriving, one hemorrhaging at every pore; one reaching new levels of growth and prosperity, one on a slippery slide of permanent decline.
— Neal R. Peirce, Washington *Post*

Writing in January of 1981, columnist Neal R. Peirce raised the prospect of an America divided by a grotesque divergence in the fates of the geographic regions. In Peirce's view, this bleak scenario could result from the continuation, or acceleration, of demographic and economic trends plainly evident during the 1970s and from the failure of federal policy to address the consequences of such trends.[1] The decade of the seventies witnessed dramatic growth in the population and economies of most southern, southwestern, and western states. Over the same period, the industrialized states of the Northeast and Midwest registered marginal gains in population and employment and suffered substantial losses in manufacturing jobs. This pattern has been reduced in the popular lexicon of regional politics to Sunbelt surge and Frostbelt decline. Such phraseology is not, as we shall see, particularly edifying, especially in light of the varied fortunes of the eleven states of the Old Confederacy.

The transformation of the "South" into the "Sunbelt" (a term evincing journalistic recognition of the increasing attractiveness of warm-weather states to people and industry) constitutes a development of more than mere semantic innovation. The South as a regional designation referred not

1. Neal R. Peirce, "Offing the Frost Belt: A Stupid Idea Whose Time Has Come," Washington *Post*, January 18, 1981, Sec. C, p. 1.

only to a particular geographic area—most often to the eleven states of the Old Confederacy—but also to a history, culture, economics, and political order that set the area apart from the rest of the nation. As Key noted in the opening chapter of *Southern Politics*, the distinctive political and economic order of the South was rooted in the "common experiences" of the eleven Confederate states from the pre–Civil War era through Reconstruction and the Populist revolt just prior to the turn of the century.[2]

The political and economic distinctiveness of the eleven southern states thus infused the term "South" with geographic and cultural precision. "Sunbelt," in contrast, is a term fraught with ambiguity, in part because characteristics of areas (climatic and otherwise) do not correspond neatly to latitude on a map. Depending on the commentator, Sunbelt may be limited to the Old South or may stretch across the entire southern half of the United States. Some would expand Sunbelt to encompass Colorado or even Washington and Oregon. Obviously, any regional classification that lumps together South Carolina and southern California within the Sunbelt may be more confusing than enlightening.[3] Yet the blurring of "South" into "Sunbelt" and the joining of Carolina and California give evidence of the reentry of the eleven states of the Old Confederacy into the political and economic mainstream of the nation. Moreover, Sunbelt itself connotes both an allure and optimism and—for the eleven states of the Old South—a shedding of a host of negative images associated with the label "South."[4]

But if the semantic transformation from South to Sunbelt signals a real and far-reaching metamorphosis in the political and economic life of the

2. V. O. Key, Jr., *Southern Politics in State and Nation* (New York, 1949), 5, 7.

3. Kirkpatrick Sale in *Power Shift: The Rise of the Southern Rim and Its Challenge to the Eastern Establishment* (New York, 1975), defined "Southern Rim" to include the states of the Old Confederacy (except Virginia) and Oklahoma, New Mexico, Arizona, southern Nevada, and southern California. The New York *Times* in a 1976 series on southern growth defined "Sunbelt" in roughly the same way, except that its version included Virginia and excluded Nevada (see "Sunbelt Region Leads Nation in Growth of Population," New York *Times*, February 8, 1976, pp. 1, 42). Ben J. Wattenberg in "The Census' Political Role," New York *Times*, January 6, 1980, Sec. E, p. 19, defined Sunbelt as "the south-and-west belt, which includes some now-and-again cold and unsunny places like Oregon and Washington."

4. On the transformation of the image of the South in the mass media, see Gene Burd, "The Selling of the Sunbelt: Civic Boosterism in the Media," in David C. Perry and Alfred J. Watkins (eds.), *The Rise of the Sunbelt Cities*, XIV, Urban Affairs Annual Reviews (Beverly Hills, 1977), 129–50.

eleven southern states, the patterns of change in the recent past do not necessarily provide ready clues to the nature of future developments in the Sunbelt. Indeed, whatever the potential applicability of Peirce's scenario of "permanent decline" in the Frostbelt—and it is unlikely—the prospect of unremitting prosperity for the Sunbelt, and the South in particular, is a gross exaggeration. This conclusion rests on the analysis of regional economic trends and their causes set out in the first section below. The second section gives brief attention to the role of federal policy in regional development in the United States, an issue raised to national prominence in the late 1970s by Frostbelt politicians who asserted that northern tax dollars were underwriting economic growth in the Sunbelt and western states. The third part of the analysis gives extended treatment to the question of whether the political culture of the Sunbelt—more than federal policy—helps to explain the economic surge of the region in the late 1960s and 1970s. Within this context, the relationship between economic development and politics receives special treatment. The economic and political future of the Sunbelt is the focus of the concluding section.

For purposes of this presentation, the designation of regions will build upon the regional definitions employed by the Bureau of Economic Analysis of the U.S. Department of Commerce. The Sunbelt will refer to the sixteen states of the Southeast and Southwest regions illustrated on the map; among these sixteen are the eleven states of the Old Confederacy.[5] Special attention is paid to the varied fortunes of these eleven states. The Frostbelt will encompass the sixteen states and the District of Columbia in the New England, Mideast, and Great Lakes regions on the map. The West will include the eleven states of the Rocky Mountain and Far West regions. (The Plains states are largely excluded from the analysis.)

ECONOMIC AND DEMOGRAPHIC CHANGE
IN THE SUNBELT, 1950–1984

Although the forces underlying the economic transformation of the Sunbelt have been at work for at least several decades, the Sunbelt surge in population growth and economic expansion is principally a phenomenon

5. *Business Week* also has defined Sunbelt in this way (see "The Second War Between the States," May 17, 1976, 92–114). C. L. Jusenius and L. C. Ledebur, in a widely cited work, define Sunbelt along the same lines, excluding Arizona and New Mexico; see their "A Myth in the Making: The Southern Economic Challenge and Northern Economic Decline," in E. Blaine Liner and Lawrence K. Lynch (eds.), *The Economics of Southern Growth* (Durham, 1977), 131–73.

POPULATION GROWTH IN THE AMERICAN STATES, 1970–1980

The figure given for each state is the percentage increase or decrease in population from 1970 to 1980, during which period the national population increased by 11.4 percent.

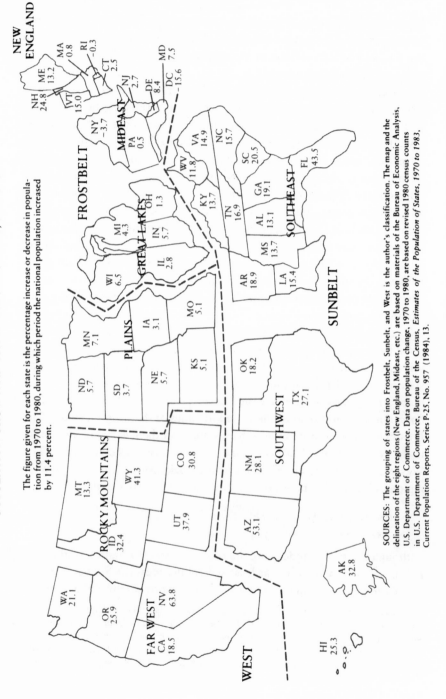

SOURCES: The grouping of states into Frostbelt, Sunbelt, and West is the author's classification. The map and the delineation of the eight regions (New England, Mideast, etc.) are based on materials of the Bureau of Economic Analysis, U.S. Department of Commerce. Data on population change, 1970 to 1980, are based on revised 1980 census counts in U.S. Department of Commerce, Bureau of the Census, *Estimates of the Population of States, 1970 to 1983,* Current Population Reports, Series P-25, No. 957 (1984), 13.

of the past ten to fifteen years.[6] From 1950 to 1970, for instance, the Sunbelt's share of the nation's population hovered around 30 percent, but by 1980 it had approached 33 percent. Only five Sunbelt states—Arizona, Florida, Georgia, Texas, and Virginia—registered a population growth rate above the national average of 13.4 percent during the decade of the sixties. In contrast, from 1970 to 1980, the population of every Sunbelt state grew at a faster rate than the national average of 11.4 percent (see map). Notably, Florida and Texas together accounted for about 44 percent of the total increase in population that occurred in the sixteen Sunbelt states during the 1970s and for half of the total increase in the eleven states of the South over the same period. Much of the growth in the population of the Sunbelt during the 1970s resulted from a net in-migration of about seven million people, who accounted for about half of the total growth of the region.[7] The impact of migration on population growth, however, varied substantially among individual states of the Sunbelt. Whereas net migration accounted for about half of the population expansion in states such as Georgia, North Carolina, South Carolina, and Virginia from 1970 to 1980, it constituted about nine-tenths of the population increase in Florida, as Table 1 shows.

The surge in population that the Sunbelt experienced during the 1970s continued during the early 1980s. From 1980 through 1984, ten of sixteen Sunbelt states showed growth rates above the national average of 4.2 percent. The six Sunbelt states with below average growth rates were Alabama, Arkansas, Kentucky, Mississippi, Tennessee, and West Virginia (of these six states, all but Arkansas and Tennessee experienced net outmigration from 1980 to 1984). Among the fast-growing Sunbelt growth states, Florida, Texas, and Arizona led the way, with increases in excess of 12 percent for the four-year period (see Table 1). As in the 1970s, Florida and Texas accounted for the lion's share of the growth (54 percent) in the population of the Sunbelt during the 1980–1984 period.[8]

Economic growth in the Sunbelt, of course, has paralleled population

6. Pre-1980 population and employment data cited in this section, except as specifically noted, were taken from U.S. Advisory Commission on Intergovernmental Relations (hereinafter ACIR), *Regional Growth: Historic Perspective*, Report A-74 (1980); and Jacqueline Mazza and Bill Hogan, *The State of the Region 1981* (Washington, D.C., 1981). Data on employment after 1980, except as noted, were derived from U.S. Department of Labor, Bureau of Labor Statistics, *Employment and Earnings*, XXXII (May, 1985), 117–45 (Annual Averages for States and Areas).

7. U.S. Department of Commerce, Bureau of the Census, *Estimates of the Population of States, 1970 to 1983*, Series P–25, No. 957 (October, 1984), 13.

8. U.S. Department of Commerce, Bureau of the Census, *State Population Estimates, by Age and Components of Change, 1980 to 1984*, Series P–25, No. 970 (June, 1985), 7.

TABLE 1
States Ranked by Largest Numerical Increase in Population,
1980–1984 and 1970–1980 (in Thousands)

	1980–1984				1970–1980	
State	Increase	Net Migration[a]	Rank	State	Increase	Net Migration[b]
California	1,955	+950	(1)	California	3,697	+1,573
Texas	1,759	+1,009	(2)	Texas	3,031	+1,481
Florida	1,229	+1,092	(3)	Florida	2,955	+2,519
Georgia	373	+182	(4)	Arizona	943	+656
Arizona	335	+207	(5)	Georgia	875	+329
Virginia	289	+131	(6)	N. Carolina	797	+278
Colorado	288	+145	(7)	Washington	719	+388
N. Carolina	283	+135	(8)	Virginia	695	+239
Oklahoma	273	+160	(9)	Colorado	680	+385
Louisiana	257	+58	(10)	Tennessee	665	+297

Sources: U.S. Department of Commerce, Bureau of the Census, *State Population Estimates, by Age and Components of Change, 1980 to 1984*, Series P-25, No. 970 (June, 1985), 2.

[a]Net migration accounted for 57 percent of the growth in Texas during the 1980–84 period. For the other Sunbelt states listed here, the percentages are as follows: Florida, 89 percent; Georgia, 49 percent; Arizona, 62 percent; Virginia, 45 percent; North Carolina, 48 percent; Oklahoma, 59 percent; and Louisiana, 23 percent.

[b]Net migration accounted for 48 percent of the growth in Texas during the 1970–80 period. For the other Sunbelt states listed here, the percentages are as follows: Florida, 85 percent; Arizona, 70 percent; Georgia, 38 percent; North Carolina, 35 percent; Virginia, 34 percent; and Tennessee, 45 percent.

increases. The Sunbelt's share of the nation's nonagricultural employment rose from less than 23 percent in 1950 to about 27 percent in 1970 to 32 percent in 1984. In absolute terms, nonagricultural employment in the Sunbelt doubled between 1960 and 1980, and the Sunbelt accounted for two-fifths of the country's growth in nonagricultural employment during that twenty-year period. Similarly, the region's proportion of national manufacturing employment increased from 18 percent in 1950 to over 25 percent in 1970 and to 30 percent in 1984.

In contrast to the patterns of growth in the Sunbelt, the population and economy of the Frostbelt have experienced rather modest growth rates in recent decades, particularly during the late 1960s and the 1970s. The

Frostbelt's share of the nation's population fell from 49 percent in 1950 to about 41 percent in 1984. From 1970 to 1980, only three Frostbelt states—Maine, New Hampshire, and Vermont—experienced population growth in excess of the national average, whereas most other states in the region grew at less than half of the national rate. New York, Rhode Island, and the District of Columbia actually lost population during the 1970s. The principal consequence of the Frostbelt's sluggish population growth, as many commentators have emphasized, was the loss of fifteen congressional seats, beginning in the 98th Congress, to southern and western states: New York alone lost five congressional seats as a result of the 1980 census.[9] From 1980 to 1984, only New Hampshire among the sixteen Frostbelt states showed a population increase above the national average.

The decline of the Frostbelt relative to other regions has been more evident in economic trends than in population patterns. The Frostbelt's share of the nation's nonagricultural employment fell from more than 57 percent in 1950 to 43 percent in 1984. Manufacturing employment in the Frostbelt, as a proportion of the national total, dropped from 68 percent in 1950 to less than 48 percent in 1984. In addition, the number of manufacturing jobs in the Frostbelt actually declined by more than 1.8 million during the 1970s and early 1980s.

Although much of the discussion of regional issues in recent years has been framed in terms of Frostbelt and Sunbelt—along the lines presented so far—this sort of dichotomy gives insufficient attention to the substantial population and economic growth that has occurred in western states. During the 1970s, for instance, the eleven states of the West in general enjoyed greater population growth than did the states in what is treated here as the Sunbelt. Population growth exceeded 25 percent in eight of eleven western states between 1970 and 1980; for the 1980–1984 period, ten of the eleven western states (all but Oregon) grew at a rate in excess of the national average. Indeed, one could make a case that the principal direction of population and economic movement in America is more westerly than southerly, particularly if the four states of the Southwest are lumped together with the eleven states of the Rocky Mountain and Far West regions (refer again to the map and Table 1).

As the economic fortunes of the Frostbelt, on one hand, and the Sunbelt and the West, on the other hand, have diverged over the past decade or two, this divergence has led to a gradual equalization of incomes among

9. See James F. Fryman, "National Reapportionment: Geographic Patterns and Implications for States," *State Government*, LVIII (Fall, 1985), 90–95.

regions. Per capita incomes in the New England, Mideast, and Great Lakes sections of the nation historically have exceeded the national average. Although per capita incomes in the Frostbelt states have continued to rise in absolute dollars, they have been declining relative to the national average, as Table 2 shows. In the Mideast, for example, per capita income in 1960 stood at 116 percent of the national average; by 1983, this figure had dropped to 110 percent. Relative per capita income in the Great Lakes region underwent a similar decline, dropping from 108 percent of the national average in 1960 to 99 percent in 1983. Relative per capita income in the New England region has moved somewhat erratically. It declined sharply between 1960 and 1970 — from 110 percent to 100 percent — and rose in the 1970s and early 1980s; by 1983, relative per capita income in New England stood at 111 percent of the national average. The recent upswing in New England, built around a vigorous high technology economy, stands out as a exception to the general pattern of decline in relative per capita income in the Frostbelt.

TABLE 2

Regional Per Capita Income as Percentage of National Average

	Actual				Projected	
	1960	1970	1980	1983	1990	2000
New England	110	100	106	111	110	110
Mideast	116	113	107	110	108	107
Great Lakes	108	104	103	99	100	100
Plains	93	95	98	97	98	99
Southeast[a]	73	82	85	87	88	90
Southwest[b]	87	89	98	97	97	98
Rocky Mountain	94	91	96	95	95	96
Far West[c]	116	111	113	110	108	107

SOURCES: U.S. Advisory Commission on Intergovernmental Relations, *Regional Growth: Historic Perspective*, Report A-74 (1980), 11; "Revised State Personal Income, 1969–80," in U.S. Department of Commerce, Bureau of Economic Analysis, *Survey of Current Business*, LXI (July, 1981), 31; "Regional and State Projections of Income, Employment, and Population to the Year 2000," *Survey of Current Business*, LXV (May, 1985), 43.

[a]The 1983 figures for each state in the Southeast are as follows: Alabama, 79; Arkansas, 77; Florida, 99; Georgia, 89; Kentucky, 80; Louisiana, 88; Mississippi, 70; North Carolina, 84; South Carolina, 79; Tennessee, 82; Virginia, 104; West Virginia, 79.

[b]The 1983 figures for each state in the Southwest are as follows: Arizona, 91; New Mexico, 83; Oklahoma, 94; Texas, 100.

[c]The figures for the Far West do not include Alaska and Hawaii.

In contrast to the overall trend of the Frostbelt, per capita incomes in the Southeast and Southwest have been rising relative to the national average in recent decades. By 1983, per capita income in the Southwest nearly equaled the national figure. Per capita income in the Southeast, the poorest area of the country, rose substantially between 1960 and 1983 both in absolute and relative terms, but it still represented only 87 percent of the national average in 1983. (In a similar vein, it might be noted that during the 1970s the poverty rate in Sunbelt states declined, although it remained well above the national average. In contrast, the poverty rate in Frostbelt states rose somewhat during the same decade.)[10]

The meaning to be attached to figures on per capita income is a matter of some dispute. Taking into account regional variation in the cost of living would tend to lower per capita incomes in the Frostbelt relative to the national average, to raise incomes in the Sunbelt, and to produce a mixed impact in the West depending on the area. Arguably, per capita incomes in various areas of the Frostbelt, when adjusted for cost of living, have dipped below the national average, whereas Sunbelt incomes approach or exceed the national average. Advocates of a strong federal program for redevelopment of the Frostbelt advance this line of reasoning, suggesting, among other measures, that federal tax rates and income support payments be adjusted to take into account regional variation in the cost of living.[11]

Alternatively, by taking per capita incomes at face value, without a cost-of-living adjustment, one could contend that the Sunbelt, despite its healthy rate of growth over the past ten to fifteen years, continues to lag behind the rest of the nation in terms of standard of living. According to

10. Sources for data on per capita income are given in Table 2. The national poverty rate was 12.5 percent in 1979; Virginia (11.5 percent) and Arizona (12.4 percent) were the only Sunbelt states with a rate below the national average, whereas Maine (12.9 percent) and New York (13.4 percent) were the only Frostbelt states with rates above the average. Rates in other Sunbelt states were 17.9 in Alabama, 18.7 in Arkansas, 13 in Florida, 16.4 in Georgia, 18.4 in Kentucky, 18.9 in Louisiana, 24.5 in Mississippi, 17.4 in New Mexico, 14.6 in North Carolina, 13.3 in Oklahoma, 15.9 in South Carolina, 17 in Tennessee, 14.8 in Texas, and 14.5 in West Virginia. U.S. Department of Commerce, Bureau of the Census, *Provisional Estimates of Social, Economic, and Housing Characteristics*, PHC80-S1-1 (1982), 36–41.

11. The ACIR, for example, estimates that adjusting per capita income in 1975 to account for regional variations in the cost of living would have lowered per capita income in New England from 103 percent of the national average to 89 percent. By the same measure, per capita income in the Mideast would have dropped from 109 percent to 100 percent; in the Great Lakes, from 104 to 102 percent; and in the Far West, from 111 to 105 percent. Per capita income in the Southeast, on the other hand, would have risen from 86 to 93 percent of the national average and, in the Southwest, from 93 to 99 percent. See ACIR, *Regional Growth*, 11.

this view, the economic transformation of the Sunbelt, far from being complete, is only beginning; by the same token, the economic decline of the Frostbelt is greatly exaggerated.[12]

Some Sunbelt states, indeed, hardly fit the stereotype of unremitting economic growth. As a group, for instance, the states of Alabama, Kentucky, Mississippi, and Tennessee had an unemployment rate above the national average for every year during the period 1979 through 1984.[13] Florida in some ways embodies the stereotype of growth, but in another way is an exception. From 1973 to 1983, Florida enjoyed an annual rate of growth in total personal income that was almost double the national average. Yet, because of the state's phenomenal population growth over the same period, per capita income stood at 99 percent of the national average in both 1973 and 1983. The Census Bureau projects that Florida will continue to experience above-average rates of growth in total income, earnings, employment, and population in the coming decades— but with the result that per capita personal income in the year 2000 will stand at only 97 percent of the national average.[14]

Such data indicate that the economic surge of the Sunbelt has been uneven and has not yet lifted the incomes of southern residents to parity with residents in other regions. On balance, however, the figures so far presented do confirm the widely publicized contrast in relative growth rates of the Sunbelt and the West versus the Frostbelt. The figures themselves, of course, do not explain the causes of the divergence in regional economic fortunes. In a cogent explanation of Sunbelt growth, Charles D. Liner noted that the American economy until well into the twentieth century was dominated by heavy industries, such as steel, that were dependent on close proximity to raw materials and to rail systems and water outlets. The requirements of these industries led to the concentration of economic activity and people in the urban centers of the Frostbelt. Growth in the post–World War II American economy, however, gradually shifted from heavy industry toward new technologies such as electronics and toward services that were "not as constrained by location of bulk

12. The contention that the contrast between Sunbelt surge and Frostbelt decline has been overdrawn is set out in some detail by Jusenius and Ledebur, "A Myth in the Making," in Liner and Lynch (eds.), *The Economics of Southern Growth*, and by Richard B. McKenzie, "Myths of Sunbelt and Frostbelt," *Policy Review*, XX (Spring, 1982), 103–14.

13. Susan Elizabeth Shank, "Changes in Regional Unemployment Over the Last Decade," in U.S. Department of Labor, *Monthly Labor Review*, CVIII (March, 1985), 21.

14. "Regional and State Projections of Income, Employment, and Population to the Year 2000," in U.S. Department of Commerce, Bureau of Economic Analysis, *Survey of Current Business*, LXV (May, 1985), 42–43.

transportation facilities." With the expansion of the national highway system, enterprises could move away from the cities and, indeed, out of the region to other areas offering inexpensive land and surplus labor willing to work for lower wages than those prevailing in the Frostbelt.[15] Thus, the "dynamics of deconcentration"—a phrase used by a presidential study commission to describe the greater mobility of firms—has spurred the economic growth of the Sunbelt in recent decades.[16]

For such "footloose industries," to use Liner's phrase, the Sunbelt has offered a variety of attractions apart from cheap land and cheap labor: favorable climate (at least after the introduction of air conditioning), low state and local taxes (discussed later), and swelling local markets for goods created by the phenomenon of growth itself.[17] Among more recent developments, the civil rights revolution of the 1960s removed from the Sunbelt the racist label long attached to the region and thus made in-migration more palatable for Frostbelt firms and individuals. Rising energy costs that greatly increased the heating bills of northern plants also have made the Sunbelt more attractive, and the presence of large reserves of oil and natural gas in the Southwest in particular have contributed significantly to the growth of the Sunbelt.

It is important to recognize, however, that the negative consequences of deconcentration—so evident in the Frostbelt—increasingly will be felt in the Sunbelt. Some southern industries, textiles for example, already are suffering from increasing competition from foreign producers; such competition is nothing more than the international extension of the deconcentration phenomenon. As one study noted:

> Although the South has benefitted from interregional economic shifts in the postwar decades, its advantages have the tendency to slip away at an even faster rate than they have from the Northwest and Midwest. For example, between 1969 and 1976, the South was the most likely region to experience the closing of a large manufacturing plant. In addition, industrial activity that was attracted to the South since the 1950s by lower wages, greater labor control, and lower energy costs now is often found relocating outside the United States to achieve even lower production costs.[18]

15. Charles D. Liner, "The Sun Belt Phenomenon—A Second War Between the States?" *Popular Government*, XLIII (Summer, 1977), 16–24, quoted at page 18. See also U.S. President's Commission for a National Agenda for the Eighties, *Urban America in the Eighties: Perspectives and Prospects* (1980), Chap. 3.

16. The term "dynamics of deconcentration" is taken from National Agenda, *Urban America in the Eighties*, Chap. 3.

17. Liner, "The Sun Belt Phenomenon," 18.

18. National Agenda, *Urban America in the Eighties*, 42.

Moreover, in terms of intraregional mobility southern cities face the same fate that has befallen Frostbelt cities, that is, the shift of people and businesses to the suburban ring. One could argue, indeed, that the perception of economic decline in the Frostbelt derives less from changes in aggregate levels of personal income, employment, and population for individual states or for the region than from the fact that the region's economic misfortunes have been so evidently concentrated in its central cities. A measure of the plight of central cities is the finding of one study that central city per capita income was less than 95 percent of suburban income in thirty-three of the thirty-four largest metropolitan areas of the Frostbelt in 1981. In contrast, per capita income in the central city stood at or above 95 percent of suburban income in fifteen of the twenty-eight largest Sunbelt metropolitan areas.[19] Whether metropolitan areas of the Sunbelt can avoid the economic and social disparities between city and suburb that have become so pronounced in the Frostbelt and in so doing avoid the wrenching political divisions that accompany such disparities will be a pressing question for the future of the Sunbelt.

Aside from the dynamics of deconcentration and other factors noted above, one other influence on southern growth has been the massive infusion of federal funds into the region from the Depression era to the present, most prominently in programs related to national defense but also in programs intended to create an infrastructure for southern economic growth — water projects, rural electrification, and highway construction. In 1960, for instance, the Sunbelt had 7,052 miles of divided four-lane highways under the federal primary system (which includes the interstate system); by 1970 the number of miles had grown to 21,607. The increase represented 44 percent of the national expansion of divided four-lane roads over the decade of the sixties and, in improving accessibility to markets within and outside the Sunbelt, contributed to the accelerated pace of southern growth in the 1960s and 1970s.[20] Federal expenditures in other programmatic areas exerted a similar influence on Sunbelt expansion.

THE FEDERAL ROLE IN SUNBELT EXPANSION

The impact of federal policies on the economic health of the nation's regions has become the central point of contention in the politics of re-

19. ACIR, *Fiscal Disparities: Central Cities and Suburbs, 1981* (August, 1984), 10–11, 52–53. The data on Sunbelt metropolitan areas exclude Jacksonville and Baton Rouge, which are consolidated city-counties. See also ACIR, *Central City-Suburban Fiscal Disparity and City Distress 1977*, Report M-119 (1980), 44–45.

20. These data were calculated from figures in U.S. Department of Commerce, Bureau of Public Roads, *Highway Statistics 1960*, Table FM-11, and U.S. Department of Transportation, Federal Highway Administration, *Highway Statistics 1970*, Table FM-11.

gional development. The conviction that the federal government, both wittingly and unwittingly, has subsidized the expansion of the Sunbelt at the expense of the North has brought together widely disparate Frostbelt interests in collective efforts to monitor and modify the effects of federal policies on regional economics. At the national level, the Northeast-Midwest Congressional Coalition was established in 1975, with 213 Democratic and Republican House members from eighteen northeastern and midwestern states (the sixteen states of the Frostbelt as defined herein, along with Iowa and Minnesota). Reapportionment in the wake of the 1980 census reduced the coalition's membership to 198. The Northeast-Midwest Senate Coalition, set up in 1978, encompasses the same states as its House counterpart. In response, there has been some effort to organize Sunbelt members of Congress, as Charles Bullock's essay in this work explains.

Historical data reveal that Frostbelt states have suffered for several decades a persistent balance of funds deficit, receiving less federal expenditures than taxes sent to Washington. Indeed, the Northeast-Midwest Institute, the research arm of the Frostbelt coalitions in Congress, estimated that the eighteen coalition states "sent $165 billion more in taxes to Washington than they got back in Federal spending" from 1975 to 1979 alone.[21] In contrast, the Sunbelt states long have enjoyed a favorable balance of funds. For example, for a time in the 1970s Mississippi received approximately $1.88 for each tax dollar; in other words, it had a ratio of expenditures to taxes of 1.88. From 1952 to 1984, however, the size of regional imbalances tended to decline (though it should be noted that data for 1979 and 1984 and figures for prior years are only roughly comparable). As Table 3 shows, the ratio of expenditures to taxes for the Southeast dropped from 1.51 to 1.12, and the ratio for the Mideast, excluding the District of Columbia, rose from .74 to .92. The Plains, Rocky Mountain, and Far West regions, though generally showing a favorable flow of funds since 1952, registered ratios of 1.09, 1.02, and 1.09, respectively, in 1984. A notable exception to the pattern of declining imbalances was the Great Lakes region, for which the ratio declined from .87 in 1952 to .71 in 1979 and .78 in 1984.[22]

Much of the imbalance in interregional "flows of funds" is attributable to the distribution of federal defense expenditures, which encompass not

21. Mazza and Hogan, *State of the Region*, 37 (emphasis omitted).
22. Sources for these data are listed under Table 2. See also Joel Havemann and Rochelle L. Stanfield, " 'Neutral' Federal Policies Are Reducing Frostbelt-Sunbelt Spending Imbalances," *National Journal*, XIII (February 7, 1981), 233–36, and Michael Lawson, "A Fiscal Note: The Flow of Federal Funds," in ACIR, *Intergovernmental Perspective*, XI (Spring–Summer, 1985), 18–19.

TABLE 3
Ratio of Federal Expenditures to Federal Revenues
for Regions of the United States, 1952 to 1984[a]

	1984	1979	1974-76	1969-71	1965-67	1959-61	1952
New England	1.07	1.09	1.01	.95	.95	1.07	.78
Mideast	1.00	1.06	.99	.89	.75	.83	.75
excluding D.C.	.92	.92	.94	.85	.72	.80	.74
Great Lakes	.78	.71	.74	.68	.64	.74	.87
Plains	1.09	1.01	.98	1.01	1.15	1.00	1.20
Southeast	1.12	1.18	1.14	1.24	1.36	1.29	1.51
Southwest	.89	1.03	1.05	1.32	1.37	1.24	1.46
Rocky Mountain	1.02	1.12	1.10	1.23	1.34	1.24	1.20
Far West[b]	1.09	1.00	1.15	1.21	1.32	1.24	1.12

SOURCES: The ratios for 1952 to 1976 were taken, with modifications, from U.S. Advisory Commission on Intergovernmental Relations, *Regional Growth: Flows of Federal Funds, 1952–76*, Report A-75 (1980), 55, 57–58. The 1979 ratios were calculated from data set out in Lillian Rymarowicz, "Tabulations: Estimated Federal Tax Payments by Residents of Individual States, Compared to Estimated Outlays in the States, Fiscal Year 1979," Library of Congress, Congressional Research Service (July 9, 1980). The 1984 ratios were calculated from data contained in U.S. Department of Commerce, Bureau of the Census, *Federal Expenditures by State for Fiscal Year 1984* (March, 1985), 1, and *Tax Features*, XXIX (April, 1985), 2. Ratios for 1984 and 1979 and those for previous years are not precisely comparable.

[a]A ratio greater than 1.00 indicates that the region (or state) receives more dollars in federal expenditures than it contributed in federal taxes. A ratio of less than 1.00 indicates that the region paid more in taxes than it received in expenditures. The states included in the various regions are noted on the map.

[b]The 1952 data exclude Alaska and Hawaii.

only spending for the operation of military installations but also the awarding of prime defense contracts. In 1984 the Frostbelt, excluding the District of Columbia, held about 41 percent of the nation's population but received less than 31 percent of federal defense expenditures. In 1984 the region contained only 20 percent of employment under the Department of Defense. The Sunbelt states, with 34 percent of the population, received the same percentage of defense spending but accounted for nearly 48 percent of Defense Department employment. The West, with 18 percent of the population, got about 28 percent of defense expenditures in 1984 and held 27 percent of Defense Department employees in 1984. California alone, however, is the principal beneficiary of so-called imbalances in the flow of defense funds; with 11 percent of the nation's population, the state received over 20 percent of defense expenditures in 1984. Among other states, Texas with 7.3 percent of defense spending and Virginia with 6.1 percent ranked a distant second and third.[23]

The apparent southern and western bias of defense expenditures generated concern among Frostbelt congressmen over the impact of the Reagan administration's plans for substantial expansion of the federal defense budget. Administration-sponsored cuts in social programs also brought charges from Frostbelt politicians that these would fall disproportionately on northeastern and midwestern states. The administration's own analysis of reductions in the 1982 budget, while conceding this point, held that the loss of federal expenditures in these states would be more than offset by the reduction in tax burden as a result of the massive 1981 tax cut.[24]

Although the data on defense expenditures and on the ratio of expenditures to taxes suggest that federal spending policies have favored the Sunbelt and West, the data themselves are open to question, given the difficulty of tracing federal expenditures to their destination or taxes from their origin. Even if the data are taken at face value, however, their significance in terms of regional development is not readily evident, since there is little agreement about the extent to which federal policies, as opposed to the dynamics of the marketplace, have contributed to current patterns of regional growth. And, of course, what a fair distribution of federal expenditures and taxes across regions would look like is subject to endless speculation and debate. U.S. Senator Daniel P. Moynihan (D-NY) has suggested that net flow of federal dollars among regions may not be so important as the purposes to which those funds are directed: "A general proposition about the political economy of New York is that the federal dollar we do receive is 'soft,' compared with the relatively 'hard' money that goes South and West. We get Food Stamps: they get infrastructure (such as water projects and defense installations)."[25]

In recent years Frostbelt states have tended to fare better than Sunbelt

23. Data on Defense Department employment in 1984 were calculated from figures in U.S. Department of Defense, *Defense/85* (September, 1985), 47–49. See also Mazza and Hogan, *State of the Region*, 100–101. Expenditure data were taken from U.S. Department of Commerce, Bureau of the Census, *Federal Expenditures by States for Fiscal Year 1984* (March, 1985), 33.

24. See U.S. Congress, Joint Economic Committee, *The Regional and Urban Impacts of the Administration's Budget and Tax Proposals* (1981), and "A Regional Tilt? Figures Don't Lie, But . . .," *National Journal*, XIII (May 2, 1981), 797.

25. Daniel Patrick Moynihan, "What Will They Do for New York?" *New York Times Magazine*, January 27, 1980, p. 32.

states in the distribution of federal grants-in-aid, programs tilted heavily toward the "soft" programs described by the New York senator. In fiscal year 1984, for example, per capita federal grant-in-aid dollars exceeded the fifty-state average in eight of the sixteen Frostbelt states. (In 1981, however, per capita aid exceeded the national average in eleven Frostbelt states.) Twelve of the sixteen Sunbelt states received fewer aid dollars per capita than the national average in 1984, whereas seven of eleven states in the West garnered per capita funds in excess of the average. It should be noted, however, that these data neither relate grant dollars received by states to taxes paid to the federal treasury nor do they reveal how much state and local governments had to spend from their own revenues to attract the federal monies they received when percentage of grant dollars received is compared to proportion of the federal tax burden; for example, nine of sixteen Frostbelt states were net gainers in 1984. Although Sunbelt states fared poorly relative to the national average in per capita aid, ten southeastern and southwestern states (the exceptions being Arizona, Florida, North Carolina, Oklahoma, Texas, and Virginia) received proportionately more aid than taxes paid.[26]

With regard to how much in-state and local matching funds is required to attract a given amount of federal aid, welfare spending in Mississippi and New York in fiscal year 1981 provides a revealing contrast. Federal reimbursement rates for Aid to Families with Dependent Children (AFDC) and Medicaid are established according to state per capita income so that the federal government pays a higher proportion of welfare costs in poor states such as Mississippi than in relatively wealthy states such as New York. AFDC and Medicaid benefits in Mississippi amounted to about $329 million in 1981, with the federal government accounting for roughly $255 million (78 percent) of this amount. AFDC and Medicaid benefits in New York totaled approximately $7.3 billion, an amount evenly divided between the federal government and New York. In other words, New York spent over $3.6 billion in state and local funds to attract an equivalent amount of federal dollars, whereas Mississippi expended about $74 million of its funds in order to draw $250 million in federal aid. This contrast appears reasonable because Mississippi is poorer than New York in terms of per capita income, tax capacity, and proportion of population below the poverty line (in 1980

26. The data on per capita grant-in-aid dollars were calculated from figures in Bureau of the Census, *Federal Expenditures by State for Fiscal Year 1984*, p. 24. Data on aid in relation to tax burden were taken from *Tax Features*, XXVI (May, 1985), 4.

the poverty rate was 24.5 percent in Mississippi and 13.4 percent in New York). Less scrutable perhaps is the fact that federal spending per person below the poverty line amounted to about $1,540 in New York and about $410 in Mississippi.[27]

Hidden in this comparison of welfare spending in Mississippi and New York are some hints about the obstacles that confronted President Reagan's "Swap Program," a 1982 plan to have the federal government take over Medicaid and give the states responsibility for AFDC, Food Stamps, and more than forty additional programs now supported by federal grants. If the federal government were to assume full authority for Medicaid, the question is which version of Medicaid it would adopt—the Mississippi variant, where outlays averaged less than $700 per recipient in 1980, or the New York version, where outlays averaged almost $2,000 per recipient.[28] The Swap Plan would have posed special problems of interstate equity, since New York in fiscal year 1984 would have given up $4 billion in Medicaid obligations while assuming $1.7 billion in AFDC and Food Stamp costs (Food Stamp benefits are fully funded, at present, by the federal government), whereas Mississippi would have been relieved of $109 million in Medicaid costs but would have taken on $293 million in costs for AFDC and Food Stamps. A new trust fund (created to finance the more than forty other programs referred to above) would have compensated states such as Mississippi for losses incurred in the swap.[29]

Whether the Swap Plan—which underwent several modifications and ultimately disappeared—would have exacerbated interstate differences in welfare benefits is an important question with respect to national poverty policy. It is also significant insofar as variation in state welfare services and expenditures can be said to influence patterns of regional economic growth—an issue dealt with in the following section.

27. This analysis duplicates the ACIR's comparison of welfare spending in Mississippi and New York in fiscal year 1976; see ACIR, *Regional Growth*, 61. Expenditure data for 1981 should be regarded as estimates and were taken or calculated from U.S. Congress, Senate Committee on Finance, *Background Material and Data on Major Federal Expenditure Programs Under the Jurisdiction of the Senate Committee on Finance* (1982), 86–87, 144–45, and House of Representatives, Committee on Ways and Means, *Background Material and Data on Major Programs Within the Jurisdiction of the Committee on Ways and Means* (1982), 375–76.

28. These data were drawn from Albert J. Davis and S. Kenneth Howard, "Perspectives on a 'New Day' for Federalism," in ACIR, *Intergovernmental Perspective*, VIII (Spring, 1982), 14.

29. "State-by-State Figures for Impact of Federalism Plan," *Congressional Quarterly Weekly Report*, XL (January 30, 1982), 182.

REGIONAL POLITICAL SYSTEMS AND ECONOMIC GROWTH

Although Frostbelt politicians and a number of scholars advance the notion that the decline of the Northeast and Midwest can be laid at the feet
of federal policy, other observers have suggested that the distinctive political outlooks of the Frostbelt and Sunbelt, more than federal policy,
explain the divergent fortunes of their economies. Sunbelt expansion and
Frostbelt contraction represent the results in an ongoing referendum
showing, according to James Ring Adams, "that Americans prefer to mi-
grate *from* states with high service levels and *to* states with low service
levels."[30] The appeal of Sunbelt states, in Adams' argument, encompasses more than good weather and the promise of nonunion labor and
low corporate taxes; the appeal embraces a wider notion of what might
be labeled the "limited state"—low taxes, limited services, and minimal
regulation of business and environment. Similarly, the unattractiveness
of Frostbelt states is tied, so this reasoning goes, to that region's pattern
of the "expansive state" or "welfare state"—high taxes, extensive services, and massive regulation of business and environment.

In terms of public sector activity, the Sunbelt states impose lower taxes
and provide a more limited array of services than their counterparts in
the Frostbelt. In fiscal year 1983, all southeastern and southwestern
states ranked in the bottom half of all fifty states with respect to per capita state and local taxes. In contrast, twelve of the sixteen states in the
New England, Mideast, and Great Lakes regions placed in the top half of
all the states in per capita taxes. To some extent these data merely reflect
the greater wealth of Frostbelt states compared with that of Sunbelt
states. But when wealth is taken into account, tax levels in Frostbelt
states still tend to be significantly higher. In 1983, ten of sixteen Frostbelt
states ranked in the top half of all states in terms of state and local taxes
per $1,000 of personal income, whereas thirteen of sixteen Sunbelt states
(all but Arizona, New Mexico, and West Virginia) placed in the bottom
half.[31]

Too little attention perhaps has been given to the impact of total state
and local taxes on persons—including personal income, sales, and property taxes—in determining interstate migration of businesses and individuals. On the other hand, too much emphasis has been devoted to the specific role that lower corporate and property taxes on businesses have in

30. James Ring Adams, "The Decadence of Federalism," *The Public Interest*, LIII (Fall,
1978), 168.
31. *Tax Features*, XXIX (February, 1985), 2.

attracting firms to particular states. Business taxes probably do not figure heavily in differential rates of regional growth for a variety of reasons. One is that most states do offer some package of tax inducements, thereby negating the impact of varying tax rates. In addition, firms will, in all likelihood, give greater weight to the quality of the site, its access to markets, and the availability of labor than to tax concessions.[32]

Available evidence does indicate, however, that levels of state and local taxation on persons differ significantly enough among states to influence locational choices of individuals and firms. A study of regional variation in state and local tax levels by the Advisory Commission on Intergovernmental Relations found wide variation across the country in the burden of state and local taxes on a couple with an income of $100,000. After allowing for the deductibility of state and local taxes for federal income tax purposes, the study determined that a couple in Detroit would pay $6,493 in state and local taxes, whereas a couple in Jacksonville would pay only $1,019. A couple in New York would pay $6,211; a couple in Houston would pay only $1,571. Although these examples highlight the extremes, they are consistent with the general pattern of lower taxes in the Sunbelt than in the Frostbelt. (To be sure, there were exceptions, with taxes in Chicago being lower than those in Atlanta, for instance.)[33]

From a policy standpoint, it is not only the differences in tax levels across cities that are important. The commission study also illustrated how deductibility of state and local taxes affects the magnitude of those differences. Without deductibility on federal income tax forms, the gap in state-local tax levels between Frostbelt and Sunbelt would be substantially greater. Before deductibility, for example, the couple in Detroit paid $12,731 in state and local taxes, versus $1,998 for the couple in Jacksonville. Not surprisingly, the Reagan administration's proposal to do away completely with the deductibility of state and local taxes aroused heated opposition from governors, such as New York's Mario Cuomo, in states that stood to lose in several ways from the end of deductibility. States like New York would have lost the tax subsidy conferred by deductibility, would have confronted greater pressure for reductions in state and local

32. See Bernard L. Weinstein and Robert E. Firestine, *Regional Growth and Decline in the United States: The Rise of the Sunbelt and the Decline of the Northeast* (New York, 1978), 134–39.

33. This and the following paragraph are based on ACIR, *Strengthening the Federal Revenue System: Implications for State and Local Taxing and Borrowing*, Report A-97 (October, 1984), esp. 41–51. See also Deborah S. Ecker and Richard F. Syron, "Personal Taxes and Interstate Competition for High Technology Industries," *New England Economic Review* (September–October, 1979), 25–32.

taxes, and would have become far less attractive as a place of residence for upper-income taxpayers. Without deductibility, New York City would not only have been threatened by Houston and Jacksonville but also—and perhaps more so—by Bridgeport, Connecticut, where the $100,000 couple would have paid nearly $9,000 less in state-local taxes. The Tax Reform Act of 1986, however, preserved deductibility for state and local income and property taxes while scrapping deductibility for state-local sales taxes.

Although states with higher levels of taxation undoubtedly provide a broader spectrum of public services than states with lower levels of taxation, extensive public services do not necessarily make a state more attractive to potential industries or residents. The expenditures of Frostbelt states and their local governments not only exceed those of Sunbelt states on a per capita basis, but they also reflect a different set of priorities. In 1982–1983 Frostbelt state and local governments, in terms of median proportion of budget expenditures, devoted less than Sunbelt states to local education, other education, and highways. On the other hand, Frostbelt states spent relatively more on welfare—a median of 14.5 percent of budgets in contrast to the Sunbelt states' expenditure of less than 10 percent.[34] Such data, though hardly conclusive, do suggest that the Sunbelt states devote a greater proportion of public resources to the creation of an economic infrastructure than do Frostbelt states. The data hint at the dimensions of the welfare burden of many Frostbelt states, which typically provide larger benefits to a greater percentage of the poor than do Sunbelt states. (Ironically perhaps, the welfare burden of Frostbelt states is, in part, the consequence of the migration of thousands of low-income southern blacks and whites to northern cities in prior decades—a movement that appeared to end in the 1970s.)

The divergence in welfare spending levels of Frostbelt and Sunbelt states may contribute to apparent differences in the characteristics of their work forces. Bernard L. Weinstein offers his impression that "the labor force in Texas seems to have more positive attitudes toward work than is the case in New York. Whether these attitudes stem from a strong fundamentalist tradition or the absence of viable alternatives to work—such as welfare or unemployment insurance—is unclear."[35] One of several studies that seem

34. Calculated from data in ACIR, *Significant Features of Fiscal Federalism 1984 Edition*, Report M-141 (March, 1985), 167–222.
35. Quoted in George Sterlieb and James W. Hughes, "Prologue: Prelude to an Agenda," in George Sterlieb and James W. Hughes (eds.), *Revitalizing the Northeast: Prelude to an Agenda* (New Brunswick, 1978), 48.

to support Weinstein's contention, done by David C. Perry and Alfred J. Watkins, compared rates of subemployment in low-income neighborhoods in nine Frostbelt and nine Sunbelt cities. The analysis found levels of subemployment—the sum of unemployed, discouraged, involuntary part-time, and low-wage workers—to be comparable for the two regions. A much larger proportion of the Sunbelt subemployed, however, were low-wage workers; the Frostbelt subemployed were more likely to be unemployed or discouraged workers and, presumably, more likely to be receiving unemployment compensation or welfare.[36]

These findings suggest that with regard to welfare spending or public services in general the Frostbelt states are to some extent victims of their own policies; high taxes, extensive public services, and liberal welfare policies discourage growth. (These findings, when viewed from a different perspective, also might indicate that unskilled workers in the Sunbelt, notwithstanding the region's economic boom, are not necessarily better off materially than their northern counterparts.) Although the pattern in the Sunbelt states of low taxes, limited services, and meager welfare spending may not be ideal public policy, it *is* conducive to economic growth.

If the pattern of low taxes and modest public services, especially social services, helps to account for the attractiveness of Sunbelt states to new businesses and new residents in recent years, the pattern is nevertheless more a contributor than a major cause of Sunbelt expansion. The Sunbelt economic advantage in low taxes and limited services—if it can be called an advantage—has existed for decades but until fairly recently was neither exploitable nor exploited by business. It would appear instead that the principal sources of Sunbelt expansion have been changing techniques of production leading to "footloose industries" and the creation of a physical infrastructure (including highways, electricity, water and sewage systems) in the Sunbelt to accommodate such industries.[37] Once the Sunbelt had developed such an infrastructure, the pattern of public sector activity of southern states undoubtedly enhanced their appeal relative to high-service, high-tax states in other regions of the country. Limited public sector activity, however, must be regarded as the last in a line of factors accounting for southern expansion in the 1960s and 1970s.

To the extent that a modest public sector has contributed to Sunbelt growth, however, one must ask what impact economic development itself will have on public sector activity in Sunbelt states in the future. Eco-

36. David C. Perry and Alfred J. Watkins, "People, Profit, and the Rise of the Sunbelt Cities," in Perry and Watkins (eds.), *Rise of the Sunbelt Cities*, 277–305, esp. 293–98.
37. Liner, "The Sun Belt Phenomenon," 18.

nomic growth generates to some degree new and unavoidable public service requirements. Sunbelt and western states, and their cities in particular,
will have to build new water and sewer systems, plus hire more teachers
and police in order to respond to the needs of growing populations. Joel
Garreau's description of the future facing Houston is illustrative.

> Civic boosters still like to recall that the first word spoken from the surface
> of the moon was not the business about the Eagle having landed. The very first
> word was "Houston?"
> But Houston in the eighties, like everything else, will be defined by far more
> down-to-earth considerations. During the good years in Houston, no one
> wanted to brake growth by taxation—not for highways, schools, police depart-
> ments, welfare structures, sewers, or water. No one in the capital of oil and gas
> wanted to face the implications of building a city even more air conditioner- and
> automobile-dependent than Los Angeles. Houston's greatest pride was in its
> dedication to a complete lack of zoning—a robust spit in the eye of pointy-
> headed urban planners. The advocates of press-on-regardless growth pointed to
> the vast wealth accruing to Houston as proof that cities like New York were
> overserviced, overtaxed, and overrated.
> Well, the news in the 1980s coming from Houston is going to be about
> whether these theories are valid. Houston has run up what residents of other—
> especially eastern—cities view as huge social debts. The lack of new freeways
> is slowly beginning to result in all-day rush hours. The lack of new water
> mains is producing breaks in overtaxed lines on an almost daily basis. The po-
> lice force is spread so thin that some businesses and some of the wealthy are
> now relying on private police forces ("site-specific enforcement") to protect
> valuable property.[38]

But the effects of economic growth on governmental activity in the Sunbelt undoubtedly will go beyond the predictable pressures to expand infrastructure and basic service activities such as police protection and schools.
An immense literature in political science, building on the work of Key in
Southern Politics, has recognized the linkages among economic development, two-party politics, and liberal public policies.[39] Although scholars
disagree about the degree to which economic development "determines"
either levels of party competition or policy outcomes, most agree that economic growth and diversification, as well as urbanization, spawn competing economic and political interests that contribute to greater party
competition and to heightened demands for public services, particularly
social services. Not incidentally, economic growth produces the tax re-

38. Joel Garreau, The Nine Nations of North America (Boston, 1981), xiii.
39. See, for example, Thomas R. Dye and Virginia Gray (eds.), The Determinants of
Public Policy (Lexington, 1981).

sources that enable governments to address these demands. In its usual formulation, this model has "explained" both the pattern of two-party politics in the industrial states of the Frostbelt and the high expenditures of these states in areas such as welfare and education. By the same token, the lack of economic diversity in the rural, agrarian South helped to account for the region's one-partyism and its meager public service levels.

Taken at face value, this line of analysis would suggest that in the future the politics and policies of Virginia and Texas, say, will more and more resemble those of New York and Illinois as economic development transforms southern politics. Undoubtedly this trend is already underway, at least in its general outlines. What is intriguing about the supposed linkage between economics and politics as applied to the Sunbelt, however, is that the region's leaders—as Garreau observed about Houston—attribute the southern surge to the skimpiness of public sector activity. What the future would appear to hold, then, is a growing conflict between a leadership wedded to a view that ties economic prosperity to low taxes and a widening array of political interests calling for increased public services and higher taxes. While the nation was mired in recession during the 1979–1982 period, this conflict was suppressed by sluggish growth in the Sunbelt itself; but the recovery of the economy and the resultant upswing in the fiscal condition of state and local governments in the region will give renewed impetus to the forces of political liberalization. These forces will include increasingly active minority interests—Hispanics in the Southwest and Florida, blacks throughout the Sunbelt—public employees' organizations, and industrial workers, although the last-named group probably will not achieve the level of unionization and thus political clout enjoyed by their northern counterparts.

CONCLUSION

Although the philosophy of the "limited state" is a pervasive influence on the politics and policies of Sunbelt states, it would appear that economic and population growth will, in the coming years, force state and local governments in the Sunbelt to undertake an expanded range of public services at higher levels of taxation. The decline in the level of federal grant-in-aid dollars will add to the demands on the public sector in Sunbelt states, perhaps most notably in the area of infrastructure development. In the late 1970s, it appeared that severance tax revenues might make the energy-rich states of the Deep South and Southwest immune to these sorts of fiscal pressures. Indeed, in 1980 four Sunbelt states—Louisiana, New

Mexico, Oklahoma, and Texas—drew one-fifth or more of their tax revenues from severance taxes.[40] Yet falling energy prices and reduced consumption led to a drop in severance tax revenues in three of these four states (all but New Mexico) from 1983 to 1984; and all four states raised sales and other taxes in 1983–1984.[41] The problems of the energy states, however, pale beside those of Sunbelt states such as Alabama and Mississippi, which hardly fit the stereotype of Sunbelt surge; as noted earlier, these states suffered severe unemployment during the early 1980s and showed a net out-migration of people.

Although governmental services will expand in many of the Sunbelt states during the 1980s, levels of public sector activity in the Frostbelt states will decline or grow very modestly as these states confront the combined pressures of sluggish economic growth, slowly rising tax revenues, and declining federal aid. This trend will be fueled by the expanding commitment of Frostbelt politicians to some elements of the philosophy of the "limited state." Tax cuts in Massachusetts and New York, for example, in the early 1980s triggered a surge in economic growth in those states; during the same period, Pennsylvania and Massachusetts made aggressive efforts to trim state welfare roles.[42]

Thus, some reduction of the gap in levels of public sector activity that now exists between Sunbelt and Frostbelt states would seem to be inevitable. This reduction would both contribute to and parallel a likely diminution in the gulf between the two rates of economic growth because market forces already are working to mitigate the Sunbelt's competitive advantage over the northern states. Not only are Frostbelt states taking stringent measures to trim the costs of government, but they also are recruiting industries more vigorously and, relative to the Sunbelt, enjoy the advantage of a large supply of skilled labor. On the other hand, the Sunbelt states, aside from confronting the prospects of rapidly rising public expenditures, will witness rising wages and expanding unionization that will reduce the southern advantage of low-wage labor. Southern and southwestern states, moreover, since 1975 have recorded a net immigration of poor persons, whereas Frostbelt states over the same period have

40. See Jerry Hagstrom, "The Severance Tax Is the Big Gun in the Energy War Between the States," *National Journal*, XIII (August 29, 1981), 1545.

41. U.S. Department of Commerce, Bureau of the Census, *State Government Tax Collections in 1984*, Government Finances GF84, No. 1 (March, 1985), 16–17, 22, 24–25, 28; ACIR, *Significant Features*, 67–69.

42. See, for example, "The Supply-Side Governors," *Wall Street Journal*, March 2, 1982, p. 30, and ACIR, *Significant Features*, 70, showing that thirteen Frostbelt states cut one or more taxes between 1981 and 1984, whereas only eight Sunbelt states did so.

had a net loss of poor; this trend represents a reversal of a decades-long pattern and clearly benefits the Frostbelt.[43]

It must be added that some major uncertainties plague the predicting of future economies of the various regions. One uncertainty is the future performance of the general economy. A second is the uncertainty surrounding the federal budgetary process; states such as Virginia, for example, that benefited tremendously from the jump in defense expenditures during Reagan's first term could be hurt by sharp reductions in military spending.

Whatever the future, by 1985 it had become clear that the economically prosperous states and the economically stagnant ones could not be divided between South and North or Sunbelt and Frostbelt. Moreover, events of the early 1980s have confounded, if not contradicted, Neal R. Peirce's ominous warning, cited at the outset, of "two Americas" split by divergent economic fortunes. The resurgent economy of New England suggested that Frostbelt revival was possible, and the sluggish economies of the South Central states indicated that the Sunbelt surge was highly uneven in impact. That the Sunbelt states are not so easily fitted into a single economic mold—or political one, for that matter—is but another sign of the observation, made earlier, that "South" and "southern" are losing their distinctiveness in the national context.

43. On the interregional movement of poor persons, see, for example, U.S. Department of Commerce, Bureau of the Census, *Geographic Mobility: March 1975 to March 1980*, Series P-20, No. 368 (1981), 129–30, and *Geographic Mobility: March 1982 to March 1983*, Series P-20, No. 393 (October, 1984), 125–29. See also John Hanly Adams, "Is the Bloom Shifting to the Frost Belt?" *Nation's Business*, LXVIII (November, 1980), 84–88.

Public Opinion in the South Today

EARL W. HAWKEY

*North and South have served each other as inexhaustible objects of
invidious comparison in the old game of regional polemics. Our faults are
as nothing, they have said over and over again, compared to theirs. . . .
Each has served the other as scapegoat for domestic
embarrassments and burdens of guilt.*

—C. Vann Woodward, *American
Counterpoint: Slavery and
Racism in the North/South
Dialogue*

The assumption that public opinion in the South is different from that in
the rest of the nation is a touchstone of popular political analysis. Although most works trace the origins of this differentiation to the Civil War
era, certain observers of the American political scene prior to that time
also saw differences between the regions. For instance, Alexis de Tocqueville drew a distinction between the culture of the New England states and
those south of the Hudson, noting, "Two branches may be distinguished
in the great Anglo-American family, which have hitherto grown up without entirely comingling; the one in the South, the other in the North."[1]
    What are we referring to when we speak of a distinctive southern cul-
ture? In a review of studies on the American South, Carole Hill lists these
unique qualities as "localism, violence, religiosity, political conservatism,
anti-semitism, anti-Catholicism, anti-unionism, poverty, racism, agrarianism, laziness, a fondness for rhetoric, romanticism, hedonism, primitive
mentality, and simple mindedness, and the dominance of the plantation
system." To this list one could add conformity of thought, courteousness, and closeness of family life.[2] But the simple fact is that many of

1. Alexis de Tocqueville, *Democracy in America* (New York, 1956), 41.
2. Carole E. Hill, "Anthropological Studies in the American South: Review and Direc-
tions," *Current Anthropology*, XVIII (June, 1977), 309–10. Wilbur J. Cash, in *The Mind*

these supposed unique qualities can be found in all regions of the country. Poverty, racism, or political conservatism, for example, are not merely southern but can be found in greater or lesser degree throughout American society.

Writing in the early 1970s Howard Zinn contended that these "unique" southern characteristics are simply characteristics of American society "writ large." And looking at the South from a historical perspective, George Mowry denied that it was ever the strange and mysterious region many authors made it out to be.[3] Comparing the South and the Midwest, he concluded that although the South was seen as deviant and the Midwest as Middle America, attitudes and practices in the two regions have been similar in the nineteenth and twentieth centuries.

A basic problem encountered in the literature on southern culture is that authors have utilized two fundamentally different approaches in studying the region. The more traditional approach has been to focus on folkways and certain norms of behavior as the sources of a unique southern world view. Southern culture thus becomes primarily a self-perpetuating, organic outcome of previous history and is not easily altered. For instance, in a group of recently published essays John Shelton Reed states, "But although many of the most dramatic cultural differences between North and South have been decreasing (it could hardly be otherwise), an accumulating body of research suggests that it is easy to overestimate the extent of cultural convergence and to underestimate the autonomy of Southern culture."[4]

One of the most influential and widely read works based on this assumed organic uniqueness is Wilbur Cash's seminal work, *The Mind of the South*. Seeking to understand southern attitudes through an analysis of life after the Civil War, Cash saw at the center of southern culture an inherent romanticism tinged with occasional appeals to violence—an emotionalism drawn often to nonrational solutions. From this came the South's religious fervor and revivalism, blatant racism, elections which revolved around charismatic personalities rather than public issues, per-

---

of the South (New York, 1941), strongly implies the presence of conformity of thought; see also Ulrich B. Phillips, "The Central Theme of Southern History," *American Historical Review*, XXXIV (1928), 30–43. John Shelton Reed, in *The Enduring South: Subcultural Persistence in Mass Society* (Lexington, 1972), considers courteousness and closeness of family life.

3. Howard Zinn, *The Southern Mystique* (New York, 1972); George E. Mowry, *Another Look at the Twentieth-Century South* (Baton Rouge, 1973).

4. See, for example, the essays on the southern regionalists in John Shelton Reed, *One South: An Ethnic Approach to Regional Culture* (Baton Rouge, 1982), 130.

sonal violence, a penchant for "lost causes," and a lack of political or class consciousness. As one critic has aptly pointed out, Cash basically hypothesized that the South had no mind at all and that southerners were ruled by their passions and prejudices.[5]

The second approach to understanding southern culture is behavioral, in that it sees southern uniqueness as primarily the result of certain demographic patterns and political/legal structures. Those who utilize this intellectual framework concede that the folkways of the region are important but are also significantly affected by modernization and development. Altering the demographic, economic, and legal structures of the South, they contend, can and will alter southern culture.

Perhaps the best example of this approach is V. O. Key's *Southern Politics*. In his analysis of the South, Key attached great importance to the political prowess of black-belt politicians who imposed their views upon the entire region through racial, political, and legal structures such as Jim Crow and the Democratic party. Southerners' strict loyalty to the one-party system had many results but primarily it "condemned them . . . to a chaotic factional politics."[6] Southern elections and governance thus revolved around personality and local politics not because of any unique regional culture or any unique personalities, but in the absence of competitive and coherent party mechanisms which would have organized political debate along more rational lines. Others have broadened Key's hypothesis to assume that no cohesive southern political culture exists beyond the region's unique socioeconomic structures and demographic patterns. The convergence of North and South in this structural sense will, they hypothesize, result in cultural convergence as well, since "similarity in socioeconomic characteristics implies similarity of values, attitudes and norms."[7]

These fundamentally different approaches set the stage for considerable controversy in the area of southern public opinion. If it is true that

5. C. Vann Woodward, "W. J. Cash Revisited," *New York Review of Books* (December 4, 1969), 28–34.

6. V. O. Key, Jr., *Southern Politics in State and Nation* (New York, 1949), 12.

7. John C. McKinney and Linda B. Bourque, "The Changing South: National Incorporation of a Region," *American Sociological Review*, XXXVI (1971), 399–412. See also Henry Savage, *Seeds of Time: The Background of Southern Thinking* (New York, 1959); Jack Bass and Walter DeVries, *The Transformation of Southern Politics: Social Change and Political Consequence Since 1945* (New York, 1976); Laurence W. Moreland, Tod A. Baker, Robert D. Steed (eds.), *Contemporary Southern Political Attitudes and Behavior: Studies and Essays* (New York, 1982), 160–82. For somewhat of a twist on this formulation see John Egerton, *The Americanization of Dixie: The Southernization of America* (New York, 1974).

the South's unique qualities can be reduced to simple structural variables such as poverty, isolation, the presence of large numbers of blacks, and a lack of educational and social opportunities, then we would expect to see great changes in southern culture over the last several decades. If, however, there is more to southern culture than the simple structural and economic constraints, if cultural norms and folkways do indeed carry regional values, then we would expect to see few changes in its fundamental character.

Because there are a large number of definitions of political culture—twenty-five according to one author—it is important to clarify which attitudes and opinions will here be considered central. In this essay *political culture* is conceptualized as the generally shared, long-lasting evaluations and expectations of individuals toward rules, institutions, and other people or groups relevant to the political system. This definition includes three core elements: orientations toward governmental structures, orientations toward others in the political system, and orientations toward one's own political activity.[8]

We will look at survey research data on a number of relevant aspects of public opinion in the South and compare these with similar data from northern respondents.[9] This will allow us to identify and explore differences between the regions in terms of political assumptions and attitudes. In attempting to gauge how the South is unique from the North we will seek some historical perspective by looking at differences in regional responses over time. This enables us to assess the effects of increasing demographic and social homogenization between the regions.

More specifically, we shall examine the ideological proclivities of both regions from 1964 through 1980 to determine whether the South has been consistently more conservative than the North. Social scientists Everett Carll Ladd and Charles Hadley in *Transformations of the American Party System* state: "The 1970s picture of the South as the most conservative region of the country leads frequently to the notion that it has always been 'to the right.' This tendency to impose the present upon the past is furthered by the recognition that majorities of southern whites histori-

8. Walter A. Rosenbaum, *Political Culture* (New York, 1975), 5–7.

9. The data used in this essay were made available by the Inter-University Consortium for Political and Social Research. The data were originally collected by the Center for Political Studies of the Institute for Social Research, University of Michigan. Neither the original collectors of the data nor the consortium bears any responsibility for the analyses or interpretations presented here. As used in this study, the South is defined as the states of the Confederacy, whereas the North is defined as those areas of the country which made up the northern forces during the Civil War period. The West is excluded from analysis.

cally have proved reactionary on civil rights."[10] They further argue that the New Deal struck a responsive chord in the radical agrarian tradition of the South and that modern conservative tendencies in the region can be seen as a reversal of past trends rather than a continuation of old ones.

Such an argument makes a great deal of sense in terms of what we know concerning the history of the South and the effects of environment upon public attitudes. From the previous essay we know that the South continues to have the lowest per capita wealth of any region of the country. Normally one would assume that such a region would be a hotbed of economic liberalism, with those in or near the poverty line favoring expansive economic policies from which they could benefit. Furthermore, if liberal attitudes in economic matters do indeed lead to liberal attitudes in other issue areas, the southerner should have a reputation for liberal economic and political attitudes. Such is not the case.

In order to understand this more fully, we shall look at attitudes toward the various levels of government in general and toward the role of government in social welfare policy in particular—key indicators of a conservative political orientation. We will also explore how northern and southern whites have changed in their attitudes toward equal rights for blacks and their feelings about blacks in general. Of critical significance here is how closely the two regions may have converged over the past two decades. Understanding this will shed light on how the racial norms and folkways of southern culture have been modified by the changing demography, economics, and political patterns in the region.

SOUTHERN CONSERVATISM

The starting point for much political commentary and analysis of the South is its "conservatism." Kevin Phillips, for example, in *The Emerging Republican Majority* speculated that because of its conservative political philosophy the South would, by the 1970s, be ripe for realignment with the Republican party.[11] On the surface there would appear to be some truth in his speculations, since over the past two decades the South has repeatedly abandoned the Democratic nominee for the presidency and given unprecedented political support to conservative Republican politicians. But it must be remembered that the entire nation gave overwhelming support to Republican nominees during the same period. How, then,

10. Everett Carll Ladd, Jr., with Charles D. Hadley, *Transformations of the American Party System* (New York, 1978), 129–30.
11. Kevin P. Phillips, *The Emerging Republican Majority* (New Rochelle, 1969).

can we ascertain whether the South has a genuine conservative tradition distinguishable from the national political culture?

A good starting point is to examine how the two regions differ in general philosophy. One measure is the Survey Research Center/Center for Political Studies (SRC/CPS) ideological placement question in which respondents are asked to place themselves on a seven-point Likert-type scale ranging from extremely conservative to extremely liberal.[12] Unfortunately, this question has only been included on the interview forms since 1972. This handicaps us considerably in our attempt to get a historical perspective on how public opinion in the South has changed over time. For this reason we have developed a derived measure of ideological predisposition from data available from 1964 through 1980, using ratings of how "warmly" respondents feel toward conservatives and liberals and combining these responses in such a way that respondents may be placed into liberal, moderate, and conservative categories. To test the validity of this procedure we compared how our derived measure categorized respondents with how they categorized themselves in three successive surveys. Although there were some inconsistencies between the two measures, we found that in general they were highly correlated — an indication that our derived measure is a good register of ideological placement.[13]

Figure 1 shows the percentage of respondents by region who are classi-

12. A Likert scale attempts to measure not only how one feels about a particular topic but also how strongly held those beliefs are. To this end respondents are given a scale of responses to a statement and are asked to agree or disagree with these responses and to state how strongly they agree or disagree. This has become a standard format in recent years for assessing the intensity of attitudes.

13. This measure is derived as follows: Respondents were asked to rate, on a scale from 0 to 100, how favorably they saw conservatives and, in a second rating, liberals. The higher the number chosen by the respondent, the more favorably they saw that particular group. Potential responses ranged from 0 (least favorable) to 100 (most favorable). For each respondent the value assigned to liberals was subtracted from the value for conservatives to form an ideological score ranging from − 100 to + 100. The scale values were then recorded into a standard tripartite classification of respondents into liberals (− 100 to − 11), moderates (− 10 to + 10), and conservatives (+ 11 to + 100).

Gamma is the statistical measure of association used here. The basic purpose for such measures is to determine how well the presence of one factor explains the presence of a second one. If the two measures classified all respondents into the same ideological categories, there would be a perfect relationship between them and Gamma would take on a value of 1. If there was no correspondence between how our derived measure classified respondents and how they classified themselves, Gamma would take on a value of 0. Hence, the relatively high values for Gamma found here (.78, .76, and .69) indicate that both measures classify individuals into ideological categories in approximately the same way.

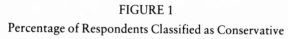

FIGURE 1

Percentage of Respondents Classified as Conservative

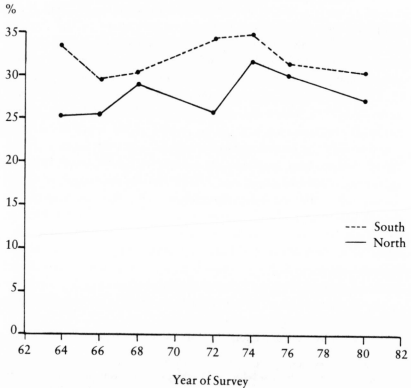

Year of Survey

fied as conservative. Throughout the sixteen-year period a slightly higher percentage of southerners have considered themselves conservative. The widest differences between the two regions occurred during the presidential election years of 1964 and 1972. Both elections were unusual in that one of the presidential aspirants was identified with an extreme ideological position. It thus would appear that such contests have a slight polarizing effect upon individual ideological placement. In more normal circumstances there seem to be only minute differences between northerners and southerners in their rates of conservative identification. In fact, there is no statistically significant difference between the two regions in either 1976 or 1980.[14]

14. In this essay a lack of statistical significance means that we cannot be certain that the relationship shown in the data is real or simply the result of random variation. In other words, the relationship between the variables is so weak that we cannot be certain it is real.

It also appears that the South has been more consistent than the North over this sixteen-year period. The data for each region reveal virtually no upward drift in conservatism by southern respondents, whereas northern respondents do exhibit a slight upward drift.[15] Thus, it would appear that the North is gradually becoming more conservative, whereas the South remains relatively steady in its ideological allegiance. This is the reverse of what would normally be expected, since the South's demographic and social convergence with the North should, according to the behavioral school, result in a convergence of attitudes as well. Instead, the North rather than the South seems to have changed.

The seeming conservative trend by northern respondents is even clearer if we look at the results of a second question that also could be considered an ideological indicator. Since 1964 respondents have been asked whether the federal government is "too powerful." We would normally expect a conservative respondent to have an inherent distrust of governmental power—especially governmental power that is distant from the control of the electorate. The results, shown in Figure 2, indicate that southerners have been fairly consistent in their attitudes toward federal power, whereas northerners' distaste for a powerful federal government has steadily increased.[16] In fact, by 1980 northerners were actually slightly more distrustful of federal power than southerners, even though this difference was not statistically significant. Since 1964, however, an increasingly large percentage of both northerners and southerners have felt the federal government was too powerful.

ATTITUDES TOWARD STATE AND LOCAL GOVERNMENT

Has the South always had a certain predisposition for local governmental institutions and a distrust of the federal government? Perhaps. Since the end of the Civil War most observers have seen a current of regional dis-

15. The method used here, as elsewhere in this essay, is a linear regression. This statistical procedure is often useful in a situation in which variables change in value across a fixed time period. In this case the regression procedure attempts to draw a straight line through the data points indicating the general relationship between the passage of time and the increasing or decreasing value of a variable. The slope of such a regression line is a measure of how quickly a value increases or decreases with the passage of time. In this case a southern slope of .01 indicates that with the passage of each year, there is an average increase of .01 percent in the percentage of respondents classified as conservatives. On the other hand, the northern slope of .21 indicates that there is, on average, a .21 percent increase in conservatism each year.

16. The method used here is the same as explained in note 15. The northern slope of 1.26 indicates an increase of 1.26 percent per year in the number of northerners who feel the federal government is too powerful, compared with an increase of only .24 percent per year in the number of southerners feeling the federal government is too powerful.

FIGURE 2

Percentage of Respondents Feeling the Federal Government
is Too Powerful

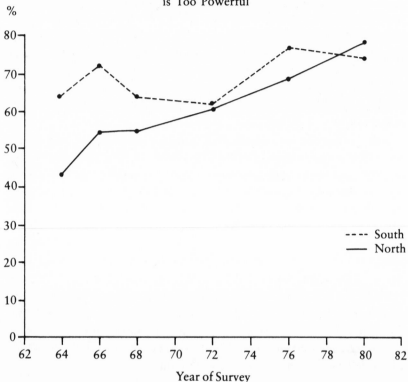

Year of Survey

trust for outside institutions. Perhaps the most obvious example is the reaction of southern governors and legislators to the integration orders issued in the decade of the 1960s. In the face of demands for integration
the southern states pleaded for relief on the basis of states' rights and asserted the doctrine of nullification. They often complained of "agitators"
who came from outside the community. Even before this, Key had noted
the strong tradition of friends and neighbors voting in the South and also
emphasized that the most important factor in determining the outcome
of statewide elections was the support of a candidate by local politicians.
Also, a great deal of the South's legal and social structure was based on
local autonomy rather than centralized control.[17]

All of these items indicate a culture that is locally oriented rather than

17. This decentralization often took the form of weak governors and a large number of
independent boards. See Part Three, and Wheat's essay in particular, for more specific information.

cosmopolitan in outlook. Thus, one would expect southerners to manifest different attitudes from those in the North toward the various levels of government. First of all, if the South is a more localistic society, we would expect southerners to exhibit greater interest in state and local politics than in national affairs. Second, we would expect that along with this greater interest would go a greater degree of satisfaction with state and local government. The evidence we shall look at to determine whether these types of attitudes are more common in the South will be somewhat scattered. However, it is substantial enough to indicate whether such differences in attitude are present.

The earliest data we have of interest in national, state, and local politics is taken from the 1952 SRC/CPS survey. In that year respondents were asked a series of questions concerning the presidential election as well as state and local contests.[18] We can see in Figure 3 that the hypothesized pattern of greater interest in state and local elections than national ones is exhibited by southern respondents. Northern respondents reacted in the opposite direction, expressing greater interest in the national election than state and local contests. However, the differentiation between the two regions was not great.

Such was also the case sixteen years later, when respondents were asked a more general question concerning how much interest they had in national, state, and local public affairs. As shown in Figure 4, southern respondents once again indicated greater interest in state and local politics than in national affairs. However, there were two significant changes from the 1952 pattern, one being that northern respondents no longer reacted in the reverse of southern respondents. In fact, the North showed very little differentiation in their interest by level of government. But it is even more noteworthy that southern respondents appear to be more interested in all types of public affairs than northerners.

This pattern is somewhat confirmed if we look at the results of a slightly different question concerning differential levels of trust and confidence at the three levels of government. Surveys from 1968 through 1976 asked respondents which level of government (federal, state, or local) they had the most faith and confidence in. Figure 5 shows the percentage of respondents who expressed greatest trust in state and local

18. The question was worded as follows: "Generally speaking, would you say that you personally care a good deal which party wins the presidential election this fall or that you don't care much which party wins? How about state and local elections? When you have state and local elections around here would you say that you care a good deal who wins or that you don't care very much who wins these elections?"

FIGURE 3

Percentage of Respondents Who Cared Who Wins National, State, and Local Elections, 1952

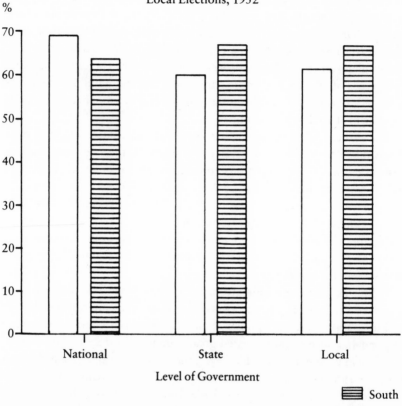

Level of Government

▤ South

☐ North

government by region. There is clearly an upward trend across the eight-year period. But what is perhaps most fascinating is the clear indication that it is the North — as it converges with the South — which is in the process of rediscovering the viability of state and local government. The data also give little evidence of a stronger localistic culture in the South than in the North during this period. If such a culture existed, a much stronger differentiation between the regions would be expected. The most that can be claimed is a rather mild preference for state and local government in the South independent of national trends. There is no statistically significant difference between North and South in their ratings of the quality of state and local government in either 1974 or 1976.

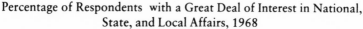

FIGURE 4

Percentage of Respondents with a Great Deal of Interest in National, State, and Local Affairs, 1968

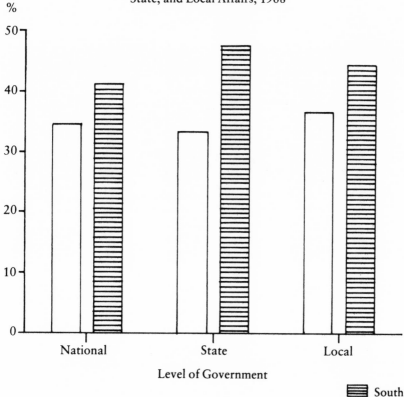

Level of Government

South

North

SOCIAL WELFARE POLICY AND AFFIRMATIVE ACTION

If a clear delineation between North and South cannot be made in the areas of general ideological orientation and attitudes toward state and local government, what about the areas of social welfare policy and equal rights/affirmative action? Can one find a unique southern political culture by looking at these specific public issues rather than at general orientations toward government?

Social welfare policy can mean a number of different things. Here we refer to individual attitudes concerning the extent of governmental action desirable to redress inequities in the social structure. Specifically, we look at questions dealing with the role of government in guaranteeing each

FIGURE 5

Percentage of Respondents with Greatest Confidence in State
and Local Government

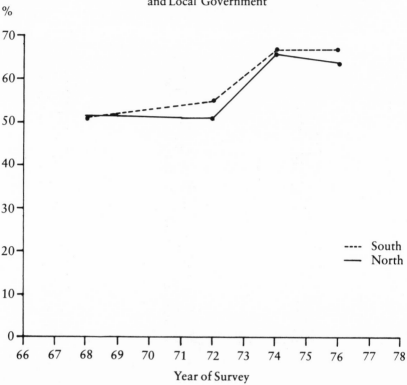

Year of Survey

person a good job and decent standard of living and also whether the
government should help minorities to improve their social and economic
positions. Those who see a more expansive role for government should
tend toward the liberal end of the ideological scale, whereas those opposed to such activities would normally be considered more conservative. Thus, if the South is a more conservative society, we would expect
to see less support for both of these forms of governmental activity than
in the North.

Figure 6 indicates that in the area of guaranteed employment there
was little convergence between North and South from 1972 through
1980. This is because the southern sample is generally less opposed to
such governmental activity, an unexpected finding in light of the normal
assumption that southern political culture is of a laissez-faire variety in

FIGURE 6

Percentage of Respondents Feeling the Government Should Not Guarantee a Job and Good Standard of Living

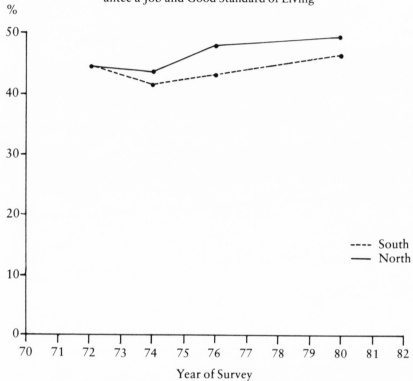

Year of Survey

---- South
— North

which each person is responsible for his or her own success or failure. Quite the opposite appears here, with southern respondents showing greater support than northerners for such activist policies. This is confirmed by similar questions asked between 1956 and 1968.[19] In all cases southern respondents were more supportive of such liberal policies than were northerners, even though the differences were relatively small.

What about governmental aid to specific racial groups in order to give them an advantage in the job market? If the South's political culture is really unique in terms of political fundamentals, we would expect to see the evidence in a question such as this. Figure 7 shows the percentage of respondents who feel that such individuals should "get along on their

19. Respondents were also questioned on government-subsidized health care and federal aid to education.

FIGURE 7

Percentage of Respondents Feeling Minorities Should Get Along
on Their Own

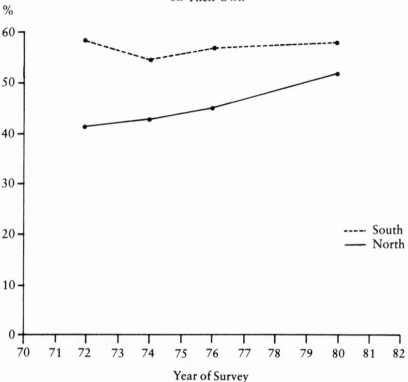

Year of Survey

own" rather than have governmental power imposed to benefit their economic positions. The patterns of response to this question from 1972
through 1980 are steady for both regions with the South always being
somewhat more opposed to such a policy than the North. However, the
percentage difference between the two regions is small.

Though it would be easy to assume that the South's greater resistance
to affirmative action is based strictly on racist sentiment among southern
whites, such is not the case. Table 1 indicates that both blacks and whites
in the South exhibit greater opposition to this concept than do their comparable racial groups in the North. The data presented are for 1980, but
the same patterns can be seen in other years as well, and it therefore
seems reasonable to conclude that they are not the result of mere statistical artifact.

TABLE 1
Percentage of Respondents Opposing Affirmative Action,
by Race and Region of Residence

	Race	
Region	Blacks	Whites
North	22%	52%
	(13)	(297)
South	33%	58%
	(20)	(165)

The responses to these two questions, as well as to others, indicate that southerners and northerners are, for the most part, quite similar in their assumptions concerning the role of government in assuring the social welfare of its citizens. They do differ slightly as to the types of situations that warrant such intervention, with the southern sample appearing more conservative than the northern one only when governmental power is used to benefit one group at the expense of another. When the use of governmental power is more generally beneficial to all individuals, the southern respondents appear somewhat less conservative than the northern.

RACIAL ATTITUDES

Virtually all would agree that nothing is of more significance to southern society than race and individual attitudes on racial matters. In fact, historian Ulrich Phillips has identified this as the central theme of southern history.[20] It is certainly, then, a critical factor in determining both the extent to which a unique southern culture exists and the degree to which southern racial opinion is independent of or susceptible to change imposed by an outside authority — in this instance the federal government. We will examine the racial theme by considering attitudes toward black integration into society as well as those of whites toward blacks in general and feelings of being threatened by the civil rights movement.

Desegregation was the major thrust of federal action in the South during the 1960s, and it was the most visible part of the struggle for equal rights. In order to see how white northerners and southerners differed over these desegregation efforts, we first consider a very general question. Every four years from 1964 through 1976 respondents were asked

20. Ulrich Phillips, "The Central Theme of Southern History."

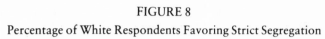

FIGURE 8

Percentage of White Respondents Favoring Strict Segregation

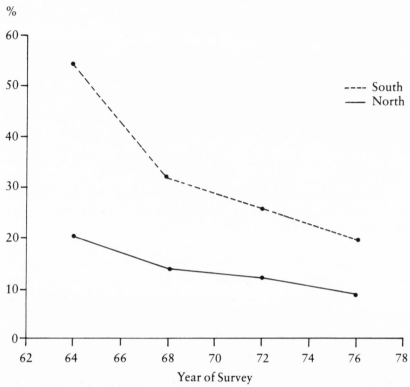

whether they were "in favor of desegregation, strict segregation, or something in between." In Figure 8, which shows the percentage of whites favoring strict segregation by region and year, a general downward trend
appears in both regions with the most precipitous decline occurring in the
southern sample. More than 50 percent of southern respondents favored
strict segregation of the races in 1964, but by 1976 less than 20 percent
did so. And though the gap between North and South on this question is
still fairly wide in 1976, it is only about a third of the difference existing
in 1964.

What processes are responsible for such a dramatic decline in segregationist attitudes? First of all, the decline appears to be of a very general
nature and not simply the result of massive change by one socioeconomic
group in the South, although the changes appeared in different groups at

FIGURE 9

Percentage of White Respondents Favoring Strict Segregation, by Age, 1976

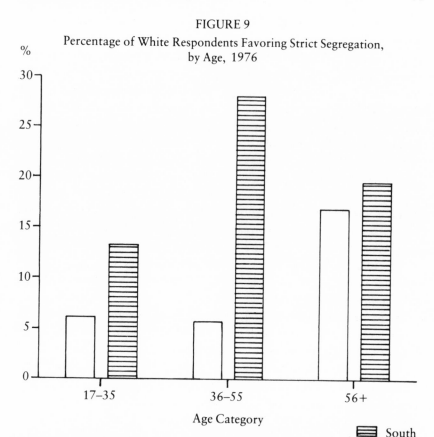

Age Category

South
North

different times. For example, for high and moderate socioeconomic groups, the most precipitous decline in support for segregation occurred between 1964 and 1968. However, for those of low socioeconomic status, the major decline occurred from 1968 through 1976. This pattern may simply reflect a two-step process in the communication of new societal norms, with social change coming first to the elites, who later communicate these new norms to the masses.

More interesting than the socioeconomic differentials are the results obtained when we subdivide our samples by age. According to Figure 9, in 1976 the greatest decline in support for segregation in the South occurred in the younger age group (thirty-five and under) and the older one (fifty-six and over). For some reason the middle-age category in the South held quite tenaciously to the segregation line. Some 28 percent of southern whites in this age group said they supported strict segregation whereas the comparable figure for northerners in that age bracket was only 5 percent. A more refined subclassification scheme indicates that those who came of legal age (twenty-one) during the 1950s are primarily responsible for this unusual bulge in the data. This leads one to speculate that a forceful and virulent socialization process took place during this decade. The older generation, having lived under a segregated system, was probably not as affected by the anti-integration hysteria prominent in the 1950s and early 1960s. For them, segregation was simply an un-questioned fact of life and not something on which strong beliefs were demanded. And those who came of age after the mid-1960s were not deeply socialized into segregationist culture, because of its collapse dur-ing the previous fifteen or so years. This generation was also not as iso-lated from national trends and ideas as previous ones. It became clear that segregation was no longer a viable position at the same time that the national media began to replace regional media as an agent of social-ization throughout the South.

Given that formalistic segregation was being rejected by a large per-centage of the population both North and South, what about less direct forms of segregation? From 1964 through 1976 respondents were asked whether "white people have the right to keep black people out of their neighborhoods if they want to; or black people have a right to live wher-ever they can afford to, just like anybody else." In Figure 10 the percent-age of white respondents by region who opposed open housing from 1964 through 1976 corresponds to the general time trends seen in the previous questions. The South experienced a much more precipitous de-cline in support for segregated housing than the North (declines of 3.62 percent per year and 1.64 percent per year respectively), which has led to a gradual convergence of the two. In 1976 some support for segregated housing patterns still existed in both regions, with about 10 percent of northern respondents and about 22 percent of southern respondents sup-porting the concept.

The responses to this question give interesting confirmation to the pat-terns of change noted previously. Figure 11, showing the percentage of white southerners (subdivided by age and year of survey) who support segregated housing, indicates better than any other item that, in fact, two processes are taking place as the two regions gradually converge in this issue. First, there is a decline in support for such racist policies among all age groups, and second, there is a clear generational differentiation as the youngest age group declines in support for such policies at a much faster

FIGURE 10

Percentage of White Respondents Supporting the Right of Whites
to Keep Blacks Out of Their Neighborhoods

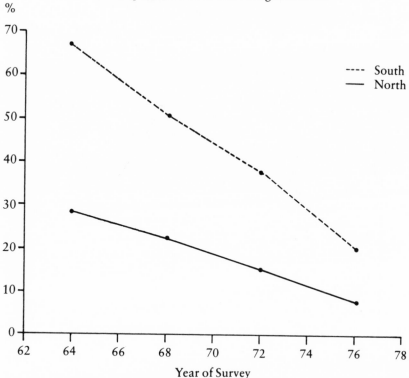

rate than the middle- and upper-age categories. From such an analysis it
is clear that complete convergence between the regions cannot occur except through generational replacement, but genuine change in attitudes
can be imposed upon a political culture irrespective of socialized attitudes, though such change appears to most affect younger individuals.

FEELINGS TOWARD BLACKS AND THE CIVIL RIGHTS MOVEMENT

One objection to our analysis so far could be that we are measuring racial
attitudes having such a low level of public acceptability that most respondents are reluctant to voice such prejudices even if they share them. To
determine whether the large decline in racist sentiment is simply a reflection of this societal pressure, we shall look as well at some more indirect
measures of racial attitudes.

FIGURE 11

Percentage of White Southern Respondents Favoring
Segregated Housing, by Age Group

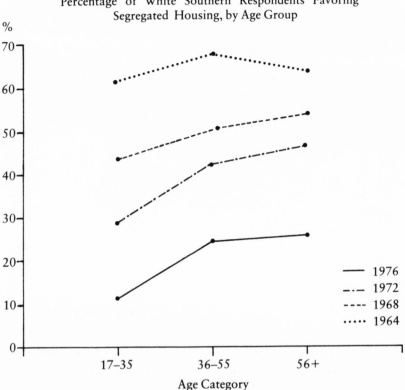

First, how do whites feel about black people in general rather than
about specific racial issues? Since 1964 the SRC/CPS surveys have included a series of "feeling thermometer" questions in which respondents
were asked to point out on a 0 to 100 scale how warmly or coldly they
felt toward certain groups. One of the groups mentioned since 1966 has
been blacks. Figure 12 shows that the mean white feeling thermometer
score for blacks is greater than 50 for both regions, indicating warm feelings toward blacks. These warm feelings increased from 1966 through
1972 when they reached their peak. After 1972 they declined contin-
uously for both regions until 1980 when they increased slightly for southern whites. More importantly, the fairly steady convergence indicated
here between the two regions from 1972 through 1976 is confirmed by
an analysis of variance tests which found regional differences in 1972,

FIGURE 12

Mean Feeling Thermometer Score for White Respondents:
Object of Questions: Blacks

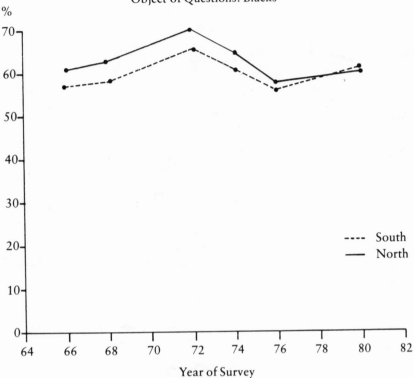

Year of Survey

1976, and 1980 to be statistically insignificant. Thus we see no significant regional differences among whites in terms of their underlying feelings about blacks in the latter two surveys.

Such is also the case in terms of white feelings of a threat from blacks
and the civil rights movement. Figure 13 shows the percentage of whites
by region who felt that the civil rights movement was pushing "too fast,"
and the pattern we see here is by now a familiar one. From the mid-1960s
through 1980 there was a steady decline in anxiety concerning the civil
rights movement, with southern white attitudes declining much more
sharply than northern ones. Also, by 1980 no statistically significant differences appear between northern and southern responses to this question. The trends we saw in our previous racially sensitive questions are

FIGURE 13

Percentage of White Respondents Who Feel Civil Rights Leaders Are
Pushing Too Fast

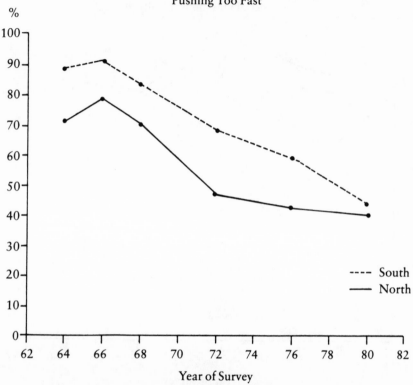

confirmed here by several less direct measures. Thus, it would appear
that white southerners have become like their northern counterparts,
though unfortunately this does not mean the elimination of racism.

CONCLUSIONS

In summary, among the mass public there is little evidence to indicate either a general southern conservatism or even a greater preference in the
South than in the North for local governmental structures. Indeed, it
would appear that North and South differ very little in these areas of
public opinion. In the area of social welfare, southerners are sympathetic
to government job programs, but not to affirmative action. Only when
looking at racial attitudes did we find firm evidence of a traditionally dis-

tinctive southern culture. However, the most massive changes in the attitudes of southerners and, to a lesser extent, of northerners occurred in this area. This leads to some important conclusions concerning the nature of southern political culture and how it may have changed over the past few decades.

First and perhaps most obvious is the way in which attitudes toward blacks and the tradition of segregation have changed over a relatively short period of time. In this regard federal policy in the South has been a dramatic success. In 1964 over 50 percent of southerners expressed a desire to live in a segregated society, whereas by 1976 less than 20 percent believed in the desirability of a racially segregated society. In a similar vein, in 1964 almost 90 percent of southern whites felt threatened by the civil rights movement and saw it as moving too quickly; by 1980 only 44 percent felt this way. Such results considerably reinforce the conclusions of the behavioral school on these issues and indicate that political culture in this area is perhaps more pliable than some would think. As political and legal structures have been changed over time, attitudes have changed to accord with these new realities. And at least for the foreseeable future most evidence points toward continued convergence with the North in terms of racial attitudes.

The second point is that we should be extremely careful in ascribing special attitudes to the South without firm evidence. In most matters region is probably not a very important variable in explaining public attitudes. With the nationalization of the mass media and social trends, both North and South now appear to react similarly rather than walking to the beat of different drummers. There may of course be slight differences in the distribution of attitudes, but we should not exaggerate the significance of these. Differences of a few percentage points do not a political culture make.

Politics and Elections PART TWO

Who would have believed it? George Wallace inaugurated in 1983 for a fourth term as governor of Alabama *with strong black support.* This was the same Wallace who had announced at another inauguration twenty years earlier, on January 14, 1963: "Let us rise to the call of freedom-loving blood that is in us and send our answer to the tyranny that clanks its chains upon the South. In the name of the greatest people that have ever trod this earth, I draw the line in the dust and toss the gauntlet before the feet of tyranny, and I say: Segregation now — segregation tomorrow — segregation forever."

Who would have believed Republicans holding one-half of the Senate seats of the Old Confederacy and some three dozen House seats, or Democratic front-runner and classic liberal Walter Mondale campaigning hard across the South in early 1983, from Biloxi, Mississippi, to Chattanooga, Tennessee, to Hawkinsville, Georgia (announcing at the latter site: "I'm the only licensed pea lice inspector ever to be elected vice president of the United States")?

Who would have believed southern elections virtually devoid of fiery orators and stump showmanship, turning instead on cool television campaigns, with even old-line southern politicos like Senator John Stennis of Mississippi succumbing and bringing in the northern media managers?

Who would have believed black mayors in Atlanta, New Orleans, Birmingham, Charlotte, and some one hundred other cities in the region, and — according to Census Bureau reports on the 1982 elections — black citizens voting at a rate higher than whites in Louisiana, South Carolina, and Tennessee, and voting at equivalent levels in Mississippi, Texas, and Virginia?

The five studies in this section attempt to explain these dramatic turnabouts from the Solid South era. T. McN. Simpson leads off with a detailed account of the intertwinings of Jimmy Carter's political career and southern politics from 1955 onward. To study Carter's progression from local officeholder to president over a quarter century is to study the transformation of southern politics as the region moved back into the national mainstream.

Black politics is the concern of the next two studies. Richard Engstrom explores the intricacies of the 1982 extension and amendment of the Voting Rights Act of 1965, the single most important piece of legislation pertaining to southern politics. Engstrom details the legislation's incredible impact and the subsequent development of black political power in the South. Ally Mack, Leslie B. McLemore, and Mary DeLorse Coleman then examine contemporary trends in black politics, discussing the key factors currently affecting participation, including the Reverend Jesse Jackson's and others' efforts at mobilization. They look at some major obstacles inhibiting black political gains in the South and close with analysis of where black politics seems to be heading.

Next is a study of partisan politics, which have always been both fascinating and baffling in the South. John Van Wingen and David Valentine begin by describing the "Solid South" and explaining how the factionalized one-party system excluded so many citizens from political life. They detail the manner in which this pattern was eroded by a host of factors, document Republican gains, and clarify why the gains have not been as great as many had predicted. Their interesting conclusion is that the South is now and will be for the foreseeable future "a one-and-a-half, no-party system."

The last essay of the section focuses on political campaigns in the region. Joseph Parker looks at the new media-oriented style of southern elections, explains the new campaign technology, and identifies major practitioners. He describes the evolution and impact of this phenomenon in two states, Louisiana and Mississippi. Finally, Parker assesses the implications of the new politics in Dixie.

Jimmy Carter and the Transformation of Southern Politics, 1953–1987

T. McN. SIMPSON III

I am a Southerner and an American.
> —Jimmy Carter, *Why Not the Best?* (1975)

When Jimmy Carter resigned from the navy and returned home upon his father's death in 1953, Sumter County, Georgia, epitomized southern politics. Malapportionment, disfranchisement, Jim Crow laws and customs, one-party solidarity in national elections, factionalism, and demagoguery —all those elements of the Solid South described so brilliantly by V. O. Key[1]—were present.

Disfranchisement and malapportionment were extreme. In the 1950 census, Sumter tallied 10,918 whites and 13,920 blacks. By a 1958 count, 3.8 percent of the blacks were registered to vote, compared with 43.4 percent of the whites.[2] Like all rural counties in Georgia, Sumter carried more weight in the General Assembly and in statewide elections than its population justified. In the state House of Representatives, Sumter County, with 24,208 people, had two seats whereas Fulton County, with 473,572 people (twenty times as many), had three. In elections for governor and United States senator, the disproportionate weight of the rural counties was even greater. For under the county unit system used in

*The author extends his thanks to the University of Tennessee at Knoxville for its support of his work on this essay through faculty research grants.

1. V. O. Key, Jr., *Southern Politics in State and Nation* (New York, 1949).
2. Margaret Price, *The Negro and the Ballot in the South* (Atlanta, 1959), 69.

the Democratic primary, each county had two unit votes for each seat in the House (thus Sumter had four unit votes and Fulton had six); and whoever received a plurality of the popular votes in a given county received all of the county's unit votes, a majority of unit votes winning nomination and election. Malapportionment in favor of rural populations, not unique to the South, was especially important there because it strengthened the courthouse gangs in counties where blacks predominated, in counties, that is, where the stakes in maintaining Jim Crow were greatest.

Since the 1930s Georgia voters had divided roughly into two groups, those supporting and those opposing the personalized faction built around Gene Talmadge (he of the red galluses), who was elected governor in 1932.[3] The son of "Old Gene," Herman, became governor in 1948, serving for several years before moving to the U.S. Senate, where he remained until a scandal over his personal use of campaign funds brought about his defeat in 1980. Sumter County, in the heart of rural, rigidly segregated South Georgia, was pretty evenly divided between the Talmadge and anti-Talmadge factions.

By mid-century powerful undercurrents were eating away at the southern politics exemplified by Sumter County, as Key acknowledges and as the essays in this volume explain. Massive numbers of blacks had been emigrating from the South to the North for decades, and from the farms to the cities. In Sumter County, the 1910 rural black population of approximately 17,000 had decreased to 7,624 by 1950, whereas the 1910 Americus black population of approximately 4,200 had increased to 5,666. While blacks were fleeing to the South's towns and cities and to the North—or being forced into this migration by agricultural mechanization—financial interests were industrializing the South. The gradually growing Sumter County city of Americus was an example of this, though Atlanta and Columbus illustrated the general development more forcefully. Another change was signaled by the television antennas sprouting from millions of roofs. Soon they would provide a mirror in which residents of Sumter County and other southerners could see themselves; later they would bring alternative cultural patterns into every home.

With the end of World War II, many returning veterans questioned southern taboos, and the pace of change quickened. Frank Myers was one of these veterans who entered politics in Sumter County. In 1948 he

3. See William Anderson, *The Wild Man from Sugar Creek: The Political Career of Eugene Talmadge* (Baton Rouge, 1975), 16–18, and Numan V. Bartley, *From Thurmond to Wallace: Political Tendencies in Georgia, 1948–1968* (Baltimore, 1970).

got elected to the Georgia House of Representatives, in 1950 he ran unsuccessfully for Congress, and in 1952 he tried to regain the Georgia House seat, advertising himself in the Americus *Times-Recorder* as "an independent candidate . . . committed to no political faction." Myers, in plain terms, was an opponent of Herman Talmadge. Earl Carter, Jimmy's father, a Talmadge supporter, ran against Myers and won. The vote was large by Sumter standards and Carter's victory was narrow — 2,177 to 1,936 — an indication that the old politics were weakening. In 1953, when Earl died and Jimmy came home, the time was nearly ripe for southern politicians to abandon the old factionalized system built upon demagoguery and racism and guide the region toward more moderate politics.

Jimmy Carter would eventually seize the moment and help carry this process along. Yet his contribution to a new, racially moderate politics did not come easily or immediately, for in the 1950s southern politics of the old style shaped politicians' careers more than politicians shaped a new politics. Carter's early career, from 1955 to 1970, illustrated this, as did George Wallace's in a more dramatic manner. Once elected governor in 1970, however, Carter pushed the transformation already under way. His election as president helped further to bring the South back into the nation.

We will examine Jimmy Carter's service on the Sumter County Board of Education (1955–1963), his activities as state senator (1962–1967), his campaigns for governor (1966 and 1970), his term as governor (1971–1975), his performance as presidential candidate and president (1972–1981), and his activities as a former president (1981–). In doing this we will assess the implications of southern politics for Carter's career and the implications of his career for southern politics.

School Board Member and Chairman: 1955–1963

By the fall of 1955, when the Sumter County grand jury appointed Carter to take the Plains seat on the county's Board of Education, the United States Supreme Court had ruled that segregation in public education was a denial of the equal protection of the laws guaranteed by the Fourteenth Amendment (*Brown* v. *Board of Education*, 1954) and that public school systems must make "a prompt and reasonable start" and move "with all deliberate speed" toward eliminating it (*Brown* v. *Board of Education*, 1955). The Supreme Court's 1955 ruling did not implement itself, of course, and Sumter County continued the South's pattern of segregation and subordination of blacks. Not for a full decade, not indeed until

1965, did the first black children enter the county's previously all-white schools.

The Sumter County school board was already dealing with issues involving "colored" schools and "white" schools when Carter joined it. His 1975 recollection that he had been on the school board for six months before he realized that black children had to walk to school whereas white children rode was inaccurate, for the minutes of his first meeting in December, 1955, show him and his colleagues discussing the need to increase the transportation of black children.[4] In subsequent meetings during the four and a half years before Carter became chairman, the board provided running water for the Plains and Leslie Negro Elementary schools, purchased a secondhand piano for the all-black high school and transferred to it several typewriters from the white high schools. Often Carter made the motions for these mundane administrative actions. In the summer of 1960, as he assumed the chairmanship, the board purchased four new typewriters and transferred four old ones to the "Colored High School," as the minutes refer to it. Separate education was never equal in Sumter County. Yet, from the perspective of respectable white Sumter citizens, if not that of Supreme Court justices or civil rights leaders, it seemed that Carter and his colleagues were making some progress.

During Carter's seven years on the school board, from December, 1955, to January, 1963, nothing happened in Sumter County's public schools comparable with the dramatic events in places like Clinton, Tennessee, or Little Rock, Arkansas.[5] In Sumter County, the most overt instances of racial conflict during this time involved Koinonia, a unique interracial farm community seven miles from Plains on the road from Americus to Dawson. Begun in 1942 as a tiny, two-family farm community whose founders interpreted Christian principles to imply pacifism, interracial fellowship, and the sharing of possessions, Koinonia had grown by 1953 to nineteen adults and twenty-two children, including at least one black couple and their four children.[6] Although not accepted in the local society, the community lived in relative peace with its neighbors until 1956, when a minor racial incident involving founder Clarence Jordan touched off a year and more of nighttime attacks by unknown persons firing rifles, shotguns, machine guns, and explosives, accompanied

---

4. Jimmy Carter, Why Not the Best? (Nashville, 1975), 66.

5. See Richard Kluger, Simple Justice: The History of Brown v. Board of Education and Black America's Struggle for Equality (New York, 1976). See also Margaret Anderson, The Children of the South (New York, 1966).

6. See Dallas Lee, The Cotton Patch Evidence (New York, 1971), 91.

by a crippling economic boycott. In 1960 the Koinonia conflict touched the school board, over which Carter presided, when the parents of several white Koinonia children appealed to the county board to intercede with the Americus school board over its refusal to allow their children to attend the city schools. The county board decided not to intercede. Carter, one of the parents told this writer many years later, "did not help us but was fair to us."

Outside of the school board, another test on the race issue that Carter faced was whether or not to join the White Citizens Council. In *Why Not the Best?* he recounted suffering "a small boycott" for being "the only holdout" when the Citizens Council movement hit Plains in the mid-1950s. He may have exaggerated the incident somewhat, since his biographer Betty Glad reports that the "townspeople do not recall it" and adds that "Carter was able to avoid taking stands on racial policies in the fifties and early sixties because he never held office at a time or in a place where he was forced to do so." He seems to concede this in *Keeping Faith*: "I was not directly involved in the early struggles to end racial discrimination, but by the time my terms as state senator and governor were over, I had gained the trust and political support of some of the great civil rights leaders in my region of the country."[7]

Although Carter did not alter the Jim Crow pattern which governed Sumter County's schools, he was a vigorous chairman. He streamlined the committee structure of the board, for example, and did his share in leading the county and city boards' joint move to consolidate the two school systems. During Carter's 1976 presidential campaign, some reporters gave him most if not all the credit for the school merger, and a few explained consolidation as his method of preparing the way for later desegregation. The evidence strongly suggests that they were wrong in both respects. State education authorities had tried before to consolidate the two systems and seem to have initiated the 1961 proposal. Furthermore, when the two boards submitted the issue to a referendum, consolidation passed overwhelmingly in the city and in most of the county precincts, demonstrating a broad base of support. It failed in the county outside the city only because the citizens of Plains and Leslie, the two communities in addition to Americus that had high schools, voted heavily against the merger. The un-

7. Carter, *Why Not the Best?*, 66–67; Betty Glad, *Jimmy Carter: In Search of the Great White House* (New York, 1980), 84–85; Jimmy Carter, *Keeping Faith: Memoirs of a President* (New York, 1982), 141–42. For alternative interpretations of Carter's character and career, see Bruce Mazlish and Edwin Diamond, *Jimmy Carter: A Character Portrait* (New York, 1979).

derstandable desire of these communities to retain their schools (and athletic teams) probably had more to do with their vote than any fear of integration, which presumably would have affected the votes of the other county communities. In any event, Jimmy Carter's old high school basketball coach, Y. T. Sheffield, now principal of Plains High School, lined up against him, along with most of his Plains constituents.

While he was on the school board it thus seems clear that Carter largely accommodated himself to Sumter County's prevailing cultural patterns. One should not forget, however, that Carter, intelligent and relatively cosmopolitan (he had been stationed, from 1946 to 1953, in Virginia, Connecticut, California, Hawaii, and New York), probably came to understand by the late 1950s what the Supreme Court's *Brown* v. *Board of Education* decision portended for Sumter County and perhaps for the future politics of the region.

Carter's work on the Sumter County Board of Education, on the Americus and Sumter County Hospital Authority, and in the Lions Club plus other organizations acquainted him with many people. He performed ably and rose rapidly in his numerous roles, and it was natural enough for some of his neighbors to think of him for higher offices. Warren Fortson, a member of the Americus school board, drove to Plains with a friend (perhaps late in 1961) to suggest that Carter challenge "Tic" Forrester, the incumbent 3rd District congressman. Carter deferred, without explanation. About the same time, when a fellow Sunday school teacher joshed that Carter would soon be tossing his hat in some elective ring, Carter flashed a smile.[8]

STATE SENATOR: 1962–1967

In 1962, the Supreme Court in *Baker* v. *Carr* brought the issue of legislative apportionment within the reach of the equal protection clause of the Fourteenth Amendment, just as it had done in 1954 with the issue of segregation. This decision affected state politics and politicians across the nation, having particular impact in states like Georgia, where correcting the urban-rural imbalance weakened white political elites.[9]

In Georgia, where Fulton County had 6 unit votes (for 556,326 residents in 1960) compared to Sumter County's 4 (for 24,652 residents) and Quitman County's 2 (for 2,432 residents), Atlanta voters challenged the

8. Interview with Warren Fortson, December 18, 1980, and interview with Clarence Dodson, March 23, 1982.
9. See Timothy G. O'Rourke, *The Impact of Reapportionment* (New Brunswick, 1980).

county unit system and the apportionment of the state legislature in federal district court and won both cases. An Americus native, Judge Griffin Bell, appointed to the court by President John F. Kennedy after managing Kennedy's successful 1960 campaign in Georgia, wrote the opinion. This decision, later upheld by the Supreme Court, destroyed the county unit system. Voting for the first time on a popular vote basis in the Democratic primary on September 12, 1962, Georgians nominated Carl Sanders for governor by a two-to-one margin. The Democratic gubernatorial nomination was still, at that time, tantamount to election.

Two days later Governor Vandiver called the General Assembly into special session for the purpose of reapportionment (although he had earlier pledged not to do so), and by October 5 a bill redistricting the state senate had become law. This nullified the results of the September 12 primary for the state senate and established a special primary for October 16. Sumter County, which had formerly rotated a senate seat with Schley County and Macon County—each occupying the seat two of every six years—would now share a senator, on a nonrotating basis, in a district with Chattahoochee, Quitman, Randolph, Stewart, Terrell, and Webster. Under the old scheme it was not Sumter County's turn to have a senator, and thus there was no obvious Sumter candidate to run in the special primary. Stewart County's Homer Moore had been selected in the September 12 primary, now nullified, and decided to run again. But because of Americus, Sumter County had a far larger population than Stewart or any other 14th Senatorial District county. The United States Supreme Court and the Georgia General Assembly, together, had handed to some aspiring Sumter County leader a golden opportunity.[10]

Jimmy Carter took it. Winning the endorsement of the Americus *Times-Recorder* and mounting a feverish ten-day friends-and-neighbors campaign, Carter pulled even with Moore by election day, only to see Quitman County, customarily rife with fraud, tip the balance against him. Carter, having placed a strong and loyal poll watcher there, sought the assistance of his Americus lawyer friend, Warren Fortson, and of an Atlanta lawyer in Griffin Bell's former law firm, Charles Kirbo. Together they succeeded in bringing the Quitman ballots before superior court Judge Carl Crow, who was from an adjoining circuit, on November 2. On Friday, November 3, four days before the general election (usually a pro forma ratification of the results of the Democratic primary), Judge Crow threw out the Quitman vote. This gave Carter the edge, by 2,788 votes

10. See Albert B. Saye, "Revolution by Judicial Action in Georgia," *Western Political Quarterly*, XVII (1964), 10–14.

to 2,703, a very light vote for seven counties with a total 1960 population of 74,533.

Moore's friends did not give up easily, and made an immediate appeal to the Quitman Democratic Executive Committee, which they controlled. They won. Carter then appealed to the state Democratic Executive Committee and its chairman, winning a ruling on Saturday, November 4, that he was the Democratic nominee. On the basis of this ruling, Secretary of State Ben Fortson (Warren Fortson's brother) instructed the ordinaries (clerks) of the seven counties to place Carter's name on the ballots in place of Moore's. Moore, supported by many established area politicians, still did not give up, and he took the case to superior court Judge T. O. Marshall, Jr., on Monday, November 6. Marshall ruled that neither Moore's nor Carter's name should appear on the following day's ballot. The ordinaries of five counties worked late into the night removing the names, according to the Americus *Times-Recorder*, but the ordinaries of two counties (Sumter and Quitman) refused to comply with Judge Marshall's order. In these clouded circumstances Moore and Carter went on the radio on Tuesday, November 7, to explain the matter as best they could and to get as many write-in votes as possible in the general election. This time Carter won by 3,013 votes to 2,182, including a lopsided margin in Quitman County of 448 to 23. Moore conceded, then threatened to contest the result, and finally gave up without contesting it. Carter, the tenacious neophyte, had won his first elective office.

The early 1960s were hectic years for the South. Desegregation of schools had proceeded so deliberately that by 1960 only 6 percent of the region's black students attended integrated classes.[11] Blacks began to press matters with direct-action strategies, engaging in lunch-counter sit-ins in 1960 and "freedom rides" (with some whites) to integrate buses and bus terminals in 1961. In January, 1961, Charlayne Hunter and Hamilton Holmes entered the University of Georgia. Riots resulted. On September 30, 1962, James Meredith enrolled at the University of Mississippi. Federal marshals were unable to control the ensuing violence, two deaths occurred, and President Kennedy sent federal troops that remained for several months.

In June, 1963, after the end of Senator Carter's first legislative session in Atlanta, Governor George Wallace symbolically blocked the schoolhouse door before standing aside, in the presence of federal officers, to allow Vivian Malone and James Hood to enroll at the University of Ala-

11. Lester A. Sobel (ed.), *Civil Rights, 1960–1966* (New York, 1967), 40.

bama. Even Carter's home county felt the impact of the civil rights movement in areas other than school desegregation. In July, 1963, blacks in Americus mounted a voter registration drive and soon expanded it to demand desegregation of a movie theater and other public facilities. Officials arrested twenty-five demonstrators. On the national scene, Martin Luther King, Jr., Atlanta born and bred, addressed not only the approximately 250,000 citizens who marched on Washington for racial justice in August, 1963, but indeed the entire country, from the Lincoln Memorial.

In January, 1964, as Carter began his second session in Georgia's General Assembly, a major civil rights bill worked its way through Congress, with the sponsorship of the new president, Lyndon Johnson, a native son of the Old Confederacy. In May and June, as Carter participated in a special session called to draft a new constitution and a new election code for Georgia, Congress debated what became the Civil Rights Act of 1964. Blacks, focusing on passage of this law and on reelecting President Johnson, tempered their demonstrations. In November a majority of whites in South Carolina, Georgia, Alabama, Mississippi, and Louisiana voted against their fellow southerner, giving Goldwater the only electoral votes he received outside his home state of Arizona.

Judging from accounts in the Americus *Times-Recorder* and the Atlanta *Constitution*, Carter had spent his first two-year term in Atlanta quietly learning the ropes and serving his constituents. In November, 1964, the same 14th District voters who deserted the Democratic presidential nominee split their votes and returned Carter, unopposed in the Democratic primary and in the general election, to a second term in the state senate. Again judging from newspaper accounts, Carter was incomparably more vigorous and publicity-conscious in his second term, and education was his chief legislative interest. Yet apparently he did not depart radically from the norms of the senate, for his colleagues in 1965 named him one of the five most outstanding senators. Carter's career as a senator was a part-time one (regular annual sessions were only about two months long), leaving him time to continue certain of his former public service activities and to add new ones. Most notable among his new activities were organizing the West Central Georgia Area Planning and Development Commission (now the Middle Flint APDC) and the Georgia Planning Association. Characteristically, he served as chairman of one and president of the other.

While Carter was making a name for himself in southwest Georgia and in Atlanta, a bill which would become the Voting Rights Act of 1965 was introduced in Congress. Blacks demonstrated for their rights even as the Congress debated the specific shape this particular bill should take. In Selma, King launched an Alabama-wide drive to register black voters. In the ensuing turmoil, a black Alabamian, Jimmie Lee Jackson, and a white Unitarian minister from Boston, James Reeb, were killed. In March, King led the famous march from Selma to Montgomery, following which a white Detroit civil rights worker and mother of five, Mrs. Viola Gregg Liuzzo, was killed. With such sacrifices the protest at Selma advanced the Voting Rights Act and the larger cause of which it was a crucial event and symbol.[12]

In the summer of 1965, race relations in Americus reached the crisis stage, as perhaps they did in America as a whole. On July 20, four black Americus women refused to leave a voting line marked "White Women Only." White officials promptly arrested and jailed them. The Americus Merchants Association recommended formation of a biracial committee, and twenty-five white businessmen, supported by the Americus Junior Chamber of Commerce, attended a civil rights rally "in the interests of harmony." County Attorney Warren Fortson participated in the biracial committee, but other political leaders, including Senator Carter, apparently avoided making a public stand. Blacks held demonstrations and vigils outside the jail and on July 28 began to picket white stores. A white youth was killed "when stones were thrown by a group of whites at a passing car driven by a Negro and shots were allegedly fired from the car."[13] On Sunday, August 1, small, integrated groups of blacks and whites tried to attend services at the First Baptist Church and the First Methodist Church. Members of the two churches turned them away.

On August 4, Governor Sanders called for mediation of the Americus conflict. Warren Fortson "called an informal biracial committee to a meeting" on the same day, but Mayor T. Griffin Walker "announced that he and other city and county officials did not support the committee." Nevertheless, on August 6, Sumter County officials appointed three black voting clerks. On the same day, by coincidence, President Johnson signed the Voting Rights Act, and Dick Gregory arrived in Americus to help round up voters. By August 9, this effort had registered 647, bringing total black registration in Sumter County to approximately 1,700 compared with approximately 7,000 white registered voters—with roughly equal numbers of blacks and whites in the county. Two weeks

12. David J. Garrow, *Protest at Selma: Martin Luther King, Jr., and the Voting Rights Act of 1965* (New Haven, 1978).
13. Sobel (ed.), *Civil Rights*, 322–24; quotations and some of the facts in this paragraph and the next also come from this source.

later, three blacks entered the formerly all-white Americus high school. Desegregation would not be easy, but for Americus and Sumter County the crisis was past.

Other events, near and far, were intertwined with those in Americus. On Sunday night, August 1, following the integrated group's effort to attend Americus churches that morning, the deacons of Plains Baptist Church—some ten miles to the west—met and agreed to ask the congregation to "instruct" ushers not to seat "agitators" for worship services.[14] Deacon Jimmy Carter was absent. On August 11, as things quieted down in Americus, a riot broke out in the Watts area of Los Angeles. Raging for five days, the violence caused an estimated thirty-four deaths and more than $40 million in property damage.[15] On August 15, in the midst of media coverage of the Watts conflagration, the Plains Baptist congregation met to vote on the "instruction" proposed two weeks before. Carter "asked the church to reject his fellow deacons' proposal and permit entry of any blacks who seemed to sincerely want to worship."[16] His plea failed, the congregation voting 54–6 to approve the deacons' request. Jimmy and Rosalynn Carter, sons Chip and Jeff, Jimmy's mother, Lillian Carter, and Homer Harris, a local farmer, were the six "no" votes.

During Carter's two terms in the Georgia Senate, the Supreme Court (through *Baker* v. *Carr, Reynolds* v. *Sims*, etc.), Congress (with the Civil Rights Act of 1964 and the Voting Rights Act of 1965), two presidents (Kennedy and Johnson), plus King and the civil rights movement, compelled the South to begin moving toward national norms of race relations. Carter was personally courageous and perhaps politically farsighted to challenge his own church congregation in the summer of 1965 on a race issue. The South's white politicians did not generally, in that season of change, act in such a manner, and it would have been suicidal for Jimmy Carter to do in the political arena anything comparable with what he did in his church. Ancient features of politics continued to shape most politicians' behavior.

In January, 1966, Carter returned to Atlanta for his fourth regular legislative session. In March, after completing it, he announced that he would seek the Democratic nomination for Congress from the 3rd District. This was an inviting race, since it was widely believed that the incumbent, Howard "Bo" Callaway, would run for governor. Callaway,

14. James Hefley and Marti Hefley, *The Church that Produced a President* (New York, 1977), 157–58.
15. Sobel (ed.), *Civil Rights*, 306.
16. Hefley and Hefley, *The Church that Produced a President*, 158.

elected in the 1964 reaction against President Johnson as Georgia's first Republican congressman since Reconstruction, seemed a good bet to lead a renascent Georgia Republican party into the executive office. If Callaway should decide to run for governor, Carter would have an excellent chance at election to Congress. But this was a race Carter was never to make.

GUBERNATORIAL CANDIDATE: 1966 AND 1970

On May 6, Calloway announced that he would run for governor. Then, on May 18, former governor Vandiver, the leading Democratic candidate, withdrew from the Democratic primary race. It was like dropping a bombshell on the Georgia Democratic party. When the smoke cleared, former governor Ellis Arnall ("tainted" by executive service in Washington and by association with national Democrats) and some half a dozen other candidates were running. Among them was Carter, who had decided to aim for governor rather than for Congress.

Given the unusual circumstances of 1966, Carter's attempt made sense, and he nearly pulled it off. As it happened, another political unknown, Lester Maddox, took an early lead in the opinion polls, barely held off Carter's fast-closing challenge for second place in the first Democratic primary (Arnall, 231,480 votes [29.4 percent]; Maddox, 185,672 [23.5 percent]; Carter, 164,562 [20.9 percent]), and defeated Arnall in the runoff Democratic primary. Considering Arnall's weakness in the runoff (Maddox, 443,055 votes; Arnall, 373,004), Carter might have been the nominee had he edged out Maddox in the first primary. And considering Callaway's and Maddox's inconclusive campaigns in the general election (Callaway, 453,665 votes; Maddox, 450,626 votes; Arnall, 51,497 write-in votes), which threw the election into the Democratic General Assembly, Carter if nominated might have been elected. Instead, Georgia suffered four years of Maddox's demagoguery, which was a mere shadow, at that, of George Wallace's in neighboring Alabama.

Within a few months of his primary loss, Carter quietly geared up his marathon campaign to become governor in 1970. Campaigning during 1967, 1968, and 1969 was a matter of speaking before men's clubs, church groups, and whoever else would give him the opportunity, and of building and maintaining contacts with hundreds of public officials in the counties, towns, and cities across Georgia.

Meanwhile, shots punctuated events, as Martin Luther King, Jr., and Robert F. Kennedy went down. The Vietnam War tore the nation apart.

George Wallace mounted a surprisingly strong presidential campaign, and the liberal wing of the national Democratic party came under increasing criticism. Richard Nixon became president. Lester Maddox appeared on television to tell the nation that what Georgia's prison system needed was a better class of prisoner. Almost unnoticed, desegregation of schools made great progress across the South. Southern blacks registered, voted, and with increasing frequency placed blacks in state legislatures and local offices.

Meanwhile, former governor Carl Sanders—who would be Carter's major opponent in 1970—flourished in Atlanta's legal community, representing the Georgia Power Company, Coca-Cola, and other corporate clients. Occasionally he visited with Hubert Humphrey or some other liberal national Democrat passing through Atlanta. In 1970, when he announced that he would run again, most of the established forces in Georgia politics supported him. Opinion polls showed that despite Jimmy Carter's impressive race against Arnall and Maddox in 1966, only a minority of Georgians recognized his name. The now-splintered Georgia Democratic party would field many candidates in the 1970 primary and Sanders looked a sure winner.

Carter surprised the field. He had already positioned himself in the center of Georgia's conservative political spectrum, using modern polling techniques to calibrate his stands, and he had built a stronger base of goodwill and support than his competitors imagined. In the closing months he adroitly adopted the posture of a "redneck" (a mild variety, to be sure) and characterized Sanders as liberal, well-to-do, and out of touch with the average Georgian. Carter, moreover, worked incredibly hard at "pressing the flesh." In the first primary he captured 388,280 votes (48.6 percent) to Sanders' 301,659 (37.8 percent). Simultaneously, only 107,555 voters participated in the Republican primary, nominating Hal Suit. The Democratic runoff primary was a breeze, with Carter taking 506,462 votes (59.4 percent) to Sanders' 345,906 (40.6 percent). In November, Carter defeated Suit by 620,419 votes (59.3 percent) to 424,983 (40.7 percent).

A great deal of foolishness has been written about the gubernatorial elections of 1966 and 1970, some of it by Carter himself. The lesson those elections offer to anyone who will study them is that an intelligent, hardworking politician could, in those troubled years, exploit the factionalism characteristic of Georgia politics and, with merely a trace of demagoguery, win the governorship. Other promising southern politi-

cians who, like Carter, won their states' governorships in 1970 included
Reubin Askew in Florida, Dale Bumpers in Arkansas, Winfield Dunn (a
Republican) in Tennessee, and John West in South Carolina.

Carter's career from his return to Plains in 1953 to his election as governor in 1970 may be interpreted in different ways. But there can be no
doubt that the Supreme Court, the president, the Congress, and the civil
rights movement lifted most of the onus of change from the shoulders of
individual southern politicians and that Carter from 1953 to 1970 experienced much good fortune. He also displayed much political skill, a
quality Henry Jackson, Hubert Humphrey, Morris Udall, and finally
Gerald Ford were to discover in 1976.

GOVERNOR: 1971–1975

For fifteen years or so, a changing southern politics had influenced Jimmy
Carter's political career. Indeed, its roiling currents had carried him
along and had helped lift him to the governorship. Now he was in a position to influence events, to influence not only the direction of Georgia
politics but of southern politics as well.

In a departure from tradition, he named a black educator, Dr. Tom
Jenkins, to the three-member Board of Pardons and Paroles on December
17, 1970, even before he took office. At his inauguration, after the all-
black Morris Brown College choir sang "The Battle Hymn of the Republic," Carter told his audience that "the time for racial discrimination is
over."

> At the end of a long campaign, I believe I know our people as well as any-
> one. Based on this knowledge of Georgians—north and south, rural and urban,
> liberal and conservative—I say to you quite frankly that the time for racial dis-
> crimination is over. Our people have already made this major and difficult de-
> cision, but we cannot underestimate the challenge of hundreds of minor deci-
> sions yet to be made. Our inherent human charity and our religious beliefs will
> be taxed to the limit. No poor, rural, weak, or black person should ever have
> to bear the additional burden of being deprived of the opportunity of an edu-
> cation, a job, or simple justice. We Georgians are fully capable of making our
> judgments and managing our own affairs. We who are strong or in positions
> of leadership must realize that the responsibility for making correct decisions
> in the future is ours. As Governor, I will never shirk this responsibility.[17]

Many white Georgians were disappointed in Carter's inaugural statement. "He ran as a conservative," they said, "when he was really a lib-

17. Frank Daniel (comp.), *Addresses of Jimmy Carter, Governor of Georgia, 1971–
1975* (Atlanta, 1975), 79–81.

eral." But other whites were happy enough to exchange Lester Maddox for Jimmy Carter, as were the 20–25 percent of the electorate who were black. Carter's treatment by the national media was unambiguously positive. Roger Mudd included him alongside Askew, Bumpers, and West on his special entitled "New Voices in the South" (March 9, 1971), and *Time* magazine put his picture on its cover to exemplify the same theme (May 31, 1971). So what in-state support Carter may have lost through his inaugural speech was offset by a gain in national attention.

Racial events during the early months of his term tested Carter's mettle. At one point a group of black protestors seized the Appropriations Committee room in the Capitol. Carter intervened in person and negotiated their grievances. When blacks and whites in Hancock County began to arm themselves with rifles and submachine guns over racial conflicts, Carter first sent an aide to deal with the matter and then went himself. He established a state Human Relations Committee to deal with issues and problems before they reached a crisis stage, and when incidents did occur, Carter used a recently created and specially trained four-man Civil Disorders Unit in the Department of Public Safety.

Carter continued his appointment of blacks, to the Board of Regents of the university system, for example, and encouraged the employment of blacks throughout state government. He arranged to hang portraits of Martin Luther King, Jr., and two Georgia black leaders from the nineteenth century, Lucy Laney and Bishop Henry McNeal Turner, in the State Capitol. On the day of the portrait hangings, Sunday, February 17, 1974, the Ku Klux Klan "helped" him, as he expressed it, "by marching around the Capitol."[18] Exploiting his role as state party leader and capitalizing on the national party's delegate selection reforms, Carter also guided the selection of an integrated delegation to the 1972 Democratic National Convention in Miami.

The crucial test in Georgia politics of Carter's anti–Jim Crow policy would come at the end of his single term as governor, in the 1974 gubernatorial election, when candidates dealt with the conservative backlash this policy occasioned. Candidates George Busbee and Bert Lance (who would later head the Office of Management and Budget for Carter in Washington), openly sought the votes of blacks and came in second and third to Lester Maddox in the first Democratic primary (Maddox, 310,384 votes [36.3 percent]; Busbee, 177,997 [20.8 percent]; Lance, 147,026 [17.2 percent]). Busbee trounced Maddox in the Democratic

18. Interview with Governor Carter, December 30, 1974.

runoff (551,106 votes [59.9 percent] to 369,608 [40.1 percent]) and beat
the Republican, Ronnie Thompson, in the general election (646,777
votes [69.1 percent] to 289,113 [30.9 percent]). Even in the aftermath of
George McGovern's electoral disaster, Georgia Democrats under Carter's leadership had integrated blacks without losing whites.

From the moment he was elected, Jimmy Carter was as active as circumstances permitted in national as well as in state politics. He participated in a November, 1970, seminar for governors-elect sponsored by
the National Governors Conference, remarking to newsmen that "if either party attempts to write off the South it will be a fatal mistake."[19] In
March, 1971, at the Democratic Governors Caucus, Carter was a member of a special committee working with Chairman Lawrence O'Brien to
strengthen the role of state officials in the national party structure. (At
the same meeting, Governors Carter, Askew, Bumpers, Hall [Oklahoma],
and West agreed to withhold commitments from candidates seeking the
nomination.) In June, as the Democratic Governors Caucus met again,
Carter was "hoping," according to newspaper accounts, "to help lead a
solid front of Democratic governors in playing a major role in selecting
the nominees at the 1972 convention."[20] At the November Southern
Governors Conference in Atlanta, the chairman, John Bell Williams of
Mississippi, said that Alabama Governor George Wallace, Congressman
Wilbur Mills, and Senator Henry Jackson were the only potential Democratic presidential contenders acceptable to the South. Carter added Senators Hubert Humphrey and Edmund Muskie, "provided that both run
'less liberal campaigns than they are now conducting.' "[21]

Carter's energetic pre-primary efforts were of little effect in the 1972
campaign. George McGovern took the lead in the primaries and held it,
despite his lack of support from southern states. Carter joined the "Stop
McGovern" movement. In late May he vowed, "We are going to stop
him," and in late June he announced that he would work to prevent Mc-
Govern's nomination on the first ballot. Few observers noticed, then or
later, that the Carters entertained McGovern and his wife overnight at the
Governor's Mansion in Atlanta just prior to the 1972 convention.[22]
Otherwise, reporters in 1976 might not have accepted his aides' claim
that their approach to McGovern four years earlier in pursuit of the vice-

19. Carter's role in the events here reported was covered by the Atlanta *Constitution*
(called, on Sunday, the Atlanta *Journal and Constitution*), November 29, 1970, Sec. A, p. 1.
20. *Ibid.*, June 22, 1971, Sec. A, p. 1.
21. *Ibid.*, November 8, 1971, Sec. A, p. 1.
22. *Ibid.*, June 27, 1972, Sec. A, p. 1.

presidential nomination had been naïve or half-hearted. McGovern's first choice, as he told this writer in 1982, was Askew, but Askew would not take it. In retrospect, McGovern concedes Carter would have been a good choice.[23] Given Carter's role in the "Stop McGovern" movement, however, McGovern went elsewhere for his running mate, to Senator Eagleton in Missouri, then Sargent Shriver when Eagleton stepped aside in the controversy over his emotional stability.

Whether the Democrats would have done any better against Nixon with Carter running for the second spot is a question thoughtful historians may pose. They probably would have still lost. But conceivably they might have won, particularly since the disastrous mishandling of the Eagleton affair would have been avoided. In any event, Carter's serious drive for the presidency began on the heels of the 1972 convention. For Jimmy Carter, the outcome of his efforts to play a role in the presidential politics of his party from November, 1970, to July, 1972, turned out to be the condition of his success in 1976. (Although it is not a perfect parallel, one is reminded of John F. Kennedy in 1956 and 1960).

Carter's anti–Jim Crow policy (as it is called here) and his effort to find a leadership role in the national Democratic party took only a fraction of his time. Indeed, these things were mostly obscured by battles with legislators and others over his program for reorganizing Georgia's executive branch. Displaying a "pragmatic temperament" and an "unorthodox legislative style" which Gary Fink has described in excellent detail,[24] Carter not only achieved the major part of his executive branch reorganization but also facilitated a reorganization of judicial administration, appointed uniformly acclaimed judges, established the Georgia Heritage Trust Fund, defeated the Corps of Engineers' Spewrell Bluff Dam project, and brought trade and investment to Georgia from other states and from abroad. None of Carter's substantial accomplishments was carried through to perfection or to everyone's satisfaction. Government policy never is. Yet Jimmy Carter showed, at least as well as Carl Sanders before him, that a Georgia governor did not have to be a demagogue and could be competent.

By January, 1975, when Jimmy Carter completed the single term then permitted Georgia governors, the Solid South was long gone from national politics and Jim Crow was flying to join the auk and the dodo.

23. Conversation with author, February 24, 1982, and George McGovern to author, July 26, 1982.

24. Gary M. Fink, *Prelude to the Presidency: The Political Character and Legislative Leadership Style of Governor Jimmy Carter* (Westport, Conn., 1980), quotations from pp. 13, 166.

Georgia's per capita personal income had reached 85 percent of the national average, and blacks, reversing their pattern of emigration, were returning to the South, participating in the Sunbelt phenomenon. Carter had contributed to these developments, perhaps most importantly through the political collaboration he engineered between blacks and whites. In so doing, he had built a record that would help in his campaign for the presidency, which few realized had already begun two and one-half years earlier, shortly after his vice-presidential bid had failed at the 1972 Democratic convention.

PRESIDENTIAL CANDIDATE AND PRESIDENT: 1972–1981

When Jimmy Carter formally announced in the fall of 1974 that he was running for president, most political observers scoffed at his presumption. Some scholars understood the national implications of the sweeping changes that had occurred in the South during the quarter-century since World War II. In his 1972 introduction to *The Changing Politics of the South*, William Havard cautiously suggested that "the South [might] preserve the distinctive qualities of its subculture and even use these qualities . . . to reconcile the races on a basis of equality," providing "an example for the national environment."[25] To the extent that this was true, a southern candidate who understood and projected this reality stood to profit. By the time Jack Bass and Walter DeVries published *The Transformation of Southern Politics* in 1976,[26] Carter was rampaging through the Democratic primaries and seemed entitled to the graceful bow they gave him in their conclusion. But their very cautious expectations indicated that only a victorious southern candidate could fully express southern politics' new opportunity. In November of 1972, the once solidly Democratic South joined the rest of America (except for Massachusetts and Washington, D.C.), in preferring the Republican candidate, Richard Nixon. Following his party's defeat, Jimmy Carter was among the governors who worked to replace Jean Westwood with Robert Strauss as chairman of the Democratic National Committee.[27] At the Democratic Governors Conference in April, 1973, Strauss named Carter to chair the party's 1974 Campaign Committee. Carter took the assignment seriously and used it not only to

25. William C. Havard (ed.), *The Changing Politics of the South* (Baton Rouge, 1972), 35–36. Other useful works on southern politics in change are Monroe Lee Billington, *The Political South in the Twentieth Century* (New York, 1975), and Numan V. Bartley and Hugh D. Graham, *Southern Politics and the Second Reconstruction* (Baltimore, 1975).

26. Jack Bass and Walter DeVries, *The Transformation of Southern Politics: Social Change and Political Consequence Since 1945* (New York, 1976).

27. Atlanta *Journal and Constitution*, December 3, 1972, Sec. A, p. 20.

help elect Democrats to Congress but also to accumulate political obligations. He also exploited the convention business of Atlanta, which was rapidly becoming one of the nation's largest convention cities, to gain exposure before many groups (and to build up mailing lists in many states). And he expanded his national contacts through continued attendance at the various governors conferences, through testimony before congressional committees, and through membership on the Trilateral Commission, often with an eye to publicity in newspapers and magazines. So the political columnists who in 1976 wrote that Jimmy Carter came out of nowhere were insensitive to the changes in southern and national politics and unmindful of Carter's tactics from 1972 on. Carter by 1976 had simply stolen a march — a long march, at that — on his rivals.

By his showing during the early caucuses and primaries of 1976, in Iowa (Carter, 27 percent; Bayh, 13 percent; others, 22 percent; uncommitted, 37 percent) and in New Hampshire (Carter, 29 percent; Udall, 24 percent; Bayh, 16 percent; Harris, 11 percent; Shriver, 9 percent), for instance, Carter proved that a southerner could do well outside the South. And by defeating George Wallace in Florida (Carter, 448,844 votes [34.5 percent]; Wallace, 396,820 [30.5 percent]; Jackson, 310,944 [23.9 percent]), he proved that a regional son of modern temperament could win in the South. Soon, despite the "Stop Carter" effort (which so resembled the 1972 "Stop McGovern" effort Carter had joined), the nomination was his. Like McGovern in 1972, Carter often overwhelmed regular state party organizations with his personal state party organizations, built much on the model of personal factions in southern state politics. Unlike McGovern, Carter avoided characterization as an extreme liberal. Indeed, by saying that he was a fiscal conservative and a civil rights liberal, he avoided both extremes and provided a poor political target for foes. In the euphoria of the New York convention in July, Carter looked like an easy winner in November, but he took no chances. He balanced his party's ticket with Walter Mondale, a liberal senator from the Midwest much better established than he with the Democratic party elite.

With the 1976 Democratic National Convention, if not before, southern politics rejoined the tumultuous American mainstream. Even if Carter and the Democrats had lost in November, the South would hardly have diverged again into a separate channel. But of course they won, if narrowly, over Ford and the Republicans (Carter, 40,831,000 [50.1 percent], 297 electoral votes; Ford 39,148,000 [48.0 percent], 240 electoral votes). All the southern states, except Virginia, were back in the Democratic camp in 1976, contributing 118 of the party's 297 electoral votes. Over the prior half-dozen years Carter had helped greatly to bring the South back into compliance with national policies and norms. In 1976 he played a major role in bringing the South back into the Democratic party.

Once Carter reached the White House, the good fortune and skill that had accompanied him from the school board to the presidency seemed to desert him all too often.[28] He surrounded himself with too many Georgians who lacked sufficient experience, he antagonized too many members of Congress, and he changed his mind often enough to seem vacillating or even weak. Double-digit inflation dogged his tracks, accompanied by persistent unemployment and energy problems. Weighing such factors heavily against his stands on human rights, women's rights, and the environment, and ignoring Carter's part in bringing the South back into the party, some Democrats rallied behind Senator Ted Kennedy's attempt to wrench the 1980 presidential nomination from him. They failed, but their move weakened his campaign and eroded the advantages of incumbency. On November 4, 1979, Iranian "students" invaded the United States Embassy in Teheran and took fifty-two Americans hostage. A rescue attempt failed, and Carter's term neared its end with the presidency hostage to an Iranian ayatollah.

In November, 1980, the voters chose Ronald Reagan (43,904,000 votes [50.7 percent]) over Carter (35,484,000 [41.0 percent]) and John Anderson, an independent candidate (5,720,000 [6.6 percent]). The distribution of Reagan's popular vote majority resulted in an electoral college landslide (Reagan, 489; Carter, 49). All southern states except Georgia were in the Republican column, very much in contrast to 1976. These results suggest that southerners were as disappointed in Carter's performance as were other Americans; that Carter had been impartial toward the nation's different regions, showing no special favors to his native South; and that presidential politics were becoming more and more nationalized, with declining regional variations.

Carter's one-term performance was not devoid of redeeming accomplishments. He furthered international concern for human rights and for international trade and cooperation of various kinds, and he greatly enhanced American prestige among African and Latin American peoples. He articulated the need of the poor and powerless for a decent standard of living and the need of everyone for peace. He signed the Panama Canal Treaties, which had eluded his predecessors, consolidated the rapproche-

28. Space does not here permit adequate discussion of the Carter administration's successes and failures.

ment with China which President Nixon had begun, and negotiated a peace treaty at Camp David between Israel and Egypt. When Carter's administration was over, he had expended no lives in military action (with the single exception of the aborted Iranian hostage rescue mission, which cost eight lives), and at the end of his term he saw all the hostages safely home. Americans are forever reassessing their former presidents, and Jimmy Carter's reputation is now improving.

CONCLUSION

On leaving the presidency, Carter said that he was assuming again the nation's highest title, that of citizen.[29] As a world citizen, he promised to speak out on such issues as nuclear disarmament, human rights, and the environment. Yet, in keeping with tradition, he gave the new president time to settle into the office before publicly addressing these matters. Carter occupied a large office on the seventeenth floor of the Richard B. Russell Building in Atlanta. He moved his presidential papers to the Old Post Office Building across the street and established his residence in Plains, where he quickly went to work on a volume of presidential memoirs.

Fifteen or sixteen months after leaving office, with *Keeping Faith* completed, Carter began to speak out, not only on the international issues he had identified in his farewell address, but on national and partisan matters as well. He distinguished his policies from those of his successor, sharply criticizing President Reagan in both domestic and foreign policy areas. Carter supported Mondale in the 1984 presidential race, making an early declaration that may have been provoked by public opinion polls showing Ted Kennedy the favorite candidate among Democrats. As early as the fall of 1982, Carter had told *Time* magazine interviewers he did not believe Kennedy could be elected, a judgment reminiscent of his 1970–1972 decision about McGovern's chances, though then he had spoken only of McGovern's unacceptability among southern voters, arguing that either party would have to win the South to win the presidency. By 1982 Carter spoke on Democratic politics in national rather than merely southern terms, assuming no differences in regional attitudes.

Meanwhile, Carter moved ahead with plans for a presidential library in Atlanta and for a center for policy studies to be sponsored by Emory University and located at the library. As two steps in these plans, Mayor

29. "Farewell Address to the Nation," January 14, 1981, in *Public Papers of the Presidents of the United States, Jimmy Carter, 1980–81* (Washington, D.C., 1982), Book III, pp. 2889–93.

Andrew Young of Atlanta (the former aide to King and former Atlanta congressman who had been Carter's U.N. ambassador), gained the city council's approval in 1982 to locate the library in the city's proposed Great Park, and Carter accepted a part-time appointment to the Emory faculty. Carter has said repeatedly that he did not intend to run again for public office (although his wife, Rosalynn, urged him to enter the Democratic race in 1984) but planned instead to complete his working life at Emory and the policy studies center. The center's work began with consultations and symposia on the Middle East (1983), on disarmament (1984 and 1985), on environment policy (1984), and on health policy (1984). In the fall of 1986, with the buildings completed, the Carter Presidential Center was formally inaugurated. The Carter Center houses, in addition to the library and the policy studies center, the Carter-Menil Human Rights Foundation, Global 2000 (another foundation with field programs already assisting governments in Africa and Asia with the problems of hunger, health, and the environment), and offices for Carter.

Carter himself travels worldwide, conversing with leaders of other countries about the world's problems and the work of the Carter Center. Since the prompt completion of his volume of presidential memoirs, he has written two other books, *The Blood of Abraham* and (with Rosalynn Carter) *Everything to Gain: Making the Most of the Rest of Your Life.* The latter, billed as a kind of how-to-do-it manual for retired people, is also an account of their continuing life together.[30]

Jimmy Carter's activities do not resemble the retirement of most recent former presidents. Instead, they seem to reflect a new stage in the political career of a former president, governor, state senator, and county school board member who, at sixty-two, is still full of energy and ideals. They also reflect ambitious efforts to place the Carter presidency in a favorable light and to use this as a foundation for further accomplishments.

30. Jimmy Carter, *The Blood of Abraham* (Boston, 1985), and Jimmy Carter and Rosalynn Carter, *Everything to Gain: Making the Most of the Rest of Your Life* (New York, 1987).

Black Politics and the Voting Rights Act, 1965–1982

RICHARD L. ENGSTROM

I don't trust white people in the South with my rights. I didn't before the [Voting Rights] Act; I don't seventeen years later.

— Vernon Jordan, president of the
National Urban League, before
the Subcommittee on Civil and
Constitutional Rights of the
House Judiciary Committee,
May 6, 1981

Voting in elections within the South is often severely polarized along racial lines. This is especially the case when black candidates and white candidates compete for the same offices.[1] When voting is racially divided, the rules under which electoral competition is structured and winners determined are a major determinant of whether minority voters are able to elect the candidates of their choice. As long as race remains a significant division within southern politics, the problem of racial discrimination within the region's electoral systems will remain an important political and legal issue.

The extent to which racial discrimination remains, or might reappear, in the southern electoral process was the central question faced by the 97th Congress (1981–1982) when it had to decide whether or not to continue the special protections against electoral discrimination contained in the Voting Rights Act. These protections apply primarily to the South

---

1. James W. Loewen, associate professor of sociology, University of Vermont, in *Hearings Before Subcommittee on Civil and Constitutional Rights of the House Committee on the Judiciary on Extension of the Voting Rights Act.*, 97th Cong., 1st Sess., 269. (Hereinafter cited as *House Hearings.*) See also Richard Murray and Arnold Vedlitz, "Racial Voting Patterns in the South: An Analysis of Major Elections in Five Cities," *Annals of American Academy of Political and Social Science*, CDXXXIX (September, 1978), 29–39.

and have been the major stimulus behind the black political advances within the region. They had been adopted initially in 1965, though only as *temporary* provisions to be in effect for five years. In 1970 Congress extended them for another five years, and in 1975 for another seven. Without further congressional action, they would have expired on August 6, 1982. Few issues have focused as directly on the question of how much southern politics has really changed than whether or not these provisions needed to be extended again in 1982.

Opponents of extension argued that the special provisions were no longer necessary. Stressing the theme of change, they argued that the South had shed its racist past and no longer needed to be singled out for special treatment. It was time, according to one congressman, for the region to be let out of "the penalty box."[2] Proponents of extension, however, focused upon the theme of continuity, and like Vernon Jordan (see epigraph), argued that southern whites still could not be trusted to keep the political system open to blacks. If federal oversight were withdrawn, history would repeat itself. Analogies frequently were drawn to the Compromise of 1877, when the soon-to-be-president Rutherford B. Hayes agreed to withdraw federal troops from the South in return for the region's electoral votes. This brought the end of Reconstruction and the return of politics "for whites only." If special federal protection were again lifted, it was argued, what had become known as the "Second Reconstruction" would also end, and blacks would again be vulnerable to racially discriminatory electoral schemes.

The continuity thesis proved dominant, for the 97th Congress—by a vote of 389 to 12 in the House of Representatives and 85 to 8 in the Senate—not only extended but also strengthened the Voting Rights Act. The special provisions were extended this time for another twenty-five years, although a more liberal (yet still demanding) procedure for permitting certain state and local governments to be released from them was added. In addition, civil rights forces won a major victory when Congress amended another part of the act to "overrule" a recent Supreme Court decision that was extremely unpopular with voting-rights attorneys. The Court in 1980 had held that plaintiffs alleging voting-rights violations could win their cases only if the discrimination was shown to be intentional.[3] This "intent" standard had been widely criticized by civil rights activists as an exceedingly burdensome and irrelevant evidentiary requirement, and they succeeded in persuading Congress to amend a previ-

2. Remarks of Congressman Henry J. Hyde (R-Ill.), *House Hearings*, 3.
3. *City of Mobile* v. *Bolden*, 446 U.S. 55 (1980), hereinafter cited as *Mobile* v. *Bolden*.

ously little-used and relatively unimportant portion of the act, section two, to make evidence of the discriminatory "effects" of an electoral scheme or procedure sufficient to establish a violation. Despite earlier expressing objections to this revision of section two, President Reagan on June 29, 1982, signed the amendments to the act.

The following examines what might be called the old and the new Voting Rights Acts. After reviewing the various provisions of the act prior to 1982 and examining the impact they have had on the racial dimension of southern politics, the focus will shift to the changes in the act that have resulted from the most recent congressional action and the expressed reasons for those changes.

THE VOTING RIGHTS ACT AND SOUTHERN POLITICS

The Voting Rights Act has frequently been described as the most effective civil rights legislation ever passed by Congress. It was initially adopted in 1965 after three previous acts aimed (at least partially) at combatting disfranchisement in the South had proved to be largely ineffectual. These acts—the Civil Rights Acts of 1957, 1960, and 1964—had attempted to strengthen federal judicial enforcement of the Fifteenth Amendment's prohibition against racially based interference with the right to vote.[4] They had empowered the United States attorney general to initiate litigation on behalf of southern blacks and authorized federal district courts, upon findings of voter discrimination in local communities, to appoint "voting referees" to register black people in those areas. This litigation-oriented approach provided little relief for disfranchised blacks, however. The cases were onerous to prepare, tended to proceed through the judicial process slowly, and often were heard by southern federal judges who had little sympathy for the plaintiffs' cases.[5] Progress in the voting-rights area was exceedingly slow. By March, 1965, the percentage of voting-age blacks actually registered in the South was still only 35.5, compared with 73.4 percent of the voting-age whites. This figure varied across the Old Confederacy, however, and in the Deep South it reached as low as 6.9 percent in Mississippi and 19.3 percent in neighboring Alabama (see Table 1). After Alabama authorities that same month responded with violence against voting-rights demonstrators in

4. The Fifteenth Amendment, ratified in 1870, states: "(1) The rights of citizens of the United States to vote shall not be denied or abridged by the United States or by any state on account of race, color, or previous condition of servitude. (2) The Congress shall have power to enforce this article by appropriate legislation."

5. See, for example, Charles V. Hamilton, *The Bench and the Ballot: Southern Federal Judges and Black Voters* (New York, 1973).

TABLE 1
Voter Registration by Race, March, 1965

	Percentage of Voting-Age Population Registered	
State	Nonwhite	White
Alabama	19.3	69.2
Arkansas	40.4	65.5
Florida	51.2	74.8
Georgia	27.4	62.6
Louisiana	31.6	80.5
Mississippi	6.7	69.9
North Carolina	46.8	96.8
South Carolina	37.3	75.7
Tennessee	69.5	72.9
Texas	—	—
Virginia	38.3	61.1
Totals	35.5	73.4

SOURCE: United States Commission on Civil Rights, *Political Participation* (Washington, D.C., 1968), 222–23. Data for Texas were not available.

Selma (violence vividly captured by the national news media), patience with the slow pace of progress was exhausted; in August Congress passed and President Lyndon Johnson signed a new act which took a dramatically different approach to the problem, the 1965 Voting Rights Act.[6]

The Southern Focus

The heart of the Voting Rights Act has been the special provisions directed at the voting-rights problem in the South. These provisions authorized the Justice Department to take new administrative actions to remedy the problem, bypassing the southern judiciary in the process. The provisions were applicable to any state, or political subdivision within a state, that satisfied two conditions. The first was that the state or local unit had maintained (as of November 1, 1964) a "test or device" as a prerequisite for voting or registering to vote. The definition of "test or device" was any requirement that a person seeking to vote "(1) demonstrate

6. For a thorough review of the events leading to the passage of the act, see David J. Garrow, *Protest at Selma: Martin Luther King, Jr., and the Voting Rights Act of 1965* (New Haven, 1978).

the ability to read, write, understand, or interpret any matter, (2) demonstrate any educational achievement or his knowledge of any particular subject, (3) possess good moral character, or (4) prove his qualifications by the voucher of registered voters or members of any other class." The second condition was that within the state or local jurisdiction less than half of the voting-age population was registered to vote as of November 7, 1964, *or* actually cast ballots in the 1964 presidential election. The determination as to whether the first condition was satisfied was to be made by the attorney general, the second by the director of the census, and both determinations were explicitly exempted from review by the judiciary. Coverage was therefore "automatic," and most of the South would be included, as had been clearly intended. Captured by this coverage formula were the entire states of Alabama, Georgia, Louisiana, Mississippi, South Carolina, and Virginia, and most (forty counties) of North Carolina. Arkansas, Florida, Tennessee, and Texas, generally considered part of the "rim" or "peripheral South" despite having been part of the Confederacy, escaped the federal net.[7]

This coverage formula triggered the special provisions of the act. One was a prohibition against any further use of any aforementioned "test or device." Another authorized the attorney general to have federal examiners sent into covered jurisdictions to register voters. The dispatching of examiners no longer required a prior judicial finding of discrimination but could now be done if the attorney general received what he considered to be meritorious complaints about voting discrimination from at least twenty residents of a political subdivision or if the attorney general himself determined that examiners were needed in order to enforce voting rights in that area. The attorney general was also authorized to have federal observers sent into the same areas as the examiners. These officers were to observe whether people entitled to vote were in fact permitted to vote and also whether the votes were being tabulated properly; they were then to report to the examiner and the attorney general.

The final special provision (section five) was a "preclearance" requirement that applied to all subsequent efforts by these jurisdictions to change their electoral laws and regulations. Any time a covered jurisdiction attempted to adopt "any voting qualification or prerequisite to voting, or standard, practice, or procedure with respect to voting" which was different from that in effect on November 1, 1964, the change could not be implemented until it was first cleared in Washington, D.C. Clearance could

---

7. Also captured by the coverage formula were Alaska, four counties in Arizona, and a single county in both Hawaii and Idaho.

Richard L. Engstrom

be attained through either the attorney general or a three-judge panel of the federal district court in Washington and was to be granted only upon a determination that the change had neither a discriminatory *purpose* nor a discriminatory *effect*. This provision was a direct response to the "legislate and litigate" strategy that had often been employed within the South. After federal courts struck down discriminatory barriers to voting, it was not uncommon for southern governments simply to adopt new, equally discriminatory devices. The result was perpetual litigation and minimal gains in black registration.[8] The electoral systems within the covered states and local subdivisions were now, however, effectively frozen and could not be changed without federal approval.

These provisions represented a dramatic new use of federal power within the region, and not surprisingly, their legality was challenged immediately. By January, 1966, the United States Supreme Court was hearing arguments by the southern states that these extraordinary, "regional" measures were unconstitutional. That Congress had exceeded its powers when it enacted them and that they impermissibly encroached upon the domain of the states and violated the equality among states within the federal system were just two of a host of arguments marshaled against them. The Court, however, rebuffed all attacks on the legislation and found the coverage formula to be "rational in both theory and practice." Each element of the formula was considered reasonably related to the problem being addressed: "Tests and devices are relevant to voting discrimination because of their long history as a tool for perpetrating the evil; a low voting rate is pertinent for the obvious reason that widespread disenfranchisement must inevitably affect the number of actual voters." As for the admittedly "stringent remedies" triggered by the formula, each was considered "a valid means of carrying out the commands of the Fifteenth Amendment." Only Justice Hugo Black, a native of Alabama and previously a staunch protector of the right to vote, sided with the opponents of the legislation, objecting to the southern states being treated as if they were "conquered provinces."[9]

As noted above, these special provisions were initially thought of as temporary measures to be dismantled once blacks were successfully integrated into the southern political process. The first scheduled expiration date was August 6, 1970, at which time a jurisdiction would be released from coverage if it could convince a three-judge panel of the federal district court in Washington, D.C., that it had not used a "test or device"

8. See William C. Havard (ed.), *The Changing Politics of the South* (Baton Rouge, 1972), 19.

9. *South Carolina* v. *Katzenbach*, 383 U.S. 301, 330, 308, 337, 360 (1966).

with either the purpose or the effect of discriminating against blacks for the preceding five years. Given that the use of these tests or devices had been suspended for five years in all jurisdictions covered by the act, these jurisdictions would meet the "bailout" criterion on August 6, 1970.

In 1970 Congress decided to continue the special provisions for another five years and therefore amended the bailout criterion to ten years without a discriminatory test or device. It also expanded the coverage formula to capture states or political subdivisions that, as of November 7, 1968, were using one of the specified tests or devices and in which less than half of the voting-age population was either registered to vote on that same date or had actually voted in the 1968 presidential election. No additional southern areas were captured by this revision, but three populous counties within the city of New York (Bronx, Kings, and New York) were now brought under the special provisions.[10]

The special provisions were extended again in 1975 for a seven-year period, when Congress made the bailout criterion seventeen years without a discriminatory test or device. The coverage formula was expanded to include states or political subdivisions which on November 1, 1972, employed a test or device and had less than half of its voting-age population either registered on that date or casting votes in the 1972 presidential election. This time, however, Congress made another important revision in the formula, to expand coverage of the special provisions to "language minorities" as well as racial minorities. This was done by adding to the list of "tests or devices" for 1972 the conduct of registration and elections in only the English language in states or local subdivisions where more than 5 percent of the voting-age population belonged to a single language minority (either American Indians, Asian Americans, Alaskan natives, or people of Spanish heritage). Specifically, if "any registration or voting notices, forms, instructions, assistance, or other materials or information relating to the electoral process, including ballots," were only in English, that jurisdiction was considered to have employed a "test or device" and therefore satisfied the first condition of the coverage formula. Areas in the South captured by this language-minority trigger were the entire state of Texas, plus five counties in Florida and another county in North Carolina.[11]

10. The revised formula also captured four election districts in Alaska (which had bailed out from its earlier coverage) and a number of local political subdivisions in Wyoming, California, Arizona, Connecticut, New Hampshire, Maine, and Massachusetts. The preclearance requirement applied to changes in the electoral systems of these units after November 1, 1968.

11. Also captured by the new coverage formula were the entire states of Arizona and Alaska and a few local political subdivisions in California, Colorado, Michigan, and South

The Impact of the Special Provisions

The impact that the Voting Rights Act has had on black participation in southern politics can be conceptualized in terms of two distinct phases — the first focusing on the issue of vote *denial,* the second on vote *dilution.* The initial focus was of course on the problem of disfranchisement. For the first few years following adoption of the act, the Department of Justice concentrated its resources on getting black people admitted to the electoral process in the covered jurisdictions, with quite impressive results. By 1967, the percentage of voting-age black people registered to vote within the covered states in the South was estimated to be 52.1, up from 29.3 percent in March of 1965, and not under 50 percent in any of the seven states—a registration of almost 1.8 million blacks (Table 2). This growing black vote, however, soon brought to the surface the problem of vote dilution. Rather than continuing to deny black people access to the ballot, schemes were developed to dilute the impact of the new black voting strength. White people were annexed to cities with substan-

TABLE 2
Black Registered Voters, 1965 and 1967

State	1965	1967	% Increase	% of Voting-Age Population, 1967
Alabama	92,737	248,432	167.9	51.6
Georgia	167,663	322,496	92.3	52.6
Louisiana	164,601	303,148	84.2	58.9
Mississippi	28,500	181,233	535.9	59.8
North Carolina	258,000	277,404	7.5	51.3
South Carolina	138,544	190,017	37.2	51.2
Virginia	144,259	243,000	68.4	55.6
Totals	994,304	1,765,730	77.6	52.1

SOURCE: United States Commission on Civil Rights, *Political Participation* (Washington, D.C., 1968), 222–23.

Dakota. The preclearance provision applied to electoral changes made after November 1, 1972, in these newly covered jurisdictions. The 1975 amendments to the Voting Rights Act also required the use of bilingual electoral material and assistance in numerous areas in the Southwest and West. On these other "language minority" provisions, see David H. Hunter, "The 1975 Voting Rights Act and Language Minorites," *Catholic University Law Review,* XXV (Winter, 1976), 250–70.

tial black populations, for example, and at-large elections were adopted
to replace election by districts. A great variety of dilutive schemes were
employed to limit the ability of black people to convert their new voting
strength into the control of (or at least influence with) elected public officials. By the late 1960s, there was what one commentator has described
as "an epidemic of dilution methods" within the covered jurisdictions.[12]

The dilution issue brought the Voting Rights Act back before the Supreme Court. In the fall of 1968, the Court was hearing complaints by
black citizens of Mississippi objecting to the implementation of three
new laws which they argued affected the electoral process in that state,
but which had not been submitted for federal preclearance as required by
section five. One of the laws allowed county boards of supervisors to be
elected at-large (countywide) rather than through districts, as had been
the practice. Another specified that the superintendent of education in selected counties could no longer be elected but would be appointed by the
county school board. The other involved restricting the requirements for
competing as an independent candidate in the state's general elections.
Attorneys for the state argued that none of these changes affected voter
registration practices and therefore that they were outside the scope of
section five. The Court, however, chose to take a more expansive view of
the section's reach and held that Congress had intended it to apply to
"any state enactment which altered the election law of a covered State *in
even a minor way.*" Specifically noting that "the right to vote can be affected by a dilution of voting power as well as by an absolute prohibition
on casting a ballot," and that electoral arrangements can be manipulated
in ways that will "nullify their [black people's] ability to elect the candidate of their choice just as would prohibiting some of them from voting,"
the Court held that any change affecting the electoral process would have
to receive section five approval. Potentially dilutive schemes, therefore,
would not be exempt from the federal preclearance requirement. As Justice Harlan stated in dissent, "A State covered by the Act must submit for

---

12. Armand Derfner, "The Implications of the *City of Mobile* Case for Extension of the
Voting Rights Acts," in *The Right to Vote* (New York, 1981), 200. See also Washington Research Project, *The Shameful Blight: The Survival of Racial Discrimination in Voting in the
South* (Washington, D.C., 1972). For evidence of the discriminatory impact of at-large elections in the South, see Richard L. Engstrom and Michael D. McDonald, "The Underrepresentation of Blacks on City Councils: Comparing the Structural and Socio-economic Ex-
planations for South/Non-South Differences," *Journal of Politics*, XLIV (November, 1982),
1088–1099, and Chandler Davidson and George Korbel, "At-Large Elections and Minority-
Group Representation: A Re-examination of Historical and Contemporary Evidence," *Journal of Politics*, XLIII (November, 1981), 982–1005.

federal approval all those laws that could arguably have an *impact on Negro voting power*."[13] The Mississippi changes, along with another in Virginia that modified the conditions under which illiterate voters could be assisted in casting their ballots, were therefore ordered to be submitted to Washington.

Following this decision, the preclearance requirement became the heart of the act. The Court soon added such changes as the relocation of polling places, municipal annexations, and representational redistricting to the list of electoral alterations requiring preclearance, and the Department of Justice refocused its resources on the enforcement of section five.[14] The number of proposed changes submitted to the department increased significantly. From 1971 through 1974, the department was receiving over nine hundred requests for preclearance annually from the southern states. After Texas was brought under the coverage of the special provisions in 1975, that number soared to several thousand every year (Table 3).[15]

The significance of this preclearance requirement cannot be overestimated. Numerous revisions in the southern electoral process which would have had deleterious effects on the black vote have been blocked. Through 1980, the Justice Department had objected to approximately 800 proposed changes (Table 4), nearly all of which were changes with dilutive potential. For example, only 9 of the objections were to changes in voter registration procedures and only 3 to reregistrations or voter purges, whereas 337 were to changes in the methods of election (*e.g.*, adopting at-large elections), 244 to municipal annexations, and 103 to revisions in the boundaries of representational districts.[16] Many of these proposed changes might otherwise have been immune to judicial invalidation, with the burden of proving discrimination resting on the shoulders of minority plaintiffs. Under the preclearance procedure, however, the state or local political subdivision enacting the change has the respon-

13. *Allen v. State Board of Elections*, 393 U.S. 544, 566, 569, 583 (1969). Emphasis added.

14. See *Perkins v. Matthews*, 400 U.S. 379 (1971), and *Georgia v. United States*, 411 U.S. 526 (1973). For a critical review of the Department of Justice's handling of section five submissions, see Howard Ball, Dale Krane, and Thomas P. Lauth, *Compromised Compliance: Implementation of the 1965 Voting Rights Act* (Westport, Conn., 1982).

15. Almost all requests for preclearance are filed with the Justice Department rather than with the federal district court in Washington, D.C., a practice that permits a jurisdiction to avoid the expense and formalities of litigation. If the department refuses to preclear a change, however, a jurisdiction may still seek approval from the district court.

16. These statistics were provided by the Voting Section of the Civil Rights Division, United States Department of Justice.

TABLE 3
Number of Voting Changes Submitted to Department of Justice for Preclearance, 1965–1980, by State

	1965	1966	1967	1968	1969	1970	1971	1972	1973	1974	1975	1976	1977	1978	1979	1980	Totals
Alabama	1	–	–	–	13	2	86	111	60	58	299	349	153	146	142	295	1,715
Georgia	–	1	–	62	35	60	138	226	114	173	284	252	242	444	371	689	3,091
Louisiana	–	–	–	–	2	3	71	136	283	137	255	303	460	254	336	356	2,596
Mississippi	–	–	–	–	4	28	221	68	66	41	107	152	114	123	112	153	1,189
North Carolina	–	–	–	–	–	2	75	28	35	54	293	125	183	156	89	158	1,198
South Carolina	–	25	52	37	80	114	160	117	135	221	201	419	299	212	138	192	2,402
Virginia	–	–	–	11	–	46	344	181	123	186	256	301	434	314	267	464	2,930
Florida	–	–	–	–	–	–	–	–	–	–	1	57	8	46	28	28	168
Texas	–	–	–	–	–	–	–	–	–	–	249	4,694	1,735	2,425	2,917	4,188	16,208
Others	–	–	–	–	–	–	23	75	34	118	133	820	379	555	350	817	3,301
Totals	1	26	52	110	134	255	1,118	942	850	988	2,078	7,472	4,007	4,675	4,750	7,340	34,798

Source: U.S. Department of Justice.

TABLE 4
Number of Voting Changes to Which Department of Justice Objected, 1965–1980, by State

	1965	1966	1967	1968	1969	1970	1971	1972	1973	1974	1975	1976	1977	1978	1979	1980	Total
Alabama	—	—	—	—	10	1	3	9	1	6	16	16	1	3	1	5	72
Georgia	—	—	—	6	—	—	12	18	15	22	83	12	34	8	5	10	225
Louisiana	—	—	—	—	2	—	36	13	6	10	5	52	1	3	—	8	136
Mississippi	—	—	—	—	4	1	19	4	7	2	17	7	8	2	3	3	78
North Carolina	—	—	—	—	—	—	10	—	—	—	8	—	37	3	1	3	62
South Carolina	—	—	—	—	—	—	—	7	7	26	4	11	8	7	7	—	77
Virginia	—	—	—	—	—	1	6	1	—	3	1	—	—	—	1	1	14
Florida	—	—	—	—	—	—	—	—	—	—	—	—	—	—	—	—	0
Texas	—	—	—	—	—	—	—	—	—	—	1	48	13	22	26	18	128
Others	—	—	—	—	—	—	—	—	1	4	3	5	2	1	1	3	18
Totals	0	0	0	6	16	3	86	52	37	73	138	151	104	49	45	51	810

SOURCE: U.S. Department of Justice.

sibility of showing that there is neither a discriminatory purpose behind it nor a discriminatory consequence likely to result from it. The Justice Department may therefore block proposed changes without reaching a positive determination of discrimination.[17] Without this preclearance requirement, it is highly unlikely that blacks in the South would have been able to convert their new voting strength into the election of black officials to the extent that they have. In 1975 the number of black elected officials in the initially covered states exceeded one thousand for the first time, and in 1980 it exceeded two thousand.[18]

As the 1982 expiration date approached and the issue of another extension of the special provisions grew more immediate, it was widely assumed that the section five preclearance requirement would occupy center stage in the forthcoming debate. In addition to the argument that a procedure as extraordinary as preclearance was no longer justified, given the integration of blacks in the southern political system, another argument began to be heard with increasing intensity—that section five had been "radically transformed" into the functional equivalent of an affirmative-action requirement. The initial purpose of the Voting Rights Act, to assure that blacks have an equal opportunity to participate in the southern electoral process, had been transformed, critics maintained, into a requirement to maximize black political strength. The act was no longer being used to combat disfranchisement but to combat any aspect of the electoral process that *disadvantaged* the black minority. "Proportional representation," it was argued, had become the standard by which electoral schemes were evaluated, and "racial quotas" were being employed in order to satisfy federal review.[19]

Much of this criticism of section five was in response to a highly publicized 1977 Supreme Court decision concerning state legislative redistricting in Kings County, New York, one of the few nonsouthern jurisdictions caught by the revised coverage formula of 1970. At issue were revisions in the redistricting plans for the New York state senate and state assembly, made after the Department of Justice in 1974 refused to preclear the new districts. The department found the nonwhite voting strength in the county to be unnecessarily concentrated in a few heavily nonwhite districts,

17. *Georgia* v. *United States*, 538–39.
18. Joint Center for Political Studies, *National Roster of Black Elected Officials* (Washington, D.C., 1975, 1980), Vols. 5, 10.
19. See, for example, Abigail M. Thernstrom, "The Odd Evolution of the Voting Rights Act," *Public Interest*, LV (Spring, 1979), 49–76, and James McClellan, "Fiddling with the Constitution While *Rome* Burns: The Case Against the Voting Rights Act of 1965," *Louisiana Law Review*, XLII (Fall, 1981), 5–75.

whereas adjoining districts had only bare majorities of nonwhites. In order to overcome the objections, the proposed district boundaries were altered so that each of the districts in which nonwhites were a population majority would be at least 65 percent nonwhite.

The revision drew an adverse response from an Hasidic Jewish community within the county. This residentially concentrated community had been located in a single assembly district and a single senate district but was now split between two districts in both the assembly and the senate plans. It therefore complained that its voting strength was being diluted so that a quota of seats controlled by nonwhites could be achieved. In *United Jewish Organizations of Williamsburg, Inc.,* v. *Carey*, however, the Supreme Court rejected this reverse discrimination claim, holding that the deliberate construction of majority black districts in order to ensure preclearance did not violate the Constitution. This was a benign use of racial data, the Court concluded, and the resulting plan was generally fair to both blacks and whites. Even if voting were racially polarized, whites would not be "underrepresented," because they were a majority in 70 percent of the legislative districts in the county, yet comprised only 65 percent of the county's population.[20]

The *United Jewish Organizations (UJO)* decision was widely reported as upholding "affirmative gerrymandering" and sanctioning an alien, "divisive" electoral system of proportional representation. This was in fact an exaggerated interpretation, for although the Court did state that it was constitutionally permissible for a state to manipulate its electoral structure to facilitate minority representation, it in no way mandated proportional representation.[21] The Court continued to use the *retrogression* principle, handed down the previous year in *Beer* v. *United States*, as its standard for preclearance under section five.[22] The Court had then held that the attorney general could object to a proposed change on the grounds that it would have a discriminatory effect only if that change would be retrogressive, that is, if it placed blacks in an electoral situation or context in which their votes would be less effective than they had been previously. If a change were not retrogressive, it could not be denied preclearance no matter how far it may have left blacks from being proportionally represented. The decisional standard, therefore, is based on the *relative*, not absolute, degree of vote dilution. In *UJO* the Court explicitly noted the plaintiffs' failure to show a violation of this rule when the

20. *United Jewish Organizations of Williamsburg, Inc.* v. *Carey*, 430 U.S. 144 (1977).
21. *Ibid.*, 167–68.
22. *Beer* v. *United States*, 425 U.S. 130 (1976).

Justice Department had objected to the districts, and they therefore failed to show that New York had been forced to do more than was required for preclearance.[23] That the retrogression standard and not a proportional standard was still the basic decisional rule after *UJO* was clarified by one of the attorneys handling preclearance matters for the Department of Justice, when he stated a few months after that case, "If a change makes something better, we're not supposed to object even if it is still not very good."[24] Despite the Court's continued adherence to the retrogression principle, however, the *UJO* decision was widely interpreted as having held that under section five minorities are entitled to representation in proportion to their numbers.

THE (NEW) VOTING RIGHTS ACT

As mentioned above, the 97th Congress made two important changes in the Voting Rights Act that would have an important impact on the racial dimension of southern politics. It extended the special provisions, including the preclearance requirement, for another twenty-five years (until August 6, 2007), although new "bailout" standards allowed governmental units to escape from coverage earlier. And a general provision of nationwide application, section two, was revised to permit voting-rights violations to be established through evidence of the discriminatory *effect* of an electoral scheme or procedure, regardless of the intent behind its use or adoption.[25]

The Special Provisions and Bailout

Opponents of the extension of the special provisions, in arguing that blacks are now fully integrated into the southern political system and therefore do not need these extraordinary protections, pointed out that voter registration among blacks within the eight southern states to which the special provisions applied ranged in 1980 from just below 50 percent of the voting-age population in Virginia, to over 70 percent in Mississippi (see Table 5). These figures, the opponents delighted in noting, compared quite favorably with those for such northern states as New York and Massachusetts, where only 46.5 and 43.6 percent, respectively, of voting-age blacks were registered in 1980. Indeed, across these

23. *United Jewish Organizations* v. *Carey*, 163.
24. Quoted in Ball, Krane, and Lauth, *Compromised Compliance*, 88. For a review of the Supreme Court's decisions involving preclearance, see Richard L. Engstrom, "Racial Vote Dilution: Supreme Court Interpretations of Section 5 of the Voting Rights Act," *Southern University Law Review*, IV (Spring, 1978), 139–64.
25. Congress also extended the bilingual election requirement through August 5, 1992.

TABLE 5
Voter Registration by Race, November, 1980

| | *Percentage of Voting-Age Population Reported Registered* | | |
State	Blacks	Whites	Difference
Alabama	62.2	73.3	− 11.1
Georgia	59.8	67.0	− 7.2
Louisiana	69.0	74.5	− 5.5
Mississippi	72.2	85.2	− 13.0
North Carolina	49.9	63.7	− 13.8
South Carolina	61.4	57.2	+ 4.2
Texas	56.4	61.4	− 5.0
Virginia	49.7	65.4	− 15.7

SOURCE: U.S. Department of Commerce, Bureau of the Census, *Voting and Registration in the Election of November, 1980*, Series P–20, No. 370 (1982), Table 5.

eight southern states, 59.2 percent of voting-age blacks were registered, which was very close to the nationwide figure of 60 percent.[26]

In addition to the data on registration, opponents of extension frequently cited the small percentage of election system changes denied preclearance under the act. Since the act was passed, almost 35,000 proposed changes had been submitted to the Justice Department, and only 2.3 percent had been refused clearance. Over 80 percent of the proposed revisions had been submitted since 1976, and of these only 1.4 percent were denied approval (see Tables 3 and 4). This, opponents suggested, reflected the new political climate in the South, a climate receptive to equal participation by black citizens.

A third set of statistics widely cited by the opponents of extension concerned the increased number of black elected officials in the affected states. In 1968, only 171 blacks were serving in elected positions in those eight states; by 1980, the number had increased over 1,000 percent, to 2,042 (see Table 6). This figure included over 100 blacks serving in state legislatures and close to 100 serving as mayors of municipalities. Clearly, the opponents claimed, with blacks being so fully integrated into the political process, it was no longer necessary to treat the South as a delinquent child.

26. U.S. Department of Commerce, Bureau of the Census, *Voting and Registration in the Election of November 1980*, Series P–20, No. 370 (1982), Table 5.

TABLE 6
Number and Percentage of Black Elected Officials, July, 1980

State	Number	Percentage of All Elected Officials	Percentage of Blacks in Total Population
Alabama	238	5.7	25.6
Georgia	249	3.7	26.8
Louisiana	363	7.7	29.4
Mississippi	387	7.3	35.2
North Carolina	247	4.7	22.4
South Carolina	238	7.4	30.4
Texas	196	0.8	12.0
Virginia	124	4.1	18.9

SOURCE: United States Commission on Civil Rights, *The Voting Rights Act: Unfulfilled Goals* (Washington, D.C., 1981), Table 2.3.

Proponents of extension, however, regarded these statistics in a radically different light. Although the figures documented impressive gains by blacks, they did not, proponents argued, justify an inference that the political process was now *equally* open to blacks. The data on voter registration showed that in all but one of the covered southern states, blacks were registered to vote at a rate substantially below that for whites (Table 5). This, it was maintained, was partly a function of deliberately restrictive registration practices still being employed in many areas, such as limiting voter registration to times and places that were very inconvenient for blacks. In addition, instances of continued harassment and intimidation of blacks attempting to register to vote were reported.[27]

As for the statistics on preclearance, proponents noted that although the rate of denials might not be high, the *number* of denials was still quite large. Approximately eight hundred proposed changes in the election systems within the covered states had been denied clearance on the ground that they would be discriminatory (or retrogressive) toward minority voters. This did not suggest, it was argued, that the political climate had been fundamentally altered. And this figure did not take into account the deterring effect of the preclearance requirement. The number of discriminatory changes that would have been adopted had federal preclearance not been required was assumed to be substantially larger.

27. See United States Commission on Civil Rights, *The Voting Rights Act: Unfulfilled Goals* (Washington, D.C., 1981), 22–28.

TABLE 7
Counties with 20 Percent or More Black Population and
No Black Elected Officials, by States, July, 1980

State	Number of Counties with at Least 20% Black Population	Counties with at Least 20% Black Population and No Black Elected Officials	
		Number	Percentage
Alabama	37	22	59.5
Georgia	107	80	74.8
Louisiana	46	7	15.2
Mississippi	65	37	56.9
North Carolina	55	23	41.8
South Carolina	40	14	35.0
Texas	28	13	46.4
Virginia	42	19	45.2

SOURCE: United States Commission on Civil Rights, *The Voting Rights Act: Unfulfilled Goals* (Washington, D.C., 1981), Table 2.5.

The data on black elected officials were also cited by the proponents of extension to show that blacks still had not been fully integrated into the southern political system. The dramatic rise in the number of black elected officials, they cautioned, should not hide the fact that black officeholders were still relatively rare. The percentage of offices filled by blacks in the covered states in 1980 ranged from 0.8 to only 7.7, despite the substantial proportions of blacks in the populations of these states (see Table 6). In six of the eight states, over 40 percent of the counties in which blacks comprised 20 percent or more of the population still did not have a single black in a county elective office (Table 7). White southerners, proponents argued, obviously were not ready to let blacks share fully in the political process. As stated in a report issued by the United States Commission on Civil Rights, "White resistance and hostility by some state and local officials to increased minority participation [is evident] in virtually every aspect of the electoral process."[28]

The proponents of extension were of course successful in persuading Congress to continue the special provisions. The efforts to eliminate or weaken the preclearance requirement never received much public support, and the focus of the debate soon shifted to the issue of revising the

28. *Ibid.*, 91.

bailout criterion. It was argued that those southern jurisdictions (especially local governmental units) that had been captured by the previous coverage formulae but were no longer engaging in racially discriminatory acts ought to be provided with a realistic chance of bailing out, something not offered in the existing standard. A 1980 Supreme Court decision, *City of Rome* v. *United States*, in which a small Georgia municipality had sought to be released from the coverage of the special provisions, was often cited. The city had been told that it was not eligible to bail out, despite judicial findings that it had not employed a discriminatory test or device for seventeen years and was not denying black people access to the ballot or preventing them from becoming candidates for office. Rome was not eligible, the Court ruled, because it was part of a covered state. No municipality (or any other local jurisdiction in Georgia) could bail out independently of the state, no matter how "clean" its own racial record may have been. Critics of the decision argued that this was unfair and noted that local units, under the existing standard, were being given no incentive to eliminate whatever discrimination might remain within their electoral systems.[29]

The new bailout criteria resulted from a compromise reached within the House Judiciary Committee and accepted on the House floor; the special provisions were made permanent (later changed to a twenty-five-year extension by the Senate), and the bailout procedure was "liberalized." Under the new standards, which took effect on August 6, 1984,[30] counties as well as states are eligible to bail out if they can satisfy two basic criteria: demonstrate a record of "good behavior" for a ten-year period and show that they have taken positive steps toward opening their electoral system to blacks. The first standard requires that for ten years no test or device has been used by the jurisdiction in a discriminatory fashion, that the courts have not found the jurisdiction guilty of any voting-rights violations, that no federal examiners have been assigned to the jurisdiction over that period, and that the jurisdiction has complied completely with the preclearance requirement, not having implemented any electoral changes without first receiving preclearance. The second standard requires the jurisdiction to have taken affirmative steps toward increasing minority participation in the electoral process. The jurisdiction must have eliminated any "voting procedure or method of election" that

29. *City of Rome* v. *United States*, 446 U.S. 156, 167 (1980).
30. A two-year delay in the implementation of the new bailout standards was adopted in order to provide the Justice Department time to prepare for the expected plethora of cases.

would result in a denial of or dilution of the vote, must have been engaged in "constructive efforts" to eliminate any intimidation or harassment of people exercising their right to vote, and must be able to demonstrate that "other constructive efforts" at facilitating black participation have been made, such as adopting more convenient hours during which people may register or appointing blacks to positions as election officials. The burden of proof on these matters is of course on the jurisdiction seeking to bail out, and the bailout standards must be met not only by that jurisdiction, but also by any smaller governmental unit within it (by all municipalities within a county and by all counties and municipalities within a state). Venue remains in the federal district court in the District of Columbia.

The new bailout provision offers covered jurisdictions a way to escape from the special provisions prior to 2007, but the standards that must be satisfied are clearly demanding. The degree to which bailout has been "liberalized," therefore, has been a matter of debate. The Senate Judiciary Committee, in its report embracing the new standards, described them as "a very substantial liberalization" and maintained that "only those jurisdictions that insist on retaining discriminatory procedures or otherwise inhibit full minority participation" will remain subject to the special provisions. Other, more conservative senators, however, have described them as creating no more than "an illusory opportunity" to escape coverage. According to the late North Carolina Senator John P. East, the "probability of a successful bail out approaches zero." The probability of any state bailing out, given that *every* unit of local government within it must meet the "clean record" test, may in fact be zero, but numerous counties (and the municipalities and school districts within them) should soon become eligible to bail out independently of their states.[31]

The Revised Section Two

Although the extension of the special provisions, even with the more permissive bailout standards, was an extremely important defensive victory for civil rights forces, the revision of section two may have been even more important. On this issue, voting-rights advocates took the offensive and demanded that changes be made in the Voting Rights Act. The target was the Supreme Court's 1980 decision in *City of Mobile* v. *Bolden*, a de-

---

31. Report of the Committee on the Judiciary, United States Senate, *Voting Rights Act Extension*, 97th Cong., 2nd Sess., Report No. 97–417, pp. 43–44, 168, 216 (hereinafter cited as *Senate Report*).

cision that voting-rights attorneys complained had placed an almost impossible burden of proof on plaintiffs in voting-rights litigation.

Bolden involved a challenge to the use of at-large (citywide) elections for selecting the city commission in Mobile, Alabama. No black had ever been elected to the commission, even though 35 percent of the city's population was black, and the plaintiffs in the case had faulted the at-large electoral system. Given the racially polarized nature of the Mobile electorate, blacks complained that it was not only impossible for a black candidate to be elected under this system, but blacks were also unable to develop effective electoral coalitions through which they could help to elect sympathetic whites to the commission. Black support for a candidate produced a white "backlash," whether that candidate was black or white. This election system, plaintiffs maintained, virtually guaranteed the election of an all-white commission with no political accountability to blacks and therefore little interest in representing the needs and concerns of the black community. Such a system, they argued, violated blacks' right to vote under the Fifteenth Amendment, their right to the "equal protection" of the laws under the Fourteenth Amendment, and also the prohibition against any denial or abridgement of the right to vote contained in section two of the Voting Rights Act.[32] Both the federal district court and the court of appeals agreed, and they mandated the adoption of single-member districts in Mobile; the Supreme Court disagreed, however, and reversed the lower courts.

The Court, in a dramatic departure from its previous voting-rights decisions, held against the plaintiffs because they had not shown a discriminatory *intent* behind the original adoption of the at-large system in Mobile in 1911 or in its continual use over the years. Both the Fourteenth and Fifteenth amendments, the Court concluded, required such a showing; proof of the racially discriminatory effects of an election scheme, though supportive of an inference of racial intent, was not a sufficient basis for invalidating the scheme. Section two of the Voting Rights Act, the Court held, was little more than a statutory restatement of the Fifteenth Amendment's prohibition on racially based interference with the franchise and, like that prohibition, required evidence of discriminatory motives to establish a violation.

Prior to *Bolden*, the litigation standard in vote dilution cases such as

32. Section two of the act stated, "No voting qualification or prerequisite to voting, or standard, practice or procedure shall be imposed or applied by any State or political subdivision to deny or abridge the right of any citizen of the United States to vote on account of race or color."

this was the "participation test," which the Court had enunciated in
Whitcomb v. *Chavis* and *White* v. *Regester*, cases involving countywide
multimember state legislative districts. As expressed in *White*: "The
plaintiffs' burden is to produce evidence to support findings that the political processes leading to nomination and election were not equally
open to participation by the group in question—that its members had less
opportunity than did other residents in the district to participate in the
political processes and to elect legislators of their choice."[33] Although the
evidentiary burden established by this standard was substantial, black
plaintiffs in the South—where it was easy to document the "hangover" effects of past discrimination (such as relatively low voter registration and
turnout among blacks) and the racially polarized nature of recent elections—were often successful in their *Whitcomb-White* based challenges
to racially dilutive electoral schemes. The intent standard, however, ele-
vated the burden of proof drastically and made litigation, according to
one voting-rights attorney, "largely useless."[34] Direct evidence of discriminatory motives is rarely available, and judges are unlikely to infer
racial intent from circumstantial evidence. The *Bolden* decision was
viewed by voting-rights attorneys, therefore, as "a severe setback" and
was said to have had an "immediate and devastating impact" on dilution
litigation as a number of post-*Bolden* cases were lost in the lower
courts.[35]

In an effort to minimize the damage to the voting-rights movement in-
flicted by *Bolden*, civil rights advocates focused on section two as a medium for "reversing" the decision. By amending that section to make evidence of discriminatory *effects* sufficient to establish a statutory violation
of voting rights, they hoped that the *Bolden* decision could be contained.
Such an amendment was accepted by the House Judiciary Committee
and passed by the entire House with relatively little debate. The new section two, as approved by the House, prohibited any "voting qualifications or prerequisite to voting, or standard, practice, or procedure" related to voting that "*results in* a denial or abridgement of" the right to

33. *Whitcomb* v. *Chavis* 403 U.S. 124, 149–50 (1971), and *White* v. *Regester*, 412
U.S. 755, 766 (1973).
34. Derfner, "Implications of the *City of Mobile Case*," 205, 206.
35. Frank R. Parker, "The New 'Results' Test of Section 2 of the Voting Rights Act: A
New Sparkle for the Crown Jewel of American Liberties," *University of Virginia Law Review*, LXIX (Spring, 1983). For additional critical commentaries on the *Bolden* decision,
see Laughlin McDonald, "The Bolden Decision Stonewalls Black Aspirations," *Southern
Changes*, II (1980), 11–17, and Richard L. Engstrom, "Racial Vote Dilution and the 'New'
Equal Protection Clause: *City of Mobile* v. *Bolden*," *American Studies*, XII (March, 1983).

vote (emphasis added). In response to criticisms that this "results" or effects standard would leave any election system in which blacks were not proportionally represented vulnerable to invalidation, the House Judiciary Committee added a "PR disclaimer" to the section, which stated, "The fact that members of a minority group have not been elected in numbers equal to the group's proportion of the population shall not, in and of itself, constitute a violation of this section."

The disclaimer clause did not satisfy many of the critics of the effects test in the Senate, however, where section two proved to be much more controversial. The more explicit disclaimer that was consequently adopted by the Senate Judiciary Committee added a codification of the *Whitcomb-White* participation test. The disclaimer now read: "A violation [of section two] is established if, based on the totality of circumstances, it is shown that the political processes leading to nomination or election . . . are not equally open . . . in that [blacks] have less opportunity than other members of the electorate to participate in the political process and to elect representatives of their choice." Although the "underrepresentation" of blacks was stated as one of the "circumstances" judges might consider, an explicit renunciation of any right to proportional representation was again included in the clause. The Senate easily defeated (by a 16 to 81 vote) an attempt to return to an intent only standard and accepted this version of section two, to which the House then also concurred.

Frank Parker, a leading voting-rights attorney, has described the revised section two as "the key feature" of the new act, one which "breathes new life" into the voting-rights movement.[36] Opponents, likewise, expect dramatic consequences and have predicted that the results test will produce more *UJO*-type "affirmative gerrymanders." Despite the disclaimer clause, which has been described as "little more than a rhetorical smokescreen,"[37] critics contend that proportional representation by race will be the result. Indeed, one commentary has even suggested that minority representation will soon be guaranteed, as was once the case "in the Parliament of Rhodesia/Zimbabwe."[38]

36. Parker, "The New 'Results' Test."
37. Report of the Subcommittee on the Constitution, in *Senate Report*, 146.
38. Peter Brimelow, "Uncivil Act," *Barron's*, January 27, 1982, p. 7. The first case involving the amended section two to reach the Supreme Court resulted in the invalidation of a number of multimember state legislative districts in North Carolina. See *Thornburg* v. *Gingles*, 106 U.S. 2752 (1986). Section two was also the basis for the invalidation of congressional districts in some southern states. See, for example, Frank R. Parker, "The Mississippi Congressional Redistricting Case: A Case Study in Minority Vote Dilution," *How-*

CONCLUSION

The debate over extending and amending the Voting Rights Act brought to the forefront the themes of continuity and change in southern politics. Although the racial dimension of southern politics has clearly undergone enormous alteration in recent years, the perception that not enough has changed remains immensely popular. Such a perception certainly dominated the congressional response to the extension issue. Civil rights forces won an impressive victory in Congress, gaining a twenty-five-year extension of the special provisions of the act (including the preclearance requirement) and creating a statutory bypass around the Supreme Court's decision in *City of Mobile* v. *Bolden.*

The role of the Voting Rights Act in facilitating the change that has occurred, and the need for continuing this special statutory protection into the immediate future, was perhaps best summarized by the president of the Southern Christian Leadership Conference in Alabama, who in testifying before the Subcommittee on Civil and Constitutional Rights of the House Judiciary Committee stated: "You've enabled us through the Voting Rights Act to begin climbing towards the top of a very deep pit. We've been climbing steadily but we have not yet reached the top. The pit is twenty feet deep. The pole, the Voting Rights Act, is only fifteen feet. We're only ten feet from the top—halfway. Taking the pole from us now—the Voting Rights Act—would cause us to descend rapidly to the bottom."[39]

---

ard Law Journal, XXVIII (1985), 397–415, and Richard L. Engstrom, "Repairing the Crack in New Orleans' Black Vote: VRA's Results Test Nullifies 'Gerryduck,' " *Publius*, XVI (Fall, 1986), 109–21.

39. Statement of Rev. John S. Nettles, state president of the Southern Christian Leadership Conference in Alabama, *House Hearings*, 851.

Current Trends in Black Politics: Prospects and Problems

ALLY MACK

MARY DeLORSE COLEMAN

LESLIE B. McLEMORE

Whatever phase of the Southern political process one seeks to understand, sooner or later the trail of inquiry leads to the Negro.
—V. O. Key, Jr., *Southern Politics*

No aspect of southern politics better illustrates the theme of "continuity and change" than the racial dimension. Since the civil rights years and the adoption of the Federal Voting Rights Act in 1965, the role of blacks in the region has changed enormously, shifting from one of "political object" to that of "political participant."[1] Black political power has forced significant alterations in the campaign strategies and policy orientations of many white politicians. And the new generation of such leaders, to be seen particularly in statewide offices within the Democratic party, is more likely to work at building biracial electoral coalitions than to engage in the "race-baiting" tactics of its predecessors.[2] Indeed, even George Wallace, who, after losing his first campaign for governor of Alabama in 1958, vowed never to be "outniggered" again,[3] was openly solicitous of black support during his successful 1982 campaign for that same office. He promised to "treat black people right" if they helped elect him governor. They did, and he immediately appointed several to high-level

1. Southern Regional Council, *The State of the South* (Atlanta, 1979), 16.
2. See, for example, Earl Black, *Southern Governors and Civil Rights: Racial Segregation as a Campaign Issue in the Second Reconstruction* (Cambridge, 1976), 336–38.
3. Robert Sherrill, *Gothic Politics in the Deep South: Stars of the New Confederacy* (New York, 1968), 267.

positions, including commissioner of revenue and commissioner of pensions and security.

Even more important than its impact on white officials is the power of the black vote to put blacks into office. In 1985 more than one-half of the nation's 6,056 black elected officials were from the South, evidence, according to some, of the region's "political modernization."[4]

Blacks without question have made tremendous advances in southern politics, but the degree to which the racial aspect of the region's political life has truly changed is debatable. The increase in black officials leveled off in the middle to late 1970s, as did black registration and turnout. Reasons for this slowdown include the dilution tactics discussed by Richard L. Engstrom in the preceding essay, the difficulty of winning white votes for black candidates, the appeal of Reagan and conservative Republicans in Dixie, and the increasing costs of campaigning. The following examination of the current state of black politics in the South will first consider officeholding, particularly the types of positions most often occupied by blacks, will then discuss the implications for southern blacks of Jesse Jackson's presidential campaign, and finally will analyze the most critical problems confronting the ongoing evolution of black political power in Dixie.

BLACK ELECTED OFFICIALS IN THE SOUTH

In 1955 in rural, black-belt Leflore County, Mississippi, fifteen-year-old Emmett Till, a black youth, was murdered in a highly publicized act of racial savagery. Today the county supervisor, tax assessor, and two school board members are black. On one infamous Sunday in 1963, Birmingham racists bombed a Baptist church and killed four little black girls. Today black Mayor Richard Arrington is serving his second term in the same Birmingham that Martin Luther King once called "the most thoroughly segregated city in America." In Memphis, where Dr. King was slain in 1968, a congressman, two state senators, five state representatives, three school board members, and seven judges are black. Dallas County, Alabama, which prior to 1965 had only 200 of the 15,000 eligible blacks registered to vote, now has, in the county seat of Selma alone, 10,500 of the 12,000 eligible black voters signed up, as well as some one dozen black officials. Montgomery, the cradle of the Confederacy, also

4. See, for example, Lorn S. Foster, "The Voting Rights Act: Black Voting and the New Southern Politics" (Paper presented to American Political Science Association, Denver, September 2–5, 1982).

TABLE 1
States with the Most Black Elected Officials, 1984

State	Black Officials	Total Population	Black Population	Percentage of Blacks in Total Population
1. Louisiana	438	4,205,900	1,238,241	29
2. Mississippi	433	2,520,638	887,206	35
3. Illinois	359	11,426,518	1,675,398	15
4. Alabama	314	3,893,888	996,335	26
5. Georgia	301	5,463,105	1,465,181	27
6. Michigan	297	9,262,078	1,199,023	13
7. Arkansas	296	2,286,435	373,768	16
8. North Carolina	294	5,874,429	1,316,050	22
9. South Carolina	263	3,121,820	948,623	30
10. California	258	23,667,902	1,819,281	8

SOURCE: Joint Center for Political Studies, *National Roster of Black Elected Officials* (Washington, D.C., 1984), 14.

has approximately a dozen blacks in office.[5] These dramatic examples show the phenomenal progress that has occurred in some of the toughest spots in the South over two decades or more.

The nationwide rate of increase in black officeholders surged in the early 1970s, reaching 26.6 percent in 1971; in the South between 1970 and 1975 the number tripled.[6] However, a significant drop-off in the nationwide rate commenced in the mid-1970s, and by 1982 the percentage of increase was at just 2.4. In 1983 the rate rose to 8.3 percent, with the largest gain occurring in the South, where the rate was 9.6 percent, which meant that 301 additional blacks were elected to office. Arkansas led the way with a remarkable 26 percent increase, the 78 new officials pushing the black total in that state to 297. According to the Voter Education Project (VEP), as of 1984, a total of 62 percent, or 3,441, of all black elected officials were to be found in the South, where a slight majority of black Americans reside.

As Table 1 indicates, of the ten states with the highest number of black elected officials, seven are in the South. Over the past two decades, the

5. Walter Leavy, "Southern Politics: A Great Change for the Better," *Ebony*, XXXIX (August, 1984), 160–61.
6. Jack Bass and Walter DeVries, *The Transformation of Southern Politics: Social Change and Political Consequence Since 1945* (New York, 1976), 50.

gains in Mississippi have led the nation. In 1964 the only 12 black elected officials in the state were the mayors and aldermen of the small all-black Delta towns of Mound Bayou and Winstonville. At that time 915,000 black citizens comprised over 40 percent of the total population and more than 70 percent in many Delta counties of the state's northwest region. By 1968 there were still only 29, but as black voter turnout surged, so did the number of officials. In 1984 the total reached 433 and included 2 state senators, 18 state representatives, 64 county officials, 21 mayors, 163 city council members, 6 other municipal officials, 1 judge, 59 justices of the peace, 6 other judicial officials, 4 sheriffs and marshals, 79 school board members, and 7 other education officials.[7]

Several dimensions of the Mississippi situation are instructive of the region as a whole. First, even with their gains, Mississippi blacks, who compose 35 percent of the state's population, hold only 8.1 percent of the elective offices. Nowhere in the South does the black share of positions reach double digits, even though 20 percent of the regional population is black and the rate is even higher in several states besides Mississippi: South Carolina, 30 percent; Louisiana, 29 percent; Georgia, 27 percent; Alabama, 26 percent; and North Carolina, 22 percent. This same disparity is even greater in the nation, with blacks holding only 1 percent of the country's 512,000 elected offices though constituting 12 percent of the population.

A second area of concern to blacks is the nature of the posts they most often occupy, for the locus of black elected officials tends to the lower rungs of the political ladder. They normally have the least visible and most insignificant posts in the electoral scheme of things, the overwhelming majority being municipal positions and educational slots, followed by judicial and law enforcement ones and county offices. (See Table 2.)

Across the South there are 1,523 black municipal officials other than mayors, 648 education officials, 364 county ones, and 287 judges and law enforcement officials. No blacks held statewide elected offices in the region until 1985, when L. Douglas Wilder was elected lieutenant-governor of Virginia. There are no black U.S. senators, and only three congressmen of 116—Harold Ford of Tennessee, Mickey Leland of Texas, and Mike Espy of Mississippi. Across Dixie 150 black-majority counties have no black representation in their state legislatures, where blacks hold less than 1 percent of the seats.

A third problem is the disparity between the high expectations of

7. Cliff Treyens, "Political Gains Have Leveled Off," Jackson *Daily News—Clarion Ledger*, July 1, 1984, Sec. H, p. 7.

TABLE 2
Black Elected Officials in Mississippi

	Number	Percentage
FEDERAL		
Representative	1	.2%
STATE		
Supreme Court	1	.2%
SUBSTATE/REGIONAL		
Circuit Court Judge	1	.2%
State Senator	2	.3%
Congressman	18	2.9%
COUNTY		
Supervisor	48	7.8%
Tax Assessor/Collector	4	.7%
Chancery Clerk	3	.5%
Circuit Clerk	3	.5%
Superintendent of Education	8	1.3%
Coroner-Ranger	2	.3%
Sheriff	3	.5%
Justice Court Judge	23	3.8%
Constable	64	10.4%
Election Commissioner	53	8.6%
School Board	98	16.0%
MUNICIPAL		
Mayor	18	2.9%
Councilman/Alderman	262	42.7%
Town Marshal	1	.2%
TOTALS	613	100%

SOURCE: Secretary of State, *List of Black Elected Officials* (Jackson, Miss., 1985).

black officeholders by their constituencies and the severe constraints often inherent in their particular posts. This is especially true of mayors. For example, none of the twenty-one mayors in Mississippi is from a town with a population greater than 5,000, and all of these towns are largely black and poor. Even in the larger cities of the South, black mayors face the disparity between high expectations and insufficient resources. The best illustration is that of Ernest "Dutch" Morial, first elected mayor of New Orleans in May, 1977, and reelected four years later. One observer describes the situation that confronted Morial:

> According to the 1980 census, New Orleans is the third largest city in the Southeast, with 557,761 people of whom 55.3 percent are black. Tourism, oil, and shipping pump billions of dollars through its economy each year, but a whopping 26.4 percent of its residents live below the poverty level, making New Orleans the third poorest large city in the U.S. One-third of the city's blacks lived in poverty in 1980, and the gap in median family income between blacks and whites ($7,598 versus $14,898) is greater in New Orleans than in any other major city.

At the very bottom of New Orleans society is a virtually unemployable underclass estimated to include 15 percent of the black community. The average black resident has less than an eighth-grade education; the schools are 85 percent black with test scores for Orleans Parish being the lowest in the state. The state constitution prohibits a city income or earnings tax, and the homestead exemption is such that only 5 percent of homeowners pay any property tax. Under Reagan federal funds were cut from $123 million in 1980 to $65 million in 1982. A long-standing pattern of tight control by a tiny economic oligarchy greatly exacerbates the problems, and one commentator concluded that Morial faced "the toughest mayor's job in the U.S."[8]

Why the leveling off of black gains in political officeholding witnessed in the 1970s and the difficulty of pushing through to larger numbers of more important ones? One factor was the leveling off of black registration and turnout during the 1970s. As Engstrom explains in his essay, the jump immediately after the Voting Rights Act was enormous, from a registration figure of 35.5 percent in 1965 to 52.1 percent in 1967. The increase crested in the early seventies and fell back to an average of some 56 percent in the middle to late years of the decade, as Table 3 makes clear.

Two political leaders helped greatly in the 1980s (one inadvertently) to rekindle the interest of southern blacks in political life. The first was Ronald Reagan, with his social welfare cuts in the 1981 budget and his slowdown—some would say rollback—on civil rights policies. The emergence of a set of southern Reaganites in both parties—people like Jesse Helms, Trent Lott, John East, Paula Hawkins, and Jeremiah Denton—

8. Monte Piliawsky, "The Limits of Power: Dutch Morial, Mayor of New Orleans," *Southern Exposure*, XII (February, 1984), 70–76. The final quotation is attributed to Bette Woode of Wellesley University.

TABLE 3
Reported Black Voter Registration in the South, 1970–1982

Year	Percentage
1970	57.6
1972	64.0
1974	55.5
1976	56.4
1978	56.2
1980	59.3
1982	56.9

SOURCE: U.S. Department of Commerce, Bureau of the Census, *Current Population Report*, Series P-25, No. 916 (1982).

also captured the attention of the black electorate, as did the support offered Reagan by Boll Weevil Democrats like Sonny Montgomery of Mississippi, Buddy Roemer of Louisiana, and Charles W. Stenholm of Texas, who gave Reagan his ideological majority in the 1981 House. In 1982, black turnout nationwide increased six points over the previous off-year elections, even though southern registration was not up. This was twice the rate of increase for whites and—as we saw—brought about a sharp increase in black elected officials in the South. The other figure who has greatly influenced the new interest in politics among southern blacks is a forty-two-year-old native of Greenville, South Carolina, to whom we now turn, the Reverend Jesse Jackson.

THE JACKSON FACTOR

"I offer myself and my service as a vehicle to give a voice to the voiceless, representation to the unrepresented, and hope to the downtrodden." From months prior to that announcement for the presidency on November 3, 1983, to his impassioned cry to the Democratic convention and the nation on July 17, 1984, to the general election of November 6, Jackson crisscrossed the South dozens of times appealing, cajoling, finally demanding that blacks sign up and turn out to vote. "God has placed us in the belly of the whale," he often told his audiences. "If we are sober, sane and sensitive, we can grab the whale by his vital organs and make him say YES when he wants to say NO." "Hands that once picked cotton," he was also fond of saying, "can now pick political leaders." One of Jackson's avowed goals was to register an additional two million blacks in the

South. Certain areas were targeted, like North Carolina, where approximately one-half of the state's 500,000 eligible black voters were unregistered and where right-wing Senator Jesse Helms had won reelection in 1978 with only slightly more than 100,000 votes. Jackson argued that it should be possible to oust people like Helms and certain southern congressmen. "Our vote can be the insecticide that destroys the Boll Weevils," he repeated across the land. A charismatic leader, Jackson engendered feelings of hope among many who previously had no inclination to participate in the political process. The NAACP, the VEP, and the Democratic party also conducted vigorous drives among black southerners in advance of the 1984 elections.

The impact on registration was phenomenal. Perhaps 750,000 southern blacks signed up, with some states experiencing major increases. One study found the following from 1982 to 1984: up 18.2 percent in Louisiana, 37.1 percent in North Carolina, 18 percent in Florida, 14 percent in South Carolina, and in the border state of Kentucky, 29.6 percent. This translated into an increase for the five-state area of 418,993 new black voters.[9] Georgia saw an increase from August, 1983, to August, 1984, of 15.6 percent, or 74,448 new black registrants, and the other states also had increases.[10]

Black participation in the Democratic party's presidential nominating process increased substantially in 1984. Although few blacks anticipated a Jackson victory, many took part in caucuses and primaries because he was a candidate. This helped push overall turnout in these forums up 4.8 percent nationwide. Not only did more blacks participate at the precinct level, but more also attended the Democratic National Convention. Whereas blacks had comprised only 2.8 percent and 10.6 percent of the delegates in 1964 and 1976 respectively, their 1984 share jumped to 17 percent.

Jackson's candidacy was successful in other ways, especially considering his lack of organization, experience, and funds, plus his being only the second of his race to make such an effort (Shirley Chisholm ran in 1972). His strongest support came from individuals under thirty and from low-income and less-educated voters, although blacks from all socioeconomic strata voted for him. Jackson's overall support divided almost equally between men and women. He won fifty-three congressional

9. "Democrats' Registration of New Voters Fails to Achieve Advantage over GOP," Washington *Post*, November 2, 1984, Sec. A, p. 23.

10. Thomas B. Edsall, "The GOP's Registration Coup," *Washington Post National Weekly Edition*, October 1, 1984, p. 6.

districts, thirty of these in the South, and was the top selection in either precinct caucuses or primaries in four southern states: Louisiana, South Carolina, Mississippi, and Virginia. Jackson was second in Texas and believes he lost Alabama and Georgia on what the media termed "Super Tuesday" only "by the margin of the crisis of confidence of our leaders."[11] He refers, of course, to the fact that some prominent blacks in the region, like Coretta Scott King and Andrew Young, Joe Reed of Alabama, and Aaron Henry of Mississippi, supported Mondale. Due to the distribution of his turnout and the party formula for awarding delegates, Jackson's actual delegate total was far lower than his share of the caucus and primary balloting. For example, in New York he got 26 percent to Hart's 27 percent, yet Hart got twice the number of delegates.

Increased black interest stimulated by Reagan's rollback on civil rights policies and Jackson's candidacy, plus the various registration efforts, brought a higher national black turnout in 1984. According to network exit polls, 10 percent of all voters were black, up one point from 1980. Selected southern precincts showed Alabama up 27 percent, North Carolina up 16 percent, and Arkansas up 8 percent. However, the figure was unchanged from 1980 in Mississippi and down in South Carolina by 3 percent.[12] The uneven regional performance may have been due to the disenchantment many blacks felt with the national ticket and platform after the Democratic convention and the effect of polls showing Reagan far ahead in the region. In terms of officeholding, blacks nationwide made no significant gains, according to an official at the Joint Center for Political Studies.[13] And in the South, the increased black registration and 90 percent black vote for Mondale-Ferraro was more than offset by the nearly 80 percent white vote for Reagan-Bush. Thus Reagan swept Dixie, jumping his percentage ten points over 1980 to 62 percent and beating his national average by three points. He won the six southern states where blacks average over a quarter of the population as follows: Mississippi, 62 percent; South Carolina, 64 percent; Louisiana, 61 percent; Georgia, 60 percent; Alabama, 60 percent; and North Carolina, 62 percent. Blacks vigorously supported many other losing candidates besides Mondale, such as Jim Hunt of North Carolina, who got over 90

11. "Jesse Jackson Speaks: 'I Could Have Won,'" *Ebony*, XXXIX (August, 1984), 166–74.

12. Juan Williams and Paul Taylor, "Blacks Reap Disappointment in Election," *Washington Post*, November 8, 1984, Sec. A, p. 46.

13. Luix Overbea, "Black Leaders Map Strategy to Broaden American Political Base," *Christian Science Monitor*, November 26, 1984, p. 9.

TABLE 4
Black Lawmakers in the South

State	1974	1983	1984	1985
Alabama	3	24	24	24
Arkansas	4	5	5	5
Florida	3	12	12	12
Georgia	16	25	26	27
Louisiana	8	13	13	18
Mississippi	1	20	20	20
North Carolina	3	12	15	16
South Carolina	3	21	20	20
Tennessee	9	13	13	13
Texas	8	13	13	14
Virginia	2	7	7	7
Totals (of 1,780)	60	165	168	176

SOURCE: Joint Center for Political Studies, *National Roster of Black Elected Officials* (Washington, D.C., 1983), xvii and 10, (1984), 10, (1985), 14.

percent of the black vote, and William Winter of Mississippi, who got over 80 percent. Black candidates also lost some crucial contests like those of Ken Mosely in South Carolina and Robert Clark in Mississippi, both thought to have good chances for Congress.

A look at the trends in the numbers of blacks elected to southern state legislatures over the past decade illustrates the leveling off of black gains. All but three states in the region—Alabama, Mississippi, and Virginia— held at least some legislative elections in 1984, yet blacks were able to increase their numbers by only three, to total less than 1 percent of the 1,780 lawmaking posts.

One of Jackson's supporters, Georgia state representative Tyrone Brooks, said prior to the election: "The Jesse Jackson campaign is a movement. We're trying to capture not only the White House, but the courthouse and statehouse. Jesse will carry other black officials with him."[14] The reasons why this did not occur point to continuing obstacles and problems constraining black gains.

14. Quoted in Rob Gurwitt, "Jackson Candidacy Alters Democratic Contests," *Congressional Quarterly Weekly Report*, XLI (November 5, 1983), 2309.

PROBLEMS AND PROSPECTS

In order to begin to understand why in 1984 blacks—approximately 18 percent of southern voters and 25 percent in several Deep South states—did so poorly in Dixie, it is useful to examine three major problems: continuing institutional constraints in the electoral system itself; racism, particularly that of the influential white generation socialized in the decade of "massive resistance" to *Brown* (1954) and to the Voting Rights Act; and inadequate resources and organization to compete in an increasingly technological and expensive southern political process.

Nineteen eighty-four saw continuing difficulties in black efforts to take even the first step toward the ballot box: registration. Our political society is unique among industrial democracies in continuing to place the burden of registration on individuals. In West Germany, for example, when a citizen becomes eighteen, he or she must register with the local government for purposes of social security coverage. This also constitutes voter registration. In Great Britain or Canada, where government or party officials register individuals in their homes, virtually everyone eligible is registered. If such schemes had been enacted in the United States, say at the time of the Voting Rights Act, much greater progress undoubtedly would have been achieved. One NAACP official estimates that fully 70 percent of registered blacks voted in 1984.[15] However, in many areas the black community had to pressure white registrars to facilitate the registration process, fighting for satellite offices and permission to sign up voters in schools, churches, shopping centers, and similar places. One of the more outlandish practices finally abolished in 1983 was the dual registration system in Mississippi whereby persons had to register at the county seat for national, state, and county elections, and at their city

15. Joseph Madison, director of the organization's Voter Education Project, quoted in Mireille Grangerois, "Jackson Urges Blacks Not to Despair," *USA Today*, November 8, 1984, Sec. A, p. 5. Much confusion persists, even in scholarly circles, as to the actual level of turnout among blacks and how effective mobilization efforts have been in this overwhelmingly poor constituency. One body of analysis, drawing on the self-reported data of the Census Bureau reports and Survey Research Center findings, holds that southern blacks turn out at a higher rate than their socioeconomic status would predict. See Sidney Verba and Norman Nie, *Participation in America* (New York, 1972). That is now being challenged. Two authors followed up to see if blacks who reported that they voted or planned to vote actually did so; they found that blacks mobilize at a lower rate than their socioeconomic status would predict. See Paul R. Abramson and William Claggett, "Race Related Differences in Self-Reported and Validated Turnout," *Journal of Politics*, XLVI (August, 1984), 719–39.

hall for municipal ones. This worked a hardship on many black poor who lacked ready access to transportation.

Racial gerrymandering, an electoral impediment all too prevalent in contests for both major and minor offices, is harder to defeat than biased registration procedures.[16] For example, in the mid-1960s officials in Mississippi split a Delta congressional district just as blacks were being enfranchised, then spent nearly $500,000 from the mid-1970s into the 1980s fighting NAACP efforts and those of other groups to restructure the boundaries to reflect the original district's large black population. The result was the 2nd District, drawn with a 54 percent black majority and 48 percent black share of the voting-age population for the 1982 race. When Robert Clark lost to Reaganite Webb Franklin by 2,914 votes, black plaintiffs persuaded a three-judge federal panel in December, 1982, that the state plan diluted the black vote. The district was re-drawn with a 59 percent black majority comprising 53 percent of the voting-age population.[17] Clark lost again in 1984, by approximately the same number of votes. Following this defeat, Clark called on the Supreme Court to act swiftly on an appeal put before it by a group of black Delta voters seeking an increase to a 65 percent black majority — still a lower percentage than that of the old Delta district prior to the Voting Rights Act.

Other institutional problems that plagued blacks in 1984 and diminished their chances were the remaining at-large elections (which are on their way out, as Engstrom explains in his essay) and the change of elective posts to appointive ones as blacks gain power. This has often happened with such positions as superintendent of education. But it wasn't so much these issues or registration problems that occasioned debate in 1984 as whether the region's partisan runoff, or second primary, was racially discriminatory.

Jackson made the runoff primary a major campaign issue and pushed an unsuccessful minority plank on it at the Democratic convention. He and others contend that this procedure, used by all southern states except Louisiana, Tennessee, and Virginia, diminishes the chances of sizable black minorities to nominate one of their own, since the white majority will vote for the white candidate in the runoff. Jackson stresses that it is no mere accident of geography or history that such systems are found

16. See Brian Sherman, "Drawing the Lines: A Primer on Reapportionment," *Southern Exposure*, XII (February, 1984), 55–60.

17. See "Mississippi Delta," in *Congressional Quarterly Special Report: The 1984 Elections, Pre-Primary Congressional Outlook*, Supp. to XLII (February 25, 1984), 388.

only in the South (plus the border state of Oklahoma) and that they were instituted with the creation of Jim Crow at the turn of the century. A recent analysis supports this charge:

Part of the impetus for establishing runoffs at that time came from white supremicists bent on discouraging blacks from voting. Black participation in primaries was already illegal in many of the states. Other states used poll taxes and literacy tests to keep blacks from voting. But some whites saw the runoff as protecting their dominance even if, as eventually happened, the courts declared the blatant tools of political segregation unconstitutional.[18]

The national Democratic party pledged at the convention to study the consequences of runoff primaries in the eight relevant states and to recommend their abolition to the state parties wherever they were found to have a discriminatory effect. Also, in March, 1984, two blacks who lost runoffs in Mississippi filed challenges to the system in federal court, and that same year South Carolina Democrats debated a compromise to allow nomination with only 40 percent of the vote.

Some blacks differ with Jackson's position. Who can forget the sad spectacle of a profusely sweating Andrew Young—who has fought all his life for civil rights—being booed by Jackson delegates as he spoke against the minority plank at the convention? Opponents note that a plurality system would have given the 1974 Georgia gubernatorial nomination to Lester Maddox over George Busbee, for Maddox led the twelve-man field with 36 percent of the vote. They also fear that if the runoff is abolished, in majority black districts a single white running against several blacks might win the nomination. And even if the abolition of second primaries should lead to more black nominees, this would only result, given current political conditions, in additional conservative, probably Republican, officeholders. This brings us to the second major obstacle restricting black gains in 1984: racial voting patterns.

Blacks confront a devilish partisan predicament within a region where

18. Phil Duncan, "Jackson's Anti-Runoff Push Divides Southern Democrats," *Congressional Quarterly Weekly Report*, XLII (May 5, 1984), 1034. According to one noted expert on southern politics, Earl Black, it is "unlikely that the use of single primaries will increase across the South." "A Theory of Southern Factionalism," *Journal of Politics*, XLV (August, 1983), 613. See also the very useful essay by Alexander P. Lamis, "The Runoff Primary Controversy: Implications for Southern Politics," *PS*, XVII (Fall, 1984), 782–87.

In August, 1985, a ruling handed down by U.S. District Judge Charles Brieant barred runoffs in New York primaries. The basis of this decision was that the 1972 runoff law was partially designed to prevent minority voters from gaining political power and to maintain the status quo of the Democratic party. The ruling is currently being appealed. Even if the ruling is upheld, a substantial increase in the number of minority office holders is unlikely, since general elections must still be won.

whites are an 80 percent majority and both parties still suffer a racist political legacy. Jackson describes it in this fashion: "You see, we're still
fighting an animal with two heads. Let us not forget that. We're still
fighting a kind of political freak."[19] In terms of the Democratic party,
blacks seem literally trapped. They are consistently the most loyal supporters of the national ticket and often comprise the critical swing group
of voters for Democratic nominees for statewide office, even though this
obviously means they never have the opportunity to support blacks—
who are not nominated—and frequently must support conservative
whites. As always, in 1984 the black vote was the margin of victory for
whites in many southern races, such as Senator Howell Heflin's reelection in Alabama and the North Carolina congressmen elected in eastern
districts having heavy concentrations of black voters.[20] And as we saw,
they provided the major bloc of support to others who lost, like Winter
and Hunt. Yet black nominees cannot count on reciprocity from whites,
who—when added to blacks—constitute an overwhelmingly Democratic
electorate. All too often black nominees receive only lukewarm support
from white party leaders, and racial patterns of voting replace white partisan loyalties. Thus, Clark blamed his second loss on "race, pure race,"
concluding: "That's it. I tried. They're not going to cross over."[21]

Even with the problems blacks face in the Democratic party, the current nature of the Grand Old Party does not invite black participation. In
his first term, for example, Reagan attempted to confer tax-exempt status on the South's segregation academies (supposedly in response to a letter of request from Congressman Trent Lott of Mississippi, the House
whip); narrowed affirmative action through joining in a Memphis, Tennessee, court challenge to limit this relief only to those who can prove
they have been personally singled out for discrimination; reshaped the
Civil Rights Commission to serve conservative ends, declaring that racial
discrimination is no longer a major problem; endeavored to gut the Vot-

19. "Jesse Jackson Speaks: 'I Could Have Won!,' " *Ebony* (August, 1984), 170.
20. This was in contrast to the defeat of three incumbent North Carolina Democrats
with few black voters in their districts. Two others from overwhelmingly white districts
barely beat weak Republican opponents. Examples in 1984 from other states where Democratic incumbents defeated credible Republican challenges due to a large black vote are
South Carolina's 6th District and Mississippi's 4th. Rob Gurwitt, "GOP Disappointed with
Gains in the House," *Congressional Quarterly Weekly Report*, XLII (November 10, 1984),
2899.
21. In Cliff Treyens, "Clark Calls for Change in 2nd District Lines," Jackson *Daily
News–Clarion Ledger*, November 9, 1984, Sec. A, p. 1.

ing Rights Act; and opposed the national holiday for Martin Luther King's birthday. In addition he slashed domestic programs for the poor and declared on at least one occasion in Georgia, "The South will rise again." Reagan's message sold well to white southerners. One study found that in 1984 it was in three formerly "Wallaceite" segregationist constituencies in Alabama, north Florida, and Louisiana that Reagan experienced his greatest gains over 1980, averaging 25 percent.[22]

In North Carolina, Helms was running far behind Hunt in the polls until he filibustered the King bill, suggesting that Dr. King was a Communist (an implication Reagan would not refute in a press conference at the time). Following this, Helms's poll ratings started to climb, leading some to liken his actions to the sixties' "stands in the schoolhouse door" by Faubus, Barnett, and Wallace. And as Charles Bullock makes clear in his essay in this volume, the civil rights scores of southern Republican House members resemble nothing so much as the racist Democratic delegations of the Solid South era from 1900 to the 1960s. Yet in 1984 their numbers increased by ten.

How does one explain this racial polarization in light of the proclamations—found often in this book as well as in others and in the media—of an increasingly deracialized public opinion in Dixie? The answer may lie in Earl Hawkey's finding that although overall public attitudes do reveal a decline in racial values, particularly among the young, a significant section of whites still holds to such orientations—the generation of Democrats intensively socialized in the 1950s and 1960s to a pronounced racism. This population cohort now dominates the region, in economics and politics, education and communications. Until their era ends, it may well be that this "two-headed animal"—the whites' unwillingness to support black Democratic nominees and their receptivity to subtle and not-so-subtle racial appeals—will continue to haunt blacks.

Among the remaining problems confronting blacks are those of trying to compete in an increasingly expensive and highly sophisticated electoral process. For example, the Republican party more than offset black registration efforts with its well-organized $11 million preelection drive, much of which was directed at the white South, where polls showed Reagan with a 2–1 lead. The party spent an average of $4.50 per new voter, and various conservative groups joined in the endeavor. The National Conservative Political Action Committee (NCPAC), for instance, funded

22. Rhodes Cook, "Reagan's Landslide Shatters Fading Democratic Coalition," *Congressional Quarterly Weekly Report*, XLII (November 17, 1984), 2939.

"Americans to Re-elect Ronald Reagan," which sent out a slick fourteen-page booklet to many white citizens in the South, stating several times the dangers posed by Jesse Jackson and "so-called" civil rights groups.[23] These combined efforts dramatically increased the numbers of whites on the rolls. Indeed, their surge outpaced in numbers, if not percentages, that of blacks: in Georgia, election-year increases were over 170,211; in Louisiana 99,169; and, in one four-county area of North Carolina, 40,844.[24] In terms of campaign funds and access to political expertise and technology, blacks can in no way compete equally with either white Democrats or Republicans. Jackson spent only some $3 million and had little staff help, no polls, and only a handful of ads, whereas Mondale's $18 million, plus untold in-kind labor union expenditures, bought a campaign with all the trimmings. The Republicans supported their state parties by spending the maximum sums permissible under the 1974 Campaign Finance Act, whereas the Democrats spent virtually nothing on their southern parties, handicapping black nominees. Helms apparently spent close to $14 million, and Webb Franklin and other Reaganites had access to ample funds and political technology. Clark was only half right in attributing his defeat to racial voting. As the newspaper headline from the state capital read the next day: "REAGAN, ORGANIZATION POWERED FRANKLIN."

This gap in resources is crucial throughout the nation and helps explain in part why 10 percent of the vote results in only 1 percent of elective offices. It is, however, particularly troublesome in Dixie. One study concluded flatly that "in the South, black representation is low primarily because blacks have fewer resources. The gaps between blacks and whites in economic and educational attainment are so great that blacks have difficulty competing politically."[25] These class differences between the races also mean that black candidates, to the degree that they represent the needs of their constituents, are liberal on economic and social welfare issues. This adds to the racial vote against their candidacy an economic bias among middle-class whites.

23. Booklet in possession of the authors. For a good account of the GOP in recent Dixie politics, see John Van Wingen and Jimmy Lea, "Reagan, Southern Republicanism, and the 1984 Election," *USA Today*, CXIII (March, 1985), 10–12.

24. Thomas B. Edsall, "The GOP's Registration Coup," *Washington Post National Weekly Edition*, October 1, 1984, p. 6, and "Democrats' Registration of New Voters Fails to Achieve Advantages over GOP," Washington *Post*, November 2, 1984, Sec. A, p. 23.

25. Albert K. Karnig and Susan Welch, *Black Representation and Urban Policy* (Chicago, 1980), 145.

CONCLUSIONS

The increased numbers of black elected officials in the South suggest that blacks have now merged into the region's political life. This is only partially true. A careful look at the actual figures reveals that although the gains have been significant, the black share of the South's authoritative decision-making positions remains far below their population share, and 1984 was anything but a growth year.

Many new black voters have turned out in the 1980s, first, in opposition to Reagan and a coterie of prominent Dixie Reaganites in both parties, and second, in support of Jesse Jackson and other black regional candidates. The impact of this increased participation cannot be measured merely in the short run. It is possible that permanent increase in political involvement at all levels might ensue and provide the base from which a new group of leaders will emerge. If so, Jackson's impact could be felt for some time.

Another potential effect of Jackson's candidacy may be to stimulate a clearer demarcation between Democrats and Republicans. During the caucuses and primaries of 1984, fewer whites participated as Democrats. If this is any indication of future trends, a greater number of conservative whites may become more closely associated with the Republican party. Also, should the Democratic party not serve as an instrument for greater black gains, community institutions such as churches and schools may be required to play more significant political roles, as they did in the heyday of the civil rights movement.

Finally, if black voters and nonvoters lose faith in politics in the face of 1984 post-election disappointments, and if that hopelessness were to persist, the political energy of recent years could dissipate.

Partisan Politics: A One-and-a-Half, No-Party System

JOHN VAN WINGEN

DAVID VALENTINE

But for all the changes that were going on and being made in Dixie,
it would still have been rash . . . to assume that the vigor had gone out of
the old pattern and that it was speedily being relegated to the limbo of
things past and done with. . . . Its power over the body of the
South would remain tremendous, even conclusive, and
would exhibit itself with great distinctiveness.
                                    —W. J. Cash, *The Mind of the*
                                    South

Electoral politics in the South is a fascinating area of study, in large part
because of the dramatic changes in the institutional rules governing elections. Electoral rules define who can run as candidates, who can vote,
and what tally produces victory. Thus, they are central to the political
process, to who gets what, when, and how. These rules have changed
more in the South since mid-century than elsewhere in the nation.

Many observers expected a correspondingly rapid change in southern
electoral politics. In particular, several predicted that the Solid South, long
the bastion of the Democratic party, would mobilize under the Republican
banner. Kevin Phillips expounded the most exuberant and confident such
prediction in 1969, and more cautious forecasts have appeared both before
and since. Although the bases for the predictions varied, essentially three
arguments emerged. Alexander Heard suggested that the urban areas
would become more Republican, a line of argument further developed by
Donald Strong; Phillips as well as James Sundquist suggested that southern
Democrats would realign to the Republican party on the basis of social issues such as race; and finally, a group of authors argued that those less
committed to the Democratic party—the independents according to E. M.
Schreiber, the split ticket voter for Charles Hadley and Susan Howell, and
the young for Raymond Wolfinger and Robert Arsenau—would begin to

swell the ranks of Republican adherents.[1] These predictions of a Republican South, first articulated in the 1950s, have yet to come true. Even after Reagan's decisive 1984 sweep of the former Confederacy, southern politics retains its decidedly Democratic flavor.[2]

The forecasts of imminent Republican dominance have not materialized, because they did not take into account the full range of the social human dynamics of partisan change.[3] Political attitudes, including partisanship, are structured through interaction with the larger environment; family, friends, school, and other agents of socialization help individuals organize the political world. Short of a full-scale social transformation and political revolution the cues provided by such agents alter very slowly.

In the South, as in no other area of the country, we have an opportunity to observe how institutions and socialization interact to fashic change. For although the region has not become a center of Republi strength, neither is it the Solid South so brilliantly described by ' Key.[4] As Bob Dylan's lyrics prophesied two decades ago, "the tin are a-changin'," and the youth of today have different attitude alterations in southern institutions drastically changed the sc   of its children. However, the process of generational replace   the old values with the new ones is slow.

To see these gradual transformations, we must first des .be the electoral rules and partisan patterns of the Solid South of the 1930s and 1940s. Then, by portraying the institutional changes of the 1950s and 1960s, we can depict the drastic alteration which led many to predict the emergence of a Republican majority in the South. Linking demographic patterns and partisan socialization, we will explain why this new majority failed to materialize. Indeed, our analysis indicates that the Republi-

1. Kevin P. Phillips, *The Emerging Republican Majority* (New Rochelle, 1969); Alexander Heard, *A Two Party South?* (Chapel Hill, 1952); Donald Strong, *Urban Republicanism in the South* (Washington, D.C., 1973); E. M. Schreiber, " 'Where the Ducks Are':· Southern Strategy Versus Fourth Party," *Public Opinion Quarterly*, XXXV (Summer, 1971), 157–67; Charles D. Hadley and Susan E. Howell, "The Southern Split Ticket Voter, 1952–1976: Republican Conversion or Democratic Decline?" in Robert P. Steed, Laurence W. Moreland, and Tod A. Baker (eds.), *Party Politics in the South* (New York, 1980); Raymond Wolfinger and Robert B. Arsenau, "Partisan Change in the South, 1952–1976," in Louis Maisel and Joseph Cooper (eds.), *Political Parties: Development and Decay* (Beverly Hills, 1978), 179–210.

2. John Van Wingen and Jimmy Lea, "Reagan, Southern Republicanism, and the 1984 Election," *USA Today*, CXIII (March, 1985), 10–13.

3. Philip E. Converse, "On the Possibility of Major Political Realignment in the South," in Angus Campbell, Philip E. Converse, Warren E. Miller, and Donald E. Stokes, *Elections and the Political Order* (New York, 1966), 212–42.

4. V. O. Key, Jr., *Southern Politics in State and Nation* (New York, 1949).

can party will probably remain the minority party in the South for some time to come.

The failure of the South to develop a thoroughly competitive two-party system, well organized at all electoral levels, means that political parties, as was the case in the Solid South, still do not provide an avenue for the disadvantaged to articulate their demands. The Republican party is a minority party, organized from the top down and very weak at the local level; the Democratic party remains dominant but highly factionalized. Consequently, images produced by media consultants, rather than issue positions articulated by competing parties, are the hallmark of contemporary southern elections (as Parker explains in the next essay in this study). The great transformation in southern electoral politics has been from the institutional exclusion of significant segments of the population to socialized inclusion into a less than meaningful mode of political participation. Elections emphasizing candidates' images at the expense of substantive issues become an important means of co-optation rather than an avenue of popular control.

INSTITUTIONAL EXCLUSION: THE SOLID SOUTH

From the turn of the century through the 1950s the electoral system of the Solid South successfully excluded by law large elements of the population. Socialization by the family, churches, schools, and peers as well as legal and economic institutions helped maintain this restrictive political system and the racism on which it was based. The adoption of laws limiting black electoral participation directly led to the development of one-party factionalism. The system also supported the persistence of poverty in the region in that wealthy elites were disinterested in bringing in jobs for poor blacks, and poor whites and blacks had no political vehicle with which to seek change. Once in place, the three interrelated institutions—Jim Crow laws, one-party factionalism, and pervasive poverty—dominated the formation of youth's attitudes toward electoral participation. Those attitudes in turn shaped the electoral politics of the 1960s and 1970s even though the institutions themselves had significantly changed.

The imposition of legal limitations upon the political rights of blacks began in earnest about 1890 and was successfully completed by the early twentieth century. A dual society was established in two steps. First, in beating back the Populist challenge, wealthy elites used race as the wedge to separate poor whites politically from their actual or potential allies—poor blacks. Second, a group of electoral "reforms" were adopted which eliminated blacks as a political force in the South. The Fifteenth Amendment to the U.S. Constitution precluded the exclusion of blacks qua blacks from general elections; but since most blacks were poor and uneducated, legally imposed poll taxes and literacy tests accomplished the same end. Surrogate restrictions upon black voting were unnecessary in primary elections. The states classified political parties as private clubs, and local party officials who were so inclined refused to give blacks a ballot; most were so inclined. This "white primary," which put Jim Crow in the voting booth, was the most important disfranchising device.[5]

Whether intentional or not, these restrictions on the political rights of blacks severely weakened all political opposition in the South. In the late nineteenth century poor whites had often supported independent Populist candidates and had even flirted with forming electoral coalitions with blacks. But such legal changes as poll taxes also excluded some poor whites, thus diluting their voting strength. In addition, the acceptance of a dual society made a poor white–black electoral alliance unthinkable. As a result, all bases for a viable second party in the South were eliminated. Both blacks and poor whites discovered that the Democratic primary, not the general election, had become the significant electoral contest. The white primary completed the disfranchisement of blacks. Jim Crow undergirded the Solid South.

As Key shows, the disfranchisement of blacks and many poor whites fragmented the Democratic party. Democrats always won the general election, but that outcome lost substantial meaning because everyone was a Democrat. Conflict within the party revolved around ephemeral factions competing in the Democratic primaries. The factions were, with few exceptions, organized around personalities rather than issues. These fluid factions fostered "friends and neighbors" voting, that is, the tendency for candidates to poll much better in and around their home counties than throughout the rest of the state; but they did not foster the articulation of alternative policy choices for the voters.[6] From the 1890s through the mid-1960s, one-party factionalism reigned supreme in the South.

5. C. Vann Woodward, *The Strange Career of Jim Crow*, (2nd rev. ed.; New York, 1966); Key, *Southern Politics*, 533–643; J. Morgan Kousser, *The Shaping of Southern Politics* (New Haven, 1974); Jerold G. Rusk, and John J. Stucker, "The Effect of the Southern System of Election Laws on Voting Participation: A Reply to V. O. Key, Jr.," in Joel H. Silbey, Allan G. Bogue, and William H. Flanigan, *The History of American Electoral Behavior* (Princeton, 1978), 198–250.

6. Key, *Southern Politics*, Chapter 14; John R. Van Wingen, "Localism, Factional Fluidity, and Factionalism: Louisiana and Mississippi Gubernatorial Contests," *Social Science History*, VIII (Winter, 1984), 3–41.

The dramatic constriction of the electorate was clearly reflected in the political agenda. Gone were the days when a coalition of lower-class blacks and whites could threaten to unite and gain governmental control. Gone, too, was any mention of the economic issues that had spurred the growth of this coalition. The primary function of governments in the South became the maintenance of the status quo. Occasionally, rabid orators preyed on the frustrations of poor whites in order to garner their vote, but once in office the factionalized legislatures ensured that the rhetoric remained symbolic. Tangible programs for meeting the real needs of the masses were rare. And southern politicians devised new types of taxes, such as the sales tax, to impose most of the tax burden upon the poor.

Thus, one-party factionalism helped ensure the continuance of the third institutional constraint—poverty. State government in the South rested on an anomaly. In order to maintain segregation, the government penetrated every aspect of southern life, from picking the textbooks that schoolchildren could read to defining who could go to the bathroom where. But at the same time, in the guise of freedom, state politicians worshiped a limited form of government when it came to providing for the public welfare. Roads, schools, and programs for the poor are traditionally the largest expenditures for state government. But in all three areas, expenditures in the southern states were significantly lower than those of the rest of the nation, at a level not explainable merely by the fact that the South was the poorest region. One-party factionalism promoted a government that would intrude itself into the daily lives of individuals to protect the status quo but, in the name of liberty, would not provide for the public welfare.

The South was poor, and its peculiar institutions, to borrow a phrase used to describe an albatross of the antebellum era, kept it so. Inadequate schools and roads impeded economic development: without skilled labor and the necessary infrastructure, the South could not grow commercially. Further, racial segregation and pervasive poverty made it an unattractive region for outsiders. Thus, the South remained insulated; "foreign" people and ideas were excluded. The term *Yankee* stood for all that was strange and different, and the contempt usually accompanying its utterance symbolized the isolation of the South.

Segregation, one-party factionalism, and poverty dominated the electoral politics of the era. And since the federal government was kept out, primarily through the power of the seniority-laden southern congressional delegation and devices such as the rule requiring two-thirds vote to nominate the presidential candidate at the national Democratic convention, these institutional arrangements molded the political socialization of young southerners. The specific direction and content of that socialization, however, depended upon who one was. For our purposes three groups merit examination, blacks, poor whites, and white Republicans.

The majority of black southerners resided in the rural areas of the so-called black belt and found life harsh. A sharecropping system supported by debtor laws tied them to the plantations where their ancestors had been slaves. Unskilled and uneducated, these people quickly learned to accept segregation and to stay out of politics. Positive political socialization about elections did not occur. Political awareness was so low that interviewers for the University of Michigan's national Survey Research Center/Center for Political Studies (SRC/CPS) election surveys of 1952 through 1960 discovered that many rural southern blacks did not understand questions concerning electoral politics. Thus, in sharp contrast to other groups in the nation, anywhere from one-quarter to one-third of southern blacks failed to respond to the standard partisan identification question, "Generally speaking, do you consider yourself a Republican, Democrat, Independent or what?"[7] Should the institutional constraints barring electoral participation be removed, this group would suddenly, en masse, be ripe for resocialization. Until such time, electoral politics would remain terra incognita.

Urban blacks, unlike their rural counterparts, were more likely to be allowed to participate and hence become socialized into politics. However, their electoral impact was inconsequential. Prior to the New Deal, urban blacks—except for those in a few well-organized political areas such as New Orleans—tended to vote Republican in national contests. Few rewards came from such loyalty though, even in states where blacks controlled the Republican organization. After 1936 more and more began to listen to the overtures of the national Democratic party, but the racist consensus of the multiple factions of the state Democratic parties blunted the utility of avid Democratic participation. Unlike the northern black, the southern urban black was not strongly committed to either party.

Poor, predominantly rural whites comprise the second important group. Their socialization was, in contrast to urban blacks', totally consistent. The Democratic party was the only party, and the only important election was the primary. Local and state candidates stumped the county

7. Paul Allen Beck, "Partisan Dealignment in the Postwar South," *American Political Science Review*, LXXI (June, 1977), 481–82.

fairs, courthouse speeches became festive occasions, and local primaries determined who controlled what. As Key said, "Politics flourished at the forks of the creek," and rural whites tended to participate more than their urban brethren.[8]

The national surveys of the 1950s reveal the overwhelmingly Democratic proclivities of native southern whites. In 1952, almost 90 percent indicated that they at least leaned toward the Democratic party. Undoubtedly, this group did not differentiate between the national and state Democratic parties, but when asked what the party meant to them, those who responded did so in terms of local, not national themes.[9] Voting turnout evidenced the distance of Washington, D.C., and the national Democratic party from the creek: the percentage of rural whites voting in the state Democratic gubernatorial primaries tended to exceed the percentage voting in the national presidential elections.[10]

The third group of importance, white Republicans, formed a distinct minority. Historical peculiarities of the Civil War produced patches of Republicanism, particularly in the mountain areas of eastern Tennessee, western Virginia, and northwestern North Carolina. These areas not only voted Republican in presidential contests but also elected Republicans to the state legislatures.[11]

Of more importance were pockets of urban Republicans. Strong found that the white upper-middle class of cities such as Birmingham usually supported Republican presidential candidates.[12] But because of the weakness or, frequently, the nonexistence of local party organizations, local Republicanism had no meaning. These presidential Republicans, as Key called them, although small in number, lived in the areas that would witness dramatic population increases in the 1960s and 1970s.

The politics of exclusion thus created a montage of institutional constraints that preserved segregation, contributed to one-party factionalism, and ensured the continuance of pervasive poverty. The socialization of the southern masses produced three important groups: the vast majority of blacks who were compelled by social and economic conditions to

8. Key, *Southern Politics*, Chapter 24.
9. Converse, "On the Possibility of Major Political Realignment," in Campbell, et al., *Elections and the Political Order*, 216–19; Jerry Perkins and Randall Guynes, "Partisanship in National and State Politics," *Public Opinion Quarterly*, XL (Fall, 1976), 376–78.
10. Key, *Southern Politics*, Chapter 23.
11. *Ibid.*, Chapter 13.
12. Strong, *Urban Republicanism*; Donald S. Strong, "Durable Republicanism in the South," in Allan P. Sindler (ed.), *Change in the Contemporary South* (Durham, 1963), 174–94.

accept segregation and were not socialized into electoral politics; the predominantly rural, poor whites who identified with the local, not national, Democratic party; and the small minority of upper-middle-class urban whites who identified with the national, not local, Republican party. The South of the 1930s and 1940s was sufficiently isolated from the rest of the country that its citizens on the whole accepted the system of political exclusion. The confluence of institutions and socialization produced and maintained the Solid South.

THE CRACKING OF THE INSTITUTIONS: THE YANKEE INVASION

Time alters most everything, sometimes slowly and imperceptibly, at other times suddenly and dramatically. The institutional constraints of segregation, poverty, and one-party factionalism began to change slowly in the 1940s, then altered dramatically in the 1960s. By 1970 the Solid South had been relegated to the history books.

The abolishment of de jure segregation, the linchpin of the Solid South, constituted the most important change. Indeed, the decline in poverty and the alteration in the nature of the party system can be traced in part to the elimination of legal segregation.

Federal intervention destroyed the dual society, with the most celebrated blows being delivered by the Supreme Court. For example, in *Smith v. Allright* (1944) the court struck down the white primary, and ten years later it ruled in *Brown v. Board of Education of Topeka* (1954) that "separate but equal" schools were inherently unequal. At the time other changes, such as the national Democratic party's abolishment of the two-thirds rule for nominating the presidential candidate, were occurring. Following Roosevelt, no president could ignore the racial issue. The national Democratic party confronted the problem in the 1940s, and Congress addressed it in the late 1950s and early 1960s.

After the 1896 Bryan debacle, the national party had tacitly agreed to let the South alone. White southern Democrats could build a society predicated upon white supremacy; in return, the South would vote solidly Democratic in presidential contests. Ironically, the New Deal, which the South supported more than any other area of the country, shattered this "gentleman's agreement." Several things occurred, but one of the most important was that northern blacks—whose numbers continually increased because of southern black migration—began to switch party allegiances in 1936, primarily because of the New Deal economic programs. This solid realignment away from the party of Lincoln into the party of FDR transformed northern urban blacks into an important voting block for the national Democratic party. In return for their support, black leaders demanded action by the federal government in the area of civil rights. Early evidence of their growing political potency was Roosevelt's creation of the Fair Employment Practices Commission during World War II. When the Democrats added a civil rights plank to the party platform in 1948, the old agreement between the northern and southern Democrats was destroyed.[13]

White southerners correctly perceived these changes as a threat to their society. In 1948 many southerners bolted the party to vote for South Carolinian Strom Thurmond, the Dixiecrat candidate who ran in protest of the party's civil rights plank. Later, in the 1950s and 1960s, southern Democrats joined northern Republicans to resist federal intervention. Clearly, southern politicians were fighting to prevent the imposition of a second reconstruction.

Everyone knows the outcome of the battle: the southern Democrats lost. The national Democratic politicos prided themselves on becoming the champions of rights for minorities, as long as the struggle was against de jure, not de facto (a troublesome northern problem), segregation. Intransigent southern whites tried legal dodges, political deals, and violence to forestall the inevitable, but by 1970 Jim Crow had slipped into his grave.

The shifting balance of power was evident by the mid-1960s. Civil rights acts were passed in 1957 and 1964. In 1964 the Twenty-second Amendment abolished the poll tax for presidential elections, and in *Harper* v. *Virginia State Board of Elections* (1966) the U.S. Supreme Court eliminated the tax for all other elections. More importantly, in 1965 Congress passed the Voting Rights Act. This act proscribed literacy tests and allowed federal marshals to monitor black registration and voting under some circumstances.

The institutional constraint of poverty also altered over these years. The story is complex, and the economic development proved to be uneven. Mississippi, for example, still remains at the bottom of almost every measure of economic well-being. The growth sprang from several sources. Deliberate federal policy, augmented by skillful senior southern congressmen sitting on key congressional committees, poured millions of dollars into the southern economy. (See O'Rourke's essay in this volume for contemporary data.) Military installations, naval shipyards, and the aerospace in-

13. Everett Carll Ladd, Jr., with Charles D. Hadley, *Transformations of the American Party System* (New York, 1978), Chapter 2; Robert J. Steamer, "Southern Disaffection with the National Democratic Party," in Sindler, *Change in the Contemporary South*, 150–73.

dustry sprouted in Dixie. At the same time, federal welfare dollars became a major component of the economy of the poorest of the southern states— as always, Mississippi, but also Alabama and Arkansas.

Not all the development depended upon infusions of federal money. Texas and Louisiana converted oil resources into revenues, whereas Florida cashed in on its sunny skies and pleasant beaches. Other areas such as Atlanta witnessed booming growth in the service sector. But whether indigenous or federally seeded, economic development brought large sums of Yankee dollars into the South. And as these dollars turned over, the racial and economic composition of the southern polity changed.

Two massive migrations accompanied the former Confederacy's dollar transfusion. History indicates that rapid development usually coincides with tragic economic dislocations. The South is no exception. Blacks had been leaving the South for decades, but with the beginning of economic development, a treacherous undertow wrenched hundreds of thousands of rural blacks off the plantations, changing their situation from bad to worse. The mechanization and chemicalization of agriculture transformed historically labor-intensive cotton and rice production into energy-intensive enterprises. The cottonpicker and crop duster replaced the field hand. Tragically, black-belt blacks were cast off the farm, where they could at least subsist, into degrading unemployment. Woefully inadequate programs for providing for the needs of this large corpus of unskilled, illiterate, unemployed, hungry blacks remained deliberately so. Many of those who could, left, catching the "freedom trains" north, hoping to find a job in the industrial cities outside Dixie.[14]

While poor blacks fled, middle-class whites moved south. These Yankees, brought in as managers and technicians to run the burgeoning military, governmental, light industrial, and service sectors, generally settled around the South's largest cities.

The inflow of middle-class whites and the outflow of poor blacks had tremendous electoral consequences. For the first time the South had a large middle class who believed that government should provide schools, roads, police and fire protection, and all the other governmental services —which is not to say social welfare programs—efficiently and effectively, with minimal corruption. These demands became a dominant force remolding southern politics. In short, the amelioration of the South's pervasive poverty brought "Yankee" ideas about the role of gov-

14. Francis Fox Piven and Richard A. Cloward, *Regulating the Poor: The Functions of Public Welfare* (New York, 1971); Nick Kotz, *Let Them Eat Promises: The Politics of Hunger in America* (Englewood Cliffs, 1969).

ernment into the heart of Dixie. Without the massive exodus of blacks, however, the voice of the new middle class might not have been heard. In the 1940s blacks potentially could have dominated politics in states such as Mississippi if they had not been excluded, for in these states they constituted a majority. By 1970, when they became enfranchised, migration patterns had reduced their proportion from slightly over half in such states to approximately a third. Direct control by blacks alone through the ballot box was no longer possible.

Economic development led as well to the demise of the last institutional constraint, one-party factionalism. Of the various types of Republicans described by Key in the late 1940s, only the small enclaves of mountain Republicans offered local opposition to the Democrats. The influx of middle-class whites altered this, for many of the immigrants were not only Yankees but were also economically conservative Republicans who settled in the very areas where presidential Republicans lived. The number of Republican newcomers was substantial: in the 1960 through 1972 nationwide SRC surveys, anywhere from one-third to one-half of those in the South professing Republican attachments grew up outside the boundaries of the former Confederacy.[15] As a result of this increase in adherents, the Republican party is now strong enough to offer serious candidates for highly publicized statewide elections in every southern state. By 1980 all of the southern states had elected at least one Republican senator or governor. Because the South now has more than one party, one-party factionalism no longer adequately describes its system of electoral politics. That institutional constraint crumbled along with the oppressive Jim Crow laws and the overwhelming regional poverty. For the second time the Yankees invaded the South and, in a manner milder than Sherman's, struck down some of the region's peculiar institutions.

SOUTHERN RESISTANCE: THE SOCIALIZATION CONSTRAINT

When the institutions of segregation, poverty, and one-party factionalism began to erode, predictions about what would happen seemed simple. Key hinted at the results.[16] The Democratic party would become liberal, aligning itself with the national Democrats to ensure support of its two largest stalwarts: blacks and poor whites. A revitalized Republican party would become the voice of economic conservatism, thus representing the growing middle class. The resulting two-party system would re-

15. Beck, "Partisan Dealignment," 480–81.
16. Key, Southern Politics, Chapter 31.

store elections to their rightful place in a democracy. The poor would have an organized avenue to articulate their needs, as would the middle class, and the winner of electoral contests would receive a clear mandate as to which direction governmental policy should proceed.

The prognosis turned out to be prescient yet inadequate. Today the right groups identify with the right parties, but the parties remain unresponsive to the needs of their constituent coalitions. The abatement of the racial issue and emergence of serious Republican opposition in statewide elections failed to ameliorate factional Democratic politics. And the Republicans, although much better organized than in the past, still constitute a minority party. Yet each year someone seems to say: "Just wait, the election results portend a healthy Republican party." Such an outcome is doubtful. Significant electoral change over the past three decades has indeed occurred, but only within the constraints of socialization. Fortunately, accurate survey information from the past eight presidential elections permit us to see what did change.[17] Four groups—blacks, pre–World War II native whites, immigrant whites, and the post–World War II generation—deserve attention.

Blacks: Democratic Mobilization

Normally, socialization into electoral politics occurs early in life. In particular, most U.S. children acquire partisan leanings, that is, the propensity to favor one or the other of the major political parties, prior to the development of the cognitive capabilities necessary for understanding the meaning of partisanship. Study after study demonstrates the importance of these socialized partisan attachments in shaping people's views of the electoral universe.[18]

These findings, of course, do not help us understand how previously excluded groups such as southern blacks will respond to politics. Figure 1 vividly demonstrates what can happen when a formerly excluded group suddenly enters the electorate. By 1960 around one-half of the southern blacks identified with the Democratic party, a figure that was steadily declining while the rate of Republican adherents increased. A large percen-

17. These data were made available by the Inter-University Consortium for Political and Social Research and were originally collected by the Survey Research Center at the University of Michigan. We are especially grateful to David Leuthold for assistance in helping us access the data at the University of Missouri. Needless to say, neither Leuthold, the consortium, nor the original collectors bear any responsibility for the analyses and interpretations presented here.

18. Bruce A. Campbell, *The American Electorate: Attitudes and Actions* (New York, 1979).

FIGURE 1

Partisan Preferences of Southern Blacks, 1952–1980

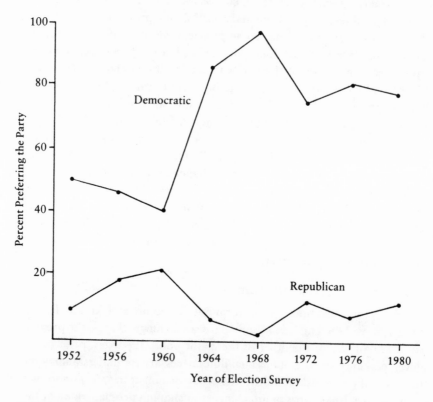

SOURCE: SRC Presidential Election Surveys

Data Points are the percentage of southern blacks responding to the partisan identification question who indicate that they at least lean toward the party.

tage (almost a third in 1960) favored neither party. In short, southern
blacks tended to be Democratic, but not overwhelmingly so.[19] After
1960, when the quest for black suffrage became a violent political issue,
partisanship took on new meaning, and almost all identified with the
Democrats.

Why at this time blacks were mobilized into the Democratic, rather

19. Bruce A. Campbell, "Change in the Southern Electorate," *American Journal of Political Science*, XXI (February, 1977), 37–64; Bruce A. Campbell, "Patterns of Change in
the Partisan Loyalties of Native Southerners, 1952–1972," *Journal of Politics*, XXXIX
(August, 1977), 730–61.

than the Republican, party is not hard to understand. Prior to the New Deal, blacks were Republicans—if they were politically socialized. But beginning in the late 1930s and the 1940s, the picture became more complex. The national Democrats sought black votes while local Democrats continued to suppress them. The Eisenhower administration muddled an already confusing situation. Buoyed in part by the Supreme Court's decision in *Brown* v. *Board of Education* (1954), Eisenhower carried black districts in New Orleans, Jacksonville, and Richmond in his 1956 campaign.[20] The following year he sent federal troops to integrate Central High in Little Rock. A distinct possibility existed for the Republican party to reap the benefit of enfranchisement.

Barry Goldwater destroyed the possibility. When he campaigned for the presidency in 1964, few doubted his stand on racial issues. Goldwater had voted against the 1964 Civil Rights Act, and honing a strategy aimed at southern whites, he often emphasized his belief in the primacy of states' rights over civil rights. The national surveys attest to the clarity of Goldwater's oratory: the percentage of Republican blacks dropped precipitously in 1964 (see Figure 1). When the Voting Rights Act passed the next year and southern rural blacks, sometimes accompanied by federal marshals, began to register, they committed themselves to the national party that helped them. By 1968 over 97 percent considered themselves Democrats.

The national Republican party, forgetting the Eisenhower experience, solidified these Democratic propensities. Ensuing presidential campaigns reflected the continual commitment to the infamous "southern strategy." Nixon, coddling the so-called silent majority, campaigned on "law and order," code words in the South (and maybe the nation) for segregation and racial suppression; Ford, while in the House, voted against the civil rights acts; and Reagan's views were reminiscent of Goldwater's. By 1980 the previously apolitical southern blacks resembled their northern brethren. Indeed, the greatest increase in participation in the 1970s was among southern blacks. Mobilization had occurred, and the politics of the times socialized them in the Democratic party.

Solid South—Generation Whites: Resistance to Conversion

Although the southern strategy adopted by Goldwater, Nixon, and Reagan cemented blacks to the Democratic party, it failed, as Figure 2 shows, to convert whites to the Republican cause, particularly at the

20. Strong, *Urban Republicanism*, 12–26.

FIGURE 2

Partisan Preference of Native White Southerners: Solid South
Generation, 1952–1980

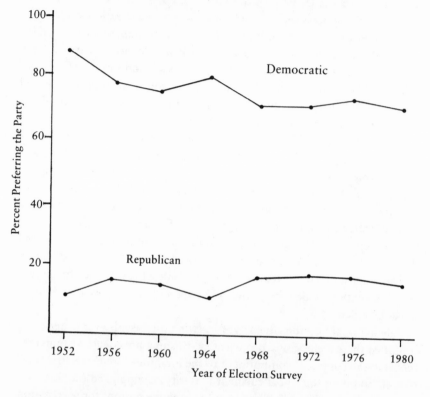

SOURCE: SRC Presidential Election Surveys
Data points are the percentage of native white southerners born prior to 1934 responding to the partisan identification question who indicate that they at least lean toward the
party.

state and local levels. The failure demonstrates how socialization can
block seemingly logical political alternatives. Whites reared in the South
prior to World War II grew up accepting segregation and one-party factionalism. But as indicated above, the focus of politics at the forks of the
creek was local rather than national. Thus, when the national Democratic party began to advocate integration, many southern whites would
vote on occasion against the Democratic presidential candidate — for
Thurmond, the Dixiecrat in 1948; for Goldwater, the Republican in
1964; and for Wallace, the American independent in 1968. Analysis of

county returns reveals high positive correlation among the percentage votes these three candidates received, and national surveys verify what most commentators believed at the time: these bolts from the national Democratic party were racially motivated.[21]

The commitments to segregation and local Democratic politics made it easy for the native southern Democrat to abandon the national party. In the Deep South, state election officials made the bolt even easier. The states that Thurmond carried in 1948 listed him as the *Democratic*, not *Dixiecrat*, candidate. Similarly, Wallace was listed as the Democratic candidate in the states that he carried. And in 1964, Alabama's ballot had no electors pledged to Lyndon Johnson, and Mississippi's Democratic leadership endorsed, en masse, Barry Goldwater. Clearly, voting against the national Democratic candidate involved little dissonance. The Solid South–generation whites remained committed Democratic racists. During the height of racial hysteria they avidly supported Democratic gubernatorial candidates such as Orval Faubus, Ross Barnett, George Wallace, Lester Maddox, and John McKeithen who rode to victory on rhetoric opposing desegregation.[22] Participation in national elections became a means for venting their ire against the Yankee invasion. Such venting in no way converted them to the GOP.[23]

White Immigrants: Republican Transplants

Jim Crow laws and one-party factionalism were unique southern institutions. Outside the South the texture of politics differed. As the Progressive reforms at the turn of the century gradually destroyed the urban machines, electoral politics revolved more and more around the quadrennial presidential elections. Unlike in the South, presidential elections, not the guber-

---

21. Louis M. Seagull, *Southern Republicanism* (New York, 1975); Philip E. Converse, Aage R. Clausen, and Warren E. Miller, "Electoral Myth and Reality: The 1964 Election," *American Political Science Review*, LIX (June, 1965), 321–36; Philip E. Converse, Warren E. Miller, Jerold G. Rusk, and Arthur C. Wolfe, "Continuity and Change in American Politics: Parties and Issues in the 1968 Election," *American Political Science Review*, LXIII (December, 1969), 1083–105.

22. Numan V. Bartley and Hugh D. Graham, *Southern Politics and the Second Reconstruction* (Baltimore, 1975), Chapter 5; William C. Havard (ed.), *The Changing Politics of the South* (Baton Rouge, 1972); Jack Bass and Walter DeVries, *The Transformation of Southern Politics: Social Change and Political Consequence Since 1945* (New York, 1976); Earl Black, *Southern Governors and Civil Rights: Racial Segregation as a Campaign Issue in the Second Reconstruction* (Cambridge, 1976).

23. Beck, "Partisan Dealignment," 477–96; Campbell, "Patterns of Change in Partisan Loyalties," 730–61; F. Glenn Abney, "Partisan Realignment in a One-Party System: The Case of Mississippi," *Journal of Politics*, XXXI (November, 1969), 1102–1106.

natorial primaries, generated the highest turnout rates. These conditions help explain how the New Deal could realign political coalitions in most of the nation. Scholars debate the how and when, but all agree that the 1930s transformed regional differences into economic differences. In state after state, the Democratic party became the party of the less fortunate. Immigrants, blacks, and blue-collar workers voted Democratic, whereas Republican candidates began to attract the professionals, managers, and business executives of the upper middle class. Those socialized in this period leaned toward the party of their parents' pocketbook.[24]

As Figure 3 indicates, many of the managers and technicians who migrated into Dixie had parents whose pocketbooks had Republican linings. The partisan composition of the whites who moved South closely resembled that of the rest of the nation, a resemblance that made them much more Republican than any other southern group except mountain Republicans.[25]

Just as the whites of the Solid South generation voted their upbringing, so too did the immigrants. Once again, dissonance was minimal even for the large number of Republican identifiers. Although local elections often lacked Republican contestants, the presidential races always had them, so the Republican transplants could vote their partisan leanings in what was to them the more important election. Further, since the immigrants moved to the areas inhabited by native presidential Republicans, the transplanted seeds began to germinate into serious Republican opposition at the state level.

The organizational effort proceeded, however, from the top down. An attractively packaged Republican candidate can beat an unpopular Democratic opponent in a well-financed statewide media campaign. But less-publicized contests present a difficulty, for even in urban areas Republicans seldom constitute a majority. As Table 1 indicates, even in the states with enclaves of mountain Republicans—that is, North Carolina, Tennessee, and Virginia—the GOP has failed to capture anything approaching a majority of the state legislative seats. By necessity, presidential politics dominates the Republican organizations.

24. Everett Carll Ladd, Jr., *American Political Parties: Social Change and Political Response* (New York, 1970); Paul Allen Beck, "A Socialization Theory of Partisan Realignment," in Richard G. Niemi and Herbert F. Weisberg (eds.), *Controversies in American Voting Behavior* (San Francisco, 1976), 396–411.
25. Beck, "Partisan Dealignment," 480–81.

FIGURE 3

Partisan Preferences of Non-Native Southerners, 1952–1980

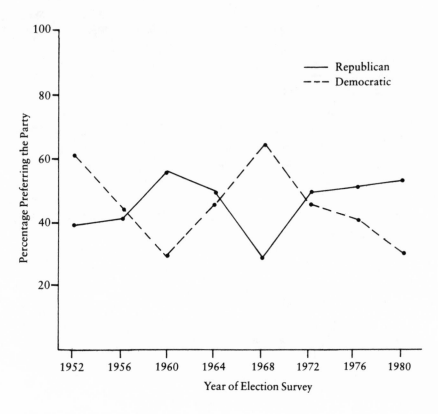

SOURCE: SRC Presidential Election Surveys
Data Points are the percentage of non-native southerners responding to the partisan
identification question who indicate that they at least lean toward the party

The Postwar Generation: Socialization Under New Institutions

Thus far we have described a three-part polyphony: blacks wedded to the
national Democratic party; rural whites of the Solid South generation
committed to the local, factionalized state Democratic parties; immigrant Republicans and native presidential Republicans glued by necessity
to the top heavy, presidential-oriented Republican parties. This new mu-
sical offering provides a different setting than the more harmonic Dixie

TABLE 1
Percentage of Republican Officeholders, January, 1983

	U.S. Senate	U.S. House	Governor	State Senate	State House
REGION					
South	50.0	29.3	18.2	13.1	17.9
Non-South	55.1	41.6	35.9	44.6	43.1
STATE					
Alabama	50.0	28.6	0.0	8.6	7.6
Arkansas	0.0	50.0	0.0	8.6	7.0
Florida	50.0	31.6	0.0	20.0	30.0
Georgia	50.0	10.0	0.0	12.5	13.3
Louisiana	0.0	25.0	100.0	0.0	9.5
Mississippi	50.0	40.0	0.0	7.7	3.3
North Carolina	100.0	18.2	0.0	10.0	17.5
South Carolina	50.0	50.0	0.0	10.9	16.1
Tennessee	50.0	33.3	100.0	33.3	38.4
Texas	50.0	18.5	0.0	16.1	24.0
Virginia	100.0	60.0	0.0	22.5	33.0

SOURCE: *Congressional Quarterly Weekly Report*, XLII (November 10, 1982), 2907, 2909, and 2910, and XLII (November 17, 1984), 2944 and 2945.

of the Solid South. One-party factionalism has been replaced by a one-and-a-half, no-party system: one-and-a-half-party because the Democrats still dominate; no-party because of the absence of well-developed party structures.[26]

The socialization of post–World War II generations varies according to which melody of the polyphony dominated where they grew up. As Table 2 shows, blacks of this age group identify with the Democratic party. Rural whites do, too, although to a lesser extent partially because of mountain Republicans. Urban whites are much more Republican. Table 3 tells the same story in a different way. Partisan inheritance is as strong in the South as elsewhere. Republicans beget Republicans, Democrats beget Democrats, and independents have both.

"The times, they are a-changin'," but the source of partisan change has

26. Everett Carll Ladd, Jr., *Where Have All the Voters Gone?* (New York, 1978); William C. Havard, "From Past to Future: An Overview of Southern Politics," in Havard (ed.), *Changing Politics of the South*, 688–729.

TABLE 2
Partisan Preferences of the Southern Postwar Generations, 1980[a]

Party Preference	Blacks	Rural Whites	Urban Whites
Republican	18.5%	29.9%	41.4%
No Preference	3.7%	11.7%	17.2%
Democratic	77.8%	58.4%	41.4%
Totals	100.0	100.0	100.0

SOURCE: 1980 SRC Presidential Election Survey
[a]Each cell entry is the percentage of the group responding to the partisan identification question who indicate that they at least lean toward the party. The postwar generations are those southerners born after 1939. *Urban* was defined as an area with a population of more than fifty thousand.

TABLE 3
Partisan Preferences of the Southern Postwar Generations
by Parental Partisan Cue, 1980[a]

	Parental Partisan Cue		
Partisan Preference	Republican	No Cue	Democratic
Republican	76%	33%	12%
No Preference	10%	33%	7%
Democratic	14%	34%	81%
Totals	100	100	100

SOURCE: 1980 SRC Presidential Election Survey
[a]Each cell entry is the percentage of the group who indicate that they at least lean toward the party. Southern postwar generations are those southerners born after 1939. Parental partisan cue is Democratic (Republican) when the respondent identifies one of his parents as being a Democrat (Republican) and the other parent as not being a Republican (Democrat). All remaining cases were classified as "No Cue."

not been conversion. Mobilization, immigration, and generational replacement slowly have made the South a much less distinct region of the country. The southern postwar generations resemble their northern cohorts much more than they resemble the Solid South generation.

Numerous statistics reveal the similarities. Greater numbers of southerners now vote in the presidential general elections than in the Democratic gubernatorial primaries. Although presidential turnout rates are still lower in the South than elsewhere, the difference is only 6 percent after one controls for educational and racial differences.[27]

Southern youth, like northern youth, are much more likely than are their parents to consider themselves independents rather than Democrats or Republicans. They also exhibit a greater propensity to behave as political independents. And the strength of their partisanship, whether measured by the partisan identification question or behaviorally, falls short of the strength of the Solid South generation.[28] All of this reflects the increasing homogeneity of the American socialization experience. The barriers ensuring southern isolation have virtually disappeared, and the attitudes of young southerners are being shaped by the same stimuli affecting young people in the rest of the nation.

CONCLUSION: LESS MEANINGFUL PARTICIPATION

We began with a portrait of the past; we conclude with speculation on the future. Ferreting out reasonable predictions is always a treacherous exercise, for unseen events have a way of making the most respected seers look fools. But barring a major catastrophe — a collapse of the southern economy, for example — we can safely make three prognostications about southern electoral politics.

The first concerns the minority party in the South. Absolutely nothing in the data indicates that the Republicans will soon shed their minority standing. Realignments in which a minority party becomes the majority party can occur in one of four ways: mobilization, migration, generational replacement, or conversion.[29] We have already examined two examples of mobilization, both involving changes in electoral laws. The first excluded blacks and poor whites through the use of literacy tests and poll taxes, thus contributing to the creation of the solidly Democratic South. The second enfranchised blacks and mobilized them into the Democratic party. Today, since there are no more groups to bring into the electorate, only institutional exclusion of predominantly Democratic groups would redound to the favor of the Republican party. Such a change in suffrage laws is highly unlikely, to say the least.

We have also encountered two examples of migration. During the 1950s and 1960s, large numbers of predominantly Democratic blacks

27. Raymond E. Wolfinger and Steven J. Rosenstone, *Who Votes?* (New Haven, 1980), 93–94.

28. Beck, "Partisan Dealignment," 477–96.

29. Jerome M. Clubb, William H. Flanigan, and Nancy H. Zingale, *Partisan Realignment: Voters, Parties, and Government in American History* (Beverly Hills, 1980).

moved out of the black belt while large numbers of northern whites who were more Republican than southerners moved into southern cities. Both movements helped the Republican party. This does not mean, however, that continued migrations would eventually lead to Republican dominance. Neither those leaving nor those entering the South differed significantly in partisan composition from those they left behind.[30] This means that a continuation of past migration trends cannot make the South any more Republican than the rest of the nation. Therein lies the rub. Nationwide, the Republicans are the minority party. (41 percent of the identifiers were Republican in 1980.[31]) The only way that migration can realign the South is if Democrats disproportionately leave and Republicans disproportionately arrive. The only observable alteration in migration patterns, however, is the drying up of the black exodus, a trend that works against southern Republicans. Indeed, in the 1970s several thousand more blacks returned to the South than left.

We have also observed the effects of generational replacement. Partisan propensities tend to be inherited.[32] Thus, the Solid South generation became Democrats, and a large percentage of white immigrants reflected parental Republicanism. The Republican party's percentage of adherents increased over the past two generations, but those increases will not lead to Republican dominance. Inheritance rates—that is, the percentage of Republicans whose children become Republican partisans and the percentage of Democrats who have Democratic children—determine the equilibrium point toward which the partisan composition of society moves. The rates in Table 3 indicate that eventually the South would become 49 percent Democratic, 40 percent Republican, and 11 percent independent.[33] With each passing generation, the size of the Republican increase will, if everything else remains the same, diminish. This, of course, ignores differences in fertility rates, but unfortunately for Republicans, the Democrats reproduce at the quicker pace.

Thus, only one way exists for the Republicans to shed their minority status in the South—they must convert large numbers of Democrats into

30. Beck, "Partisan Dealignment," 481.
31. Paul R. Abramson, John H. Aldrich, and David W. Rohde, *Change and Continuity in the 1980 Election* (Washington, D.C., 1982), 160–65.
32. M. Kent Jennings and Richard G. Niemi, *Generations and Politics: A Panel Study of Young Adults and Their Parents* (Princeton, 1981), Chapter 4.
33. The equilibrium point is found by solving the equations $a*R + b*I + c*D = R$, $d*R + e*I + f*D = I$, $g*R + h*I + i*D = D$, and $R + I + D = 100$, for R, I, and D. R represents the percentage of Republican identifiers, I the percentage of independent identifiers, and D the percentage of Democratic, with a, b, c, d, e, f, g, h, and i being the cell entries in Table 3.

Republicans who will support local as well as national GOP candidates. Massive conversions have occurred, for example, during the Civil War, when the Republican party emerged, and during the New Deal realignment. All of the research indicates, however, that such massive transfers of party allegiance require two conditions: the presence of highly salient issues dividing the populace and a large group with weak partisan attachments who will on the basis of the issues transfer their allegiance from the majority party to the minority party.[34] Race and economics are the salient issues of the South, and the postwar generations are the group with weak partisan attachments.

But massive conversion of this group to the Republican party appears unlikely. Two things augur against it. First, the race issue is not terribly salient to the youth of either party. Second, Republicans tend to be more conservative on economic issues than do Democrats. Thus, the GOP faces the classic dilemma of a minority party.[35] Before it can possibly convert Democrats, it must become more liberal on the economic issues. To do so, however, would upset Republican party activists and make the Republicans look more like the Democrats, thus removing any incentive for young Democrats to abandon their party. This dilemma has sharply divided the southern Republican state parties, as was evident by the schisms during the 1976 Ford-Reagan nomination battles and Reagan's quick dismissal of Bill Brock, who as national Republican committee chairman had sedulously been trying to recruit blacks into the Republican ranks. The southern strategy avidly pursued by Republican presidential candidates will help elect Republican presidents but will not stimulate the emergence of a viable two-party system in the southern states.

The data merit a prognostication about the Democratic party as well. Key had hoped that if race could be removed as the raison d'être of southern politics and if Republicans could begin offering competition in statewide elections, the Democratic party would become less factionalized and hence more responsive to the people's needs. Jim Crow is dead, and although vestiges of race still dominate issues such as redistricting, the racial issue is not salient for the youth. Also Republican opposition flourishes in contests for gubernatorial and national senatorial and House offices. But, as of yet, the Democratic parties in the southern states remain fragmented. Incredibly, Bradley Canon found that the degree of fragmentation actually increased in the period 1960–1978 over 1932–1959

34. Beck, "A Socialization Theory of Partisan Realignment."
35. Samuel Lubell, *The Future of American Politics* (Garden City, 1951), Chapter 11; Ladd, *American Political Parties*, 1–11.

even though the Republican party was reviving and race was being eclipsed as *the* issue in southern politics.[36] As long as the state legislatures remain over two-thirds Democratic, no reason exists for the Democrats to coalesce. Barring the emergence of a cataclysmic event alluded to earlier, the South will remain a one-and-a-half, no-party system. The Republicans will be the top-down minority party, and the Democrats will be as fragmented as before.

Which brings us to our last prediction. Two beliefs animated those who risked their lives in the civil rights movement. The first was an article of faith that the politics of exclusion was evil and thus had to be destroyed. The second was a hope that inclusion of all in the polity would make the government responsive to the voice of the people. The most evil aspects of racism have disappeared. The lynchings and the political violence of infamous groups such as the KKK have subsided. The vitriolic, disparaging, spiteful rhetoric of gubernatorial campaigns has evaporated. The hates, doubts, and self-destructiveness that fed the dual society and became the theme of so many of the South's great novels have dissipated. The civil rights movement exorcised the demon of race.

A truly responsive governmental system failed, however, to materialize. The one-and-a-half, no-party system has made electoral participation less and less meaningful. The declining strength of partisan attachments, the substanceless media-produced campaigns,[37] the increasingly bureaucratic state governments,[38] the multitude of governors committed to administrative reform rather than policy reform,[39] all of these mitigate against responsible party government.

This is ironic. Key lamented how the institutions of the Solid South prevented the development of a two-party system through which the poor could articulate their demands. After decades of turmoil following *Smith* v. *Allright,* all can now participate. But the victory is pyrrhic. The one-and-a-half, no-party system is nowhere near as oppressive as one-party factionalism, but its benign neglect still provides no avenues for articulating demands. Inclusion into electoral politics has been less meaningful than many had hoped. The ballot box has become increasingly a means of co-optation, not citizen control. Modernity's alienation has supplanted racism's guilt, *A Confederacy of Dunces* supplanting *To Kill a Mockingbird.*

36. Bradley Canon, "Factionalism in the South: A Test of Theory and Revisitation of V. O. Key, Jr.," *American Journal of Political Science,* XXII (November, 1978), 33–57.
37. See essay by Joseph B. Parker in this volume.
38. See essay by Edward M. Wheat in this volume.
39. See essay by Larry Sabato in this volume.

New-Style Campaign Politics: Madison Avenue Comes to Dixie

JOSEPH B. PARKER

When you're down to one or two candidates, the one with the cleverest ads, with the freshest slogans, catchy slogans and the money and symbols is going to win. We have now what might be called Miller Time politics.

—Ralph Nader
"McNeil/Lehrer News Hour"
November 29, 1985

When a poor man stops by, I tell him to give his money to the Cancer Society, where a small amount of money might do some good. I firmly believe that poor people should not be allowed to run for public office.

—Campaign consultant Hal Evry,
quoted in David Chagall, *The New Kingmakers* (1981)

Proclamations of a "New South" and a "changing South" have been made for so long and so often that it is easy to understand why many skeptics are leery of such assertions. Yet, a defensible claim can be made that in the realm of political campaigning the last quarter century has indeed produced a very different South. The states that formed the Confederacy were once recognized for a special brand of flamboyance in their politics and their politicians. Most did not have meaningful two-party systems after the virtual elimination of Republicans and defeat of the Populists just prior to the turn of the century. Various forms of factional competition prevailed in the region, and silver-tongued orators, race-baiters, and showmen flourished in that sometimes amorphous factionalism. Their performances on the stump frequently became legend both at home and around the nation. According to V. O. Key, Jr.: "Individualistic or disorganized politics places a high premium on demagogic qualities that attract voter attention. Party machinery, in the advancement of leaders, is apt to reject those with rough edges and angular qualities out of preference for more conformist personalities. Perhaps the necessities of an unorganized politics—lacking in continuing divisions of the electorate and in continuing collaboration of party workers—provide partial explanation for the rise to power of some of the spectacular southern leaders."[1]

1. V. O. Key, Jr., *Southern Politics in State and Nation* (New York, 1949), 304–305.

Products of the region who became nationally known as "characters" include Theodore "The Man" Bilbo, James K. "The White Chief" Vardaman, "Big Jim" Eastland, and Ross Barnett in Mississippi; "Uncle Earl" and Huey "Kingfish" Long in Louisiana; Tom Watson, Eugene ("Old Gene") and Herman Talmadge, and Lester Maddox (whose political symbol was the ax handle with which he barred blacks from his cafe) in Georgia. Others include "Cotton Ed" Smith, "Pitchfork Ben" Tillman, and "Ole Strom" Thurmond in South Carolina; "Kissing Jim" Folsom, and the "Fightin' Gov" George Wallace, in Alabama; "Ma" and "Pa" Ferguson and W. Lee "Pappy" O'Daniel in Texas; and Orval Faubus in Arkansas.[2] All of these personalities shared certain characteristics. Their appeal was charismatic, each had a uniquely flamboyant campaign style, and each received his or her strongest support from rural whites.

Prior to the television era, candidates for statewide office had to go to the voters at "the forks of the creek," as Key said, to solicit support. This took the form of stumping—a mobile campaign not unlike the traveling circus, the old-time patent medicine salesman, or the traveling tent revival preacher. Candidates for major offices frequently spent several months stumping their state. They would make several stops each day, frequently in the heat of summer. This went on day after grueling day.[3] For a candidate to hope for success, he had to be a good performer on the stump both to draw crowds and to convince his audiences of his meritorious qualities. This system of campaigning may very well have produced more entertainment than enlightenment. But in its behalf it must be said that it allowed the voters to see candidates "in the flesh." In the same way that stage performances by actors are more difficult and demanding than movies or television, with their numerous retakes, stumping was a more

---

2. For the reader who is interested in colorful personalities in southern politics, a number of substantial biographical works are available. Some of these are: William Anderson, *The Wild Man from Sugar Creek: The Political Career of Eugene Talmadge* (Baton Rouge, 1975); Marshall Frady, *Wallace* (New York, 1970); Bruce Galphin, *The Riddle of Lester Maddox* (Atlanta, 1968); A. Wigfall Green, *The Man Bilbo* (Baton Rouge, 1963); William F. Holmes, *The White Chief: James Kimble Vardaman* (Baton Rouge, 1970); Sam Kinch and Stuart Long, *Allen Shivers: The Pied Piper of Texas Politics* (Austin, 1974); Alberta M. Lachicotte, *Rebel Senator: Strom Thurmond of South Carolina* (New York, 1966); A. J. Liebling, *The Earl of Louisiana* (Baton Rouge, 1970); Seth Shepard McKay, *W. Lee O'Daniel and Texas Politics* (Lubbock, 1944); Francis B. Simkins, *Pitchfork Ben Tillman: South Carolinian* (Baton Rouge, 1944); T. Harry Williams, *Huey Long* (New York, 1971). See also Robert Sherrill, *Gothic Politics in the Deep South: Stars of the New Confederacy* (New York, 1968), for interesting accounts of several old-time politicians.

3. For an entertaining account of old-style campaigning, see Elizabeth Mullener, "Stumping with Uncle Earl: Adventures Along the Campaign Trail in the 1930s," *Dixie Magazine*, New Orleans *Times-Picayune/States Item*, August 22, 1982.

direct and less packaged form of appeal to voters than is modern television campaigning. There were no retakes and no film editing.

As the changing economics and demographics of the South since World War II have made the South more like the rest of the nation, the uniqueness of its political style has eroded. Political consultants and professionally orchestrated campaigns came to the South in the 1960s and the 1970s. Since most southern states had little in the way of party organization and competition and some did not even have enduring factions within the Democratic party, the region provided a political setting quite conducive to the new media-based and candidate-centered campaigns.

> Campaign consultants are not new, as Larry Sabato points out: There have always been political consultants in one form or another in American politics, but the campaign professionals of earlier eras were strategists without benefit of the campaign technologies so standard today. Usually, too, consultants were tied to one or a few candidates, or perhaps to a state or local party organization. Before consulting became a full-time profession, lawyers were assigned campaign management chores since they had flexible work schedules as well as the personal finances and community contacts to do the job properly. The old-time press agent, usually a newspaperman familiar with the locale, was also a crucial and influential figure in campaign organization. But in most cases these lawyers and press agents were only functionaries when compared to party leaders and organization bosses who wielded far greater authority in political matters.[4]

The changed nature of campaigning has not developed in a uniform fashion across the South or across the nation. Variations still exist, but as pollster Patrick Caddell comments: "I can see from the beginning of the decade [1970s] when I started to the end of the decade that the regional differences [in campaigning]—which are still there to some extent—have narrowed. The country has become more homogeneous."[5] Campaigns today are more likely to reveal the style of the strategist and/or the media expert than they are to reflect a regional flavor.

Of course, the services of political consultants are expensive, as are the technologies they apply. Although the South has been the poorest region of the nation during much of the twentieth century, this has not held back the development of modern campaigning. Energy-rich states like Louisiana and Texas have had enormous sources of money for the conduct of professionally directed campaigns. And even in the poor states, expensive, professional, media-oriented campaigns have rapidly become

    4. Larry J. Sabato, *The Rise of Political Consultants: New Ways of Winning Elections* (New York, 1981), 10.
    5. *Ibid.*, 312.

the order of the day as the key economic interests seek to exercise political influence. In fact, since strong party organization is more likely in industrialized, higher-than-average per capita income states,[6] poorer states with weak parties frequently produce more extravagant spending on media-based and candidate-centered campaigns. In effect, an inverse relationship often develops between the wealth of a state and the level of campaign spending.

A variety of factors—television, computers, the weakness of political parties, urbanization—have combined to increase the demand for specialized campaign consultants and also to increase the variety of specialties. New specialists continue to appear. More stringent campaign finance–reporting laws of recent years have spawned accountants who provide financial management and record-keeping services to campaigns, and skyrocketing campaign costs have spawned fund-raising consultants.

The four most important categories of campaign consultants are strategists (or generalists), media specialists, pollsters, and direct-mail experts. Ideally a modern campaign should have all four of these, but many do not. Media specialists have become the superstars of consultants and frequently sell themselves as strategists as well. Most can also provide direct-mail service but rarely so effectively as the consultant whose domain is direct mail.

As the nature of campaigning changed, a different, more polished type of politician began to emerge, and those politicians whose careers have spanned several decades, such as John Stennis, Herman Talmadge, Strom Thurmond, and George Wallace, have adjusted their campaign style to fit the changed times. Stennis, for example, who traditionally used a casual and folksy campaign style and who had encountered little opposition after his first race, at the age of eighty-one faced the challenge of a thirty-four-year-old Republican in his reelection bid in 1982. He was persuaded by Senate colleague Russell Long that modern campaigns require a sophisticated media orientation. Thus, on this occasion Stennis employed a media-based campaign for the first time in his political career, using Washington-based pollster Peter Hart and media expert Ray Strother. (Strother is also Washington-based but had only recently relocated his operation from Louisiana, where most of his campaign work has been done.)[7] Strother's television ads effectively portrayed the aging senator as a Washington legend. His promotional spots showed a vigorous, energetic, experienced "senator's senator," working through the

6. Thomas R. Dye, *Politics in States and Communities* (Englewood Cliffs, 1977), 97–99.
7. *Wall Street Journal*, September 16, 1982; Jackson *Clarion-Ledger*, September 6, 1982.

night to hammer out legislation in committee. These and other factors enabled Stennis to coast to victory with 64 percent of the vote.

An examination of professional campaigning in selected Louisiana and Mississippi gubernatorial races will illustrate the development of this new political style in Dixie over the past two decades. There is no claim that the patterns of campaign activity in these states represent a microcosm of the South; indeed, little, if anything, is uniform in the region, and these contiguous states have experienced divergent patterns in the growth of campaign consultants and their uses. However, these two Deep South states reflect two general patterns in the evolution of modern campaigning. Louisiana was among the first states to become fully enmeshed in the merchandising of candidates and is therefore quite representative of the more urban and affluent southern states. Mississippi has moved along this path at a much slower pace and is perhaps representative of the poorer and more traditional states. Hence a general description of the evolution of campaigning in the two states may indicate developments that are paralleled in a general way in other southern states.

PROFESSIONAL CAMPAIGNING IN THE SOUTH: THE CASE OF LOUISIANA

Professional campaign consultants emerged relatively early in Louisiana. New Orleans, a center of banking, commerce, and tourism, was a major birthplace for the new campaigning, which even predated in its origins the diffusion of television in the state.

In 1946 a young returning army officer, DeLesseps S. Morrison, defeated the incumbent mayor and boss of the well-established political machine, Robert S. Maestri. Morrison did so with the help of transplanted Yankee advertising specialist Scott Wilson.[8] A native New Yorker, Wilson was a journalist turned public-relations and advertising specialist who had gotten his first campaigning experience in one of Fiorello La Guardia's races in the early 1930s, when as a young reporter he was contributed by his employer to the campaign in lieu of money. Wilson was a jack-of-all-trades in campaign consulting—strategist, planner, writer, commercial artist, and, when television emerged, media specialist. He was good at all of these but never restricted himself to political campaign consulting. Instead he continued to operate a full-service advertising agency, and his political contacts almost certainly enhanced his advertising business.

Wilson proved in Morrison's 1946 campaign that many of the tech-

8. Joseph B. Parker, *Reform Politics in New Orleans: The Morrison Era* (Gretna, La., 1974), 67–69.

niques of commercial advertising could be applied to political campaigns. His success stimulated the development of Louisiana political consultants in two ways. It set standards in the use of new campaign techniques, and it encouraged public-relations specialists to expand their activities into the campaign area. By the mid-1960s a group of Louisiana political consultants with expertise in media-based campaigning emerged. Along with Wilson there was Max Fetty in New Orleans, Jim Carvin in Lake Charles, Sandy Kaplan and Gus Weill in Lafayette, and Ed Reed in Baton Rouge. All were public-relations generalists who branched out. During the 1970s the community of consultants grew substantially in responses to the demand in races for both major and minor offices. Those who went off on their own after apprenticeships under one of the first generation of consultants include Bill Allerton, Rusty Cantelli, Jimmy Farwell, and Ron Fauchaux (all based in New Orleans).

At about the same time that media consultants and strategists were emerging, there was an increasing awareness of the need for polling information in the formation of campaign strategy. Dallas pollster Alex Louis, of Louis, Bowles, and Grace, Inc., began polling extensively in Louisiana in the 1950s. He established a reputation for accuracy and integrity, which helped to increase the demand for polling. In the late 1960s and early 1970s four key pollsters emerged: James Chubbuck, Edward Renwick, and Joe Walker in New Orleans, plus Verne Kennedy in Alexandria. All quickly earned a name for themselves and were widely used in Louisiana campaigns. Chubbuck left the polling business in 1975 to become administrative assistant to United States Senator J. Bennett Johnston, and in 1978 he became chief political troubleshooter for New Orleans Mayor Ernest Morial. Still in New Orleans, Renwick and Walker have continued to be successful pollsters with enough work on just Louisiana campaigns to make going out of state largely unnecessary. Kennedy moved his polling operation to Jackson, Mississippi, when he became president of Bellhaven College. (He left Bellhaven in 1986 to devote his full-time effort to polling.) However, his firm still does extensive polling in Louisiana as well as in approximately twenty other states. Kennedy's clients are largely Republicans and conservative Democrats.

The 1963 Governor's Race: The Beachhead

The election that first established professional campaigning statewide in Louisiana was the governor's race of 1963–1964. In this campaign all the serious candidates had professional polls conducted and employed media strategists. John J. McKeithen's media strategist was a young public-relations man, Gus Weill, DeLesseps Morrison employed Max Fetty, and

Gillis Long had Jim Carvin as his strategist with special concern for newspaper, radio, and television advertising.

In this race the old factional division begun in the late 1920s between Longs and anti-Longs disintegrated. There were two major Long faction candidates in the first primary, Gillis Long and McKeithen, and two major anti-Long candidates, Robert F. Kennon and Morrison. But a combination of circumstances blurred the old factional division in such a way as essentially to destroy it as a factor in Louisiana politics.[9] This was also the last campaign in which stumping was used extensively. For as long as anyone could remember, the accepted practice was for gubernatorial candidates to barnstorm the entire state beginning around July 4 of each election year. A candidate carried with him an extensive entourage including his entire "ticket" plus a band. The latter was almost always the hillbilly (nowadays called country and western) variety in North Louisiana. In South Louisiana a Cajun band might be employed instead. Such an aggregation required a sizable number of vehicles, sound equipment, and personnel. By 1963–1964 this had become a very expensive operation, requiring approximately $1,000 per day.[10]

This campaign marked the real beginning of thirty-second and sixty-second statewide promotional spots targeted at particular segments of the electorate. Television had been used in a somewhat haphazard fashion prior to this time, with candidates generally buying thirty minutes of time when campaigning in a city with a television station and making what amounted to a stump speech via television.

The campaigns of all major candidates were characterized by friction between the new breed of media-oriented campaign professionals and the traditionalists within their camps. These were not battles between amateurs and professionals but rather between two kinds of political professionals. One group consisted of veteran campaigners (traditionalists) who either had been involved in several winning campaigns or had been elected to office several times themselves. The other group (merchandisers) had training and experience in public relations and advertising and were convinced that the time had come for their techniques to be applied in political campaigns. This division was compounded by a generation gap, with the advertising specialists generally much younger than the other group. In both the Long and Morrison campaigns, the traditionalists within each camp succeeded in gaining the upper hand and scrapping

9. Perry H. Howard, *Political Tendencies in Louisiana* (Rev. ed.; Baton Rouge, 1971), Chapter 10.
10. Interview with Jim Carvin, campaign consultant, June 8, 1982.

campaign themes and strategies developed by the professional advertisers. At this stage the newer group did not have sufficient credibility to win such battles, but their input into campaigns was vastly greater than it had been before, and they thus established a beachhead for the professional consultants and their media-based campaigning.

For the remainder of the 1960s and throughout the 1970s, the status of the new professionals was on the rise. The demise of Long versus anti-Long factionalism destroyed much of the grass-roots political organization that had existed in Louisiana for more than three decades. Stumping virtually died, and newspaper advertising diminished substantially as campaigns were increasingly conducted via television and radio.

Since the late 1960s serious candidates for statewide offices and for most local positions in larger urban areas have had professional polls conducted before making their decision to run or developing a campaign strategy. It is now established practice for a candidate for governor to have a benchmark poll, then to have virtually continuous tracking polls conducted in the course of a campaign. The utility of polling is now so well established that candidates for relatively minor offices feel obligated to employ a pollster.

More important than pollsters are the media experts, who have become the new men of power in Louisiana politics. In races for major offices, a candidate's media consultant draws nearly as much interest as does the candidate. To be taken seriously and to be able to raise adequate money to make a serious race, particularly for governor, a candidate is expected to employ a top-rated media consultant. If there are more candidates than there are major-league in-state media consultants, candidates bring in out-of-staters. But since no out-of-state media consultant has been involved in a successful gubernatorial campaign, candidates generally prefer the homegrown variety. All the elements of this new-style media-based campaigning were present in the dramatic and expensive race for governor in 1979.

The 1979 Governor's Race: Professional Campaigning Enshrined

In 1979 the six major candidates in the "open election" for governor, with their media consultants were:

Lieutenant Governor Jimmy Fitzmorris (D): Rusty Cantelli (New Orleans)

Secretary of State Paul Hardy (D): Gus Weill and Ray Strother (Baton Rouge)

House Speaker E. L. "Bubba" Henry (D): Charles Gugginheim (Washington, D.C.)

Public Service Commissioner Louis Lambert (D): Jim Carvin (New Orleans)

Senate President Edgar "Sonny" Mouton (D): David Garth (New York)

Congressman David Treen (R): Jimmy Farwell and Ronald Fauchaux (New Orleans)

This extensive array of viable candidates and top media specialists was unprecedented in Louisiana history.

The Treen campaign jumped the gun with television spots six weeks to two months ahead of the traditional starting point of a campaign, setting off an orgy of television campaigning and, of course, spending. When the dust settled in November and Treen had defeated Lambert in the general election, these six candidates reported expenditures of $20,624,539.[11] Louisiana campaign finance reporting legislation is riddled with loopholes, and informed sources contend that real spending was probably nearer $30,000,000.

The campaign had all the trappings of a modern professionally operated voter appeal — slick media plus "telephone banks, mass mailings, campaign parties, literature, buttons, billboards, yard signs, bumper stickers, and computers."[12] In the course of the race some shuffling of media consultants occurred, the most notable move being the eventual firing of David Garth by Senator Mouton. The hiring of Garth, a highly successful New Yorker who had never previously worked in Louisiana, had created quite a stir at the time. There was friction from the beginning between Garth and Charles Roemer, chief of administration in the outgoing administration of Governor Edwin Edwards, who was a fundraiser and strategist for Mouton. (Roemer had his own campaign consulting operation, built largely around computers.) Garth subscribes to some campaign theories that are highly unorthodox to Louisianians. He does not, for example, believe in the use of bumper stickers and yard signs, which in Louisiana comes close to being against motherhood and the church. And his media ads were viewed as too tame. "Garth used his standard brand of television for Mouton," wrote political journalist Iris Kelso of New Orleans. "It was plain.

11. Public Affairs Research Staff, *The Great Louisiana Spendathon* (Baton Rouge, 1980), 2.
12. *Ibid.*, 1.

No pretty pictures, no gimmicks."[13] In surveys conducted to get voter reaction to all the candidates' television ads, it was discovered that Garth's got the lowest positive reaction from voters.[14] Roemer finally won the battle for control of the Mouton campaign, and Garth went back to New York after a few unimpressive weeks in Louisiana politics. Roemer's agency, assisted by Gens Valleley and Associates of Boston, took over the campaign's media and print operations.

Louis Lambert's campaign also did a lot of shuffling. Lambert began the campaign with Jim Carvin as his chief strategist and media expert, but he also employed media man Robert Squier of Washington late in the primary campaign. Squier was on a hot roll after victories in the Kentucky gubernatorial campaign of John Y. Brown and the Mississippi campaign of William Winter. Additionally, Matt Reese of Washington was employed at a cost of over $500,000 to provide campaign organization, targeting, and get-out-the-vote (GOTV) services. After Lambert emerged by a narrow margin as one of the general election candidates, he split with Carvin by mutual agreement. Lambert stuck with Squier for a brief time before dismissing him and employing the Baton Rouge firm of Weill and Strother, which had handled Paul Hardy in the primary. (In political campaigns, as in athletic contests, it is hard to follow the game without a program.) Thus, as in earlier races the out-of-state media consultants did not meet with much success in Louisiana. Garth and Squier were dismissed in the course of the campaign, and Charles Gugginheim's candidate, E. L. Henry, ran a poor fifth.

The 1983 Governor's Race: Battle of Titans and Bucks

Even before the vote counting was completed in the 1979 governor's race, campaign watchers were looking forward to 1983. Although immensely popular, Edwin Edwards was prohibited from seeking a third term in 1979, but he made clear his intentions to reapply for his old job after sitting out a term. In fact, Edwards began his campaign as he was leaving office. When he opened his Baton Rouge law office in 1980, he had a helicopter pad installed to enhance his availability for speaking engagements. Speaking, organizing, and fund-raising were thus worked into his lucrative law practice.

By the spring of 1983 the race was on, with the incumbent Republican

13. Iris Kelso, "The Image Makers," New Orleans *Times-Picayune/States Item*, September 11, 1979.
14. Interview with Edward Renwick, pollster, June 23, 1982.

governor facing the former two-term Democratic governor. Edwards had a substantial war chest, and though Treen faced some problems raising money because of his low standing in the polls, no one doubted that an incumbent governor would be able to raise big bucks. The usual assortment of consultants was employed. Edwards' team included Bill Hamilton (Washington), polling; Edwards and Funkerson (Baton Rouge), media; Matt Reese and Associates (Washington), organization, targeting, and get-out-the-vote services; Dino Seder (Washington), media "negatives"; and Jim Carvin, strategy. The media firm was Edwards' daughter Vicki's operation, an interesting family arrangement. Seder was employed early in the campaign to produce television spots that would counter the highly negative tone of the Treen campaign. As the campaign unfolded, it was obvious that Seder's negatives would not be needed, so Edwards decided not to run them. Treen's pollster was Verne Kennedy of Jackson, Mississippi, and his media work was done by Gus Weill and Associates of Baton Rouge.

The campaign disappointed no one looking for a show. It was a circus of media campaigning, fund-raising, and spending. The two candidates reported spending nearly as much as six had in 1979 — Edwards $12,362,652, and Treen $6,276,141.[15] Treen's reported total was certainly held down by the fact that he trailed in widely publicized polls throughout the campaign. Edwards ended the campaign, which he won by a near 2–1 margin, with debts approaching $5,000,000.[16] He then proved how easy it is, and even fun, to pay off campaign debts if you are elected governor of Louisiana with such a margin, by sponsoring a ten-day fund-raising trip to Paris for over five hundred people. (He also hit the dice table at Monte Carlo for $10,000 during the trip.) Treen's debt of $692,000 was much more difficult to retire. In January, 1986, he still owed $151,500,[17] no doubt reaffirming what astute observers have always known about the enthusiasm of campaign contributors for winners and their lack of enthusiasm for losing causes.

PROFESSIONAL CAMPAIGNING IN THE SOUTH:
THE CASE OF MISSISSIPPI

The emergence of professionally conducted campaigns was later coming and slower to develop in Mississippi than in Louisiana. Professional cam-

    15. Public Affairs Research Staff, *Financing the 1983 Gubernatorial Campaign* (Baton Rouge, 1984), 3.
    16. *Ibid.*
    17. New Orleans *Times-Picayune/States Item*, January 18, 1986.

paign consultants made their first major entry into Mississippi politics in the gubernatorial campaign of 1971, and their significance has increased with each statewide campaign since. However, in contrast to Louisiana, a homegrown establishment of campaign consultants has not developed. In races for governor and United States Senate seats most candidates have come to rely on out-of-state consultants, and each campaign seems to reemphasize the conventional wisdom that a serious candidate for these offices should employ outsiders. Jackson particularly has a number of sizable public-relations and advertising agencies capable of conducting effective campaigns, but these firms have commercial concerns as their principal clients. Politicians complain that the firms do not devote sufficient time and talent to political clients and lack expertise in placing political advertising. These criticisms are probably valid, but such failings are also understandable. Banks, savings and loans, electrical power utilities, and department stores are the bread and butter of advertising firms on a year-round basis, whereas political campaigns last only for a brief interlude. Jackson, in contrast to cities like New Orleans and Baton Rouge, cannot support a community of full-time campaign consultants. It would be penny-wise and pound-foolish for an advertising firm to neglect its dependable permanent clients on behalf of a transient political client.

Another factor holding back the development of in-state consultants is that the timing of the governor's race helps attract some of the nation's leading campaign consultants at bargain prices. Few other states hold statewide election at this time, and odd-numbered years produce no races for the United States Congress. It is a slack period for campaigns, and coming so close to national elections, it provides tune-up opportunities for consultants.

The 1971 Governor's Race: The First Invasion

The first campaign consultant to make a splash in Mississippi politics was DeLoss Walker of Memphis, who was engaged by Jackson attorney William Waller in the 1971 governor's race. Waller, who had run very poorly four years earlier, was impressed by Walker's role in the election of a virtually unknown small-town lawyer, Dale Bumpers, to the Arkansas governorship. Waller hoped that Walker could do the same for him, and, in fact, he did. Walker used essentially the same campaign strategy that had worked for Bumpers, and Waller's opponents discovered too late for any good purpose that many of his television and radio promotional spots were exactly the same as those used in the Bumpers campaign except for the substitution of Waller's name and face for Bumpers'.

Waller's major opponent, Lieutenant Governor Charles Sullivan, was the projected favorite at the outset of the campaign. The Sullivan campaign employed for its media work Goodwin Advertising of Jackson, which brought political strategist Bill Spell into the firm for this campaign. Spell, an attorney, had strong connections with the Citizens Council in the 1950s and 1960s. Since the early 1960s Senator Stennis had employed Spell to shore up his wavering support by using the council as protection against the possibility of opposition from the flamboyant racist Ross Barnett. Spell returned from Washington for the Sullivan campaign. He cast Sullivan, who had solid gray hair which was bleached even lighter, in a white suit to match his white hair. This crude symbolism aimed at the white electorate backfired first with recently enfranchised black voters, whose new significance had escaped Spell. And then in the course of the campaign one of Sullivan's opponents, Edwin Lloyd Pittman, labeled him the "Man from Glad" after the then much-used promoter of Union Carbide's plastic garbage bags. The derisive label stuck, and it hurt.

The 1971 campaign turned out to be a mismatch between the teams of Waller and Walker versus Sullivan and Spell. It was a case of the new politics of media techniques winning out over the old ways of Mississippi campaigning.

Walker was widely acclaimed for his genius in electing Waller governor. This conventional wisdom was so prominent that even Senator James O. Eastland, who had the nearest thing to a political machine that Mississippi has known in recent times, employed Walker for media work in his 1972 reelection campaign. Walker portrayed the somber Eastland with a cheery smile in campaign posters tacked onto light poles and pine trees, and according to one wag, "no one recognized him." Eastland's employment of Walker was a strong signal to other politicians that an out-of-state consultant was not only acceptable but perhaps necessary.

The 1975 Governor's Race

The 1975 governor's race brought more consultants into the state. The major candidates hired the following consultants:

Gilbert Carmichael (R): Walter DeVries (Wrightsville Beach, N.C.), strategy; David Hughly (Meridian, Miss.), media; Manion Mullican (Frank, W.Va.), campaign organization; Richard Wirthlin

(Santa Ana, Calif.), polling; Edward Grief and Associates (New York), fund-raising.

Maurice Dantin (D): DeLoss Walker and Associates (Memphis), strategy and media; polling subcontracted by Walker.

Cliff Finch (D): Bill Jones of Viewpoints (Montgomery, Ala.), strategy and media; Oliver Quayle and Associates (New York), polling.

William F. Winter (D): Maris, West, and Baker (Jackson), media; Peter Hart and Associates (Washington), polling.

Out-of-state consultants gained new credibility in this campaign in large part because of the successful Finch campaign. Finch began with less than 10 percent name recognition but ultimately was elected in a race that portrayed him as the workingman's candidate, with a black lunch box as his symbol. Finch, in reality a well-heeled tort-liability lawyer who had learned to operate a bulldozer in his younger days, engaged in a variety of "work days." Starting with a day as a bulldozer operator, he went on to pump gas, sack groceries, operate a fork lift, cut pulpwood, and do many other jobs. These "work days" were transformed into very effective television promotional spots as well as favorable, free media coverage. Once again, observers of Mississippi politics marveled at the wonders of an out-of-state consultant, in this case Bill Jones.

Carmichael used a Mississippi advertising agency for his media work but had an army of outside figures for the other phases of his campaign. Although defeated, Carmichael's 46 percent of the vote was a twentieth-century high for a Republican running for state office—another plus for the out-of-state consultants.

William Winter, a strong favorite to win the governorship, used a Jackson advertising agency for his media. That firm was blamed for the inane slogan "William Winter—He's for Real" as well as a generally less imaginative media campaign than Finch had. Winter's campaign gave new credibility of a negative sort to the out-of-state media experts.

The 1979 Governor's Race: The Great Invasion

All is transitory in the world of politics, and the 1979 gubernatorial campaign brought new consultants to challenge the performance of those who had established themselves. The serious candidates for governor and their consultants were as follows:

Leon Bramlett (R): Gordon Marks and Associates (Jackson), media; Stuart Stevens (Washington), strategy; Lance Terrance (Houston), polling.

Gilbert Carmichael (R): Douglas Bailey (McLean, Va.), media; Walter DeVries (Wrightsville Beach, N.C.), strategy; The Creative Group (Jackson), organization; Robert Teeters of Market Opinion Research (Detroit) and Lance Terrance (Houston), polling.

Charles Deaton (D): Larry Painter & Associates (Jackson), media and strategy.

John Arthur Eaves (D): Steve Patterson (Jackson), management and strategy; Dozier, Summer and Berry (Tulsa)/Hammon and Willard (Jackson), cooperative venture, media; Jack Friend and Associates (Mobile), polling.

Evelyn Gandy (D): John Davis (Washington), organization and management; Rusty Cantelli of Cantelli, Killeen, and Shaumburg (New Orleans), and Goodwin Advertising (Jackson), media; no polling.

James H. Herring (D): Tommy Giordino (Pearl, Miss.), management and strategy; Cook, Reuf, Spann, and Weisner (Columbia, S.C.), and David Brown and Associates (Jackson), media; Bill Hamilton and Staff (Chevy Chase, Md.), polling.

William F. Winter (D): Robert Squier of The Communications Company (Washington), strategy and media; Maris, West, and Baker (Jackson), print media and some radio; Peter Hart and Associates (Washington), polling; Binns and Associates (Dallas) fund-raising.

This lineup of out-of-state consultants broke all previous records. It also resulted in new highs in spending, with Carmichael, Eaves, Herring, and Winter reaching the $700,000–$1,000,000 category. Leon Bramlett was defeated in the Republican primary, in which only approximately 40,000 votes were cast; yet he reported spending $284,880. (As in Louisiana, reported spending is notoriously understated in Mississippi.)

Only two of the serious candidates began the campaign with Mississippi media consultants. However, three of the candidates—Eaves, Gandy, and Herring—who started with out-of-state media consultants dismissed them in the course of the campaign. In each case the candidate switched to an in-state advertising agency or to in-house media production. The motivation for switching in the case of the Gandy campaign was lack of adequate financial resources to continue use of the New Orleans firm of Cantelli, Killeen, and Shaumburg. In the case of the Eaves and Herring campaigns the cause was dissatisfaction with the performance of the media consultant. In both cases strong differences over strategy and tactics arose between the candidate and his close advisors on one hand and the media consultants on the other. This kind of dissension is a fairly normal outgrowth of the competing voices heard in a campaign and is especially common when things are not going well. The likelihood of dissension is further magnified when a media consultant is an out-of-stater. The consultant frequently is inclined to feel that he knows a great deal more about how to conduct a successful campaign than does the candidate, and he can generally point to successes in other states. The candidate and his supporters, especially those who are investing money in the campaign, look upon the consultant as a foreigner who does not grasp the subtleties of the state's politics. A homegrown political consultant has the advantage of being able to claim an understanding of the idiosyncrasies of state politics, whether he does in fact or not.

Nonetheless, the 1979 campaign brought new prestige to out-of-state consultants. The winning campaign of William Winter was attributed to his pollster, Peter Hart, and his media consultant, Robert Squier. After unsuccessful races for governor in 1967 and 1975, he had virtually abandoned hope of achieving the governorship. At the brink of the qualifying deadline he decided, on the basis of urging from longtime supporters, to commission a poll by Peter Hart. The results not only convinced Winter to make a last-hour entry into the race but also provided the basis of the successful campaign strategy.

Hart's polling showed that of Winter's three main opponents in the Democratic primary, the strongest was Evelyn Gandy, the incumbent lieutenant governor. It further showed that Gandy had two liabilities: she was identified with the Finch administration, in which she had served, and she was a woman. Winter, therefore, would be the candidate of change and of masculinity.[18]

Squier, making his first entrance on the Mississippi campaign stage, was employed as the strategy and media consultant to make those themes of change and macho effective with the voters. The Winter campaign was new to Mississippi in the number and diversity of radio and television commercials. Instead of the usual fifteen to twenty ads of a typical campaign, "Squier produced seventy . . . most of them with a specific audience and time slot in mind."[19] Many of those promotional spots were aimed at saying that Mississippi could not afford to have a woman governor, but doing so with sufficient subtlety not to offend the sensitivities of

18. Nicholas Lemann, "No, Seriously, I Want You to Look at the Camera and Say, 'Ride with Me, Wyoming!'," *Washington Monthly*, XII (July–August, 1980), 13.
19. Sabato, *The Rise of Political Consultants*, 183.

viewers. Stressing in his radio and television spots that the governorship is the "toughest job in Mississippi," Squier consistently placed Winter in masculine environments—sawmills, heavy-equipment repair shops, and truck stops. Most attention has been devoted to a spot which put "Winter out in the midst of a National Guard battlefield maneuver. With the rumble of tanks in the background and military true grit filling the screen the candidate solemnly intoned, 'The governor is the commander-in-chief of the National Guard. He's ultimately responsible for how it performs. The Guard is the first line of national defense.' "[20] This spot was just one of many aimed at pointing up the masculine character of the governor's duties. Several writers outside of Mississippi have taken note of its effectiveness in pointing up "the governorship ain't no woman's work" theme, but none has mentioned that the preceding four years—in which Gandy had been lieutenant-governor—had seen unusually blatant, even by traditional standards, political involvement in National Guard promotion decisions. It was in fact a good two-for-the-price-of-one blow at femininity and corruption.

Other spots had a "narrow-casting" focus to specific groups of voters including persons employed in the lumber industry, the oil and gas industry, and agriculture. One of the Winter spots aimed at blacks created a stir in the campaign brain trust: "Several of William Winter's campaign aides objected to the airing of one of Robert Squier's spots . . . because it featured a relaxed black worker who continued to recline as Winter spoke to him. The fear was that blacks would see the portrayal as demeaning and suggestive of slothfulness, but when a group of black voters viewed all of Winter's commercials, they chose the one in question as their favorite. Squier said that black observers approvingly saw the black man as declaring 'I'm laying right here, whitey. In the old days I had to get on my feet for you, but I don't have to anymore.' "[21] There is little question about the superiority of the Winter media work as compared with that of his opponents. Squier's ads were technically good and carefully targeted.

However, the credit given to Hart and Squier has been excessive, and Winter probably would have been elected in 1979 without either. He was known throughout the state from four previous statewide campaigns, and he had extremely loyal supporters in every area. In his two previous races for governor he had been defeated by a racist (John Bell Williams in

20. *Ibid.*, 127. See also Lemann, "No, Seriously," 13, and "Robert Squier's Media Miracles in Dixie," *Campaigns and Elections*, I (Summer, 1980), 34.
21. Sabato, *The Rise of Political Consultants*, 139.

1967) and by a new-face, outsider type (Cliff Finch in 1975). Both turned out to be rather incompetent governors. Finch, in fact, was erratic and an embarrassment to the state. Many observers felt that by 1979 Mississippi voters were inclined to cast their ballots for the candidate who had not resorted to demagoguery in the days of hostility between the races and who had generally been thought of as "too progressive" by Mississippi standards—Winter. Also, many Mississippians are very defensive about their image in the Union and are greatly concerned with the " 'Today Show' interview variable," thus casting their ballots for candidates who will not embarrass Mississippi on national television. Winter filled the bill as an experienced and articulate municipal-bond attorney. No doubt Hart and Squier added points, but their contribution has been inflated in its recounting. Fred Barnes, citing the Winter campaign, suggests that consultants are consistently given more credit than they deserve in victorious campaigns. He lays much of the blame for this hyperbole upon journalists.[22] This campaign nevertheless effectively reinforced the already established notion that a serious candidate for a major office should retain nationally recognized media and polling consultants.[23]

CONSEQUENCES OF PROFESSIONAL CAMPAIGNING

What has been the impact of campaign consultants and their new campaign techniques? Some are obvious; others are more difficult to detect. More time will be required before the full effect of these campaign technologies are understood.

One outgrowth is a diminished regional flavor to campaigns in the South. Consultants borrow freely from one another, and many have clients in several states or throughout the nation. Naturally there are some parochial appeals in the state campaigns, but more and more the distinctions from state to state have been blurred, with television as the prime vehicle for campaign messages prepared by consultants whose scope and perspective are national.

A second obvious impact of professional campaigning is the rapid rise in costs that has paralleled its evolution. The high costs of consultants and their technologies have spawned new experts. Direct-mail specialists

22. Fred Barnes, "The Myth of Political Consultants," *New Republic* (June 16, 1986), 17.

23. The next race, in 1983, saw new pollsters and consultants (like Dick Morris, Pat Caddell, and Robert Goodman), new highs in spending—over $5 million—and new lows in mudslinging. The latter occurred when the Republican candidate, Leon Bramlett, charged the eventual winner, Bill Allain, with homosexuality. For a brief account of the issue of homosexuality in the campaign, see Stephen A. Salmore and Barbara G. Salmore, *Candidates, Parties, and Campaigns* (Washington, D.C., 1985), 174–75.

are used extensively to raise funds, now there are also fund-raising consultants, and the services of both are likely to be in increasing demand. The skyrocketing expenses incurred in professional campaigning may explain the noticeable increase in the number of millionaires elected to office in the past decade. Dolph Biscoe and William Clements in Texas, Fob James in Alabama, Lamar Alexander in Tennessee, and Edwin Edwards in Louisiana are examples. The ability of a candidate to campaign on his own money provides a substantial advantage. It is especially important to be certain of money early in a campaign to nail down consultants and to purchase prime radio and television time. A wealthy candidate can do those things with ease. In U.S. Senate races in 1982, 20 percent of all campaign contributions came from candidates themselves, up from 8 percent four years earlier.[24] The appraisal of wealth in politics by consultant Hal Evry is no doubt extreme, but a considerable thread of truth runs through his statements: "In any election, the golden rule applies. He who has the gold rules. The more money a candidate spends, the more likely he is to win. . . . Studies show that the candidate who outspends his opponents wins four out of five times. . . . Being rich is not just an advantage, it's virtually a prerequisite for most offices today. . . . We made a rule that anybody walking into our office had to have half a million dollars in assets before we would even talk to him."[25] Court interpretations of federal laws limiting campaign contributions have excluded contributions by a candidate to his own campaign from these limits, thereby providing a substantial advantage to the wealthy.

Perhaps more disturbing than the trend toward millionaires in politics is the necessity for nonwealthy candidates to raise vast amounts of money. Basically, three legal approaches can be used. One is the traditional pursuit of "fat cat" dollars in races other than those for national office, in which contributions are limited by law. This usually comes in the form of large contributions from persons who have a major stake in governmental policies. Traditionally, big contributions have come from certain businesses: banking, construction, trucking, railroads, gambling, utilities, coal, oil, gas, timber, auto dealerships, and insurance. Most big contributors expect a favorable return on their investment. Godfrey Hodgson suggests a conservative bias in the funding and use of new campaign technology: "Insurgents were less likely to be able to afford lavish

24. Ibid., 100.
25. David Chagall, The New Kingmakers (New York, 1981), 298–99.

media campaigns than incumbents, and liberals less likely to be able to afford them than conservatives."[26]

The serious potential for scandal in high-stakes campaign financing was revealed in an FBI "sting" operation during the 1979–1980 Louisiana governor's race. Convicted as a result of this operation were reputed Mafia boss Carlos Marcello and Charles Roemer, former commissioner of administration under Governor Edwin Edwards. Marcello and Roemer were charged with engaging in a bribery-kickback scheme with the latter using his position and influence to gain a lucrative state insurance contract for a Marcello company. Roemer, who was recorded on tape accepting a $25,000 bribe, contended that he was at that time raising campaign funds for gubernatorial candidate Edgar G. Mouton and that he was only stringing the FBI undercover agent along in hopes of substantial financial support for Mouton's campaign. A trial jury did not accept this defense as credible.[27] The case points up the blurred line between contributions and bribes. With the rapid rise of campaign costs, enormous temptation exists for candidates and their supporters to resort to unethical and illegal schemes to raise the funds necessary for a modern campaign.

Another way of funding campaigns, particularly for U.S. House and Senate seats, is through political action committees (PACs), which are on the rise in the South as in the rest of the nation. A look at the ten biggest spenders among the region's PACs in 1981–1982 is instructive.[28]

	Total Spending 1981–82	Direct Contributions to Candidate 1981–82
National Congressional Club	$10,404,521	$235,263
C-TAPE–Associated Milk Producers, Inc.	$1,611,630	$962,450
Texas Medical Association	$1,061,845	$8,752
Dairymen, Inc.–SPACE	$867,519	$226,193

26. Godfrey Hodgson, *All Things to All Men: The False Promise of the American Presidency* (New York, 1980), 169.

27. New Orleans *Times-Picayune/States Item*, August 4, 1981. Marcello was heard to lament on the tapes that despite his heavy investments, Louisiana politicians were such scoundrels they wouldn't stay bought; they were untrustworthy and unreliable.

28. Bill Hogan and Diane Kiesel, "Money Business: PACs in the South," *Southern Exposure*, XII (February, 1984), 99–104.

Florida Medical Association	$712,628	$71,740
Elect–Alabama Farm Bureau	$659,430	$29,975
Tenneco Good Government Fund	$499,651	$454,150
American Family PAC	$335,613	$232,775
Sunbelt G.G.C.–Winn Dixie Stores	$319,863	$256,000

These contributions went largely to reelect incumbents serving on committees dealing with taxes; sugar and tobacco price supports plus other agricultural subsidies; medical, airline, and banking deregulation; and migrant labor laws, among other things. The six Senate races in the South in 1980–1981 found four incumbents ranking in the top ten nationally for PAC contributions:

Lloyd Bentsen (D-Tex.) $800,443

Robert C. Byrd (D-W. Va.) $710,541

Paul S. Tribble, Jr. (R-Va.) $671,016

James R. Sasser (D-Tenn.) $641,970

In the same years, eight House incumbents in the region got over $200,000 from PACs.

William Chappel, Jr. (D-Fla.) $284,116

Stanford Parris (R-Va.) $277,383

William Philip Gramm (D-Tex.) $269,870

Jim Wright (D-Tex.) $255,065

Jack Brooks (D-Tex.) $241,055

Martin Frost (D-Tex.) $233,914

John L. Napier (R-S.C.) $230,494

Frank Wolf (R-Va.) $233,565

The national activity of PACs has been extensively publicized in a wide variety of vehicles, but their activity at the state and local levels has not been studied extensively. Studies of several states indicate that the role of PACs in funding state legislative campaigns, especially those of incumbents and legislative leaders, has paralleled the national pattern.[29]

The third approach to raising big money is to employ the direct-mail technique, aimed at relatively small contributors. The hallmark of direct-mail fund-raising is a shrill appeal to save the world from the menace of the opponent the mailing is trying to defeat. More extensive use of direct-mail fund-raising is likely to lead to increasingly nasty and bitter cam-

29. Nicholas Henry, *Governing at the Grassroots* (Englewood Cliffs, 1984), 79–80; Salmore and Salmore, *Candidates, Parties, and Campaigns*, 201.

paigns largely focused on divisive social issues. Sabato's evaluation is that the recurrent themes of direct mail are "emotionalism, personalization, and gimmickery. The copy tends to be negative, sometimes vehemently so, particularly when a well-known incumbent is the target. The difficulty in triggering contributions using simple print media alone encourages exaggerated drama, intimacy, and urgency."[30] Perhaps this is why right-wing candidates and causes have had more success in direct-mail fund-raising than have moderate candidates.

Another impact of the new campaigning is upon the recruitment of candidates. Style and image take on great importance in campaigns that rely heavily on the visual media. In a pioneering work on the topic Dan Nimmo suggested that the day might come when consultants recruited candidates on the basis of their marketability.[31] The general pattern is still for candidates to seek the services of consultants, but the top media consultants are very selective about which candidate they sell their services to. Nonincumbents are particularly disadvantaged by consultants' selectivity. "Because in most races challengers are assumed to be the underdogs, and consultants' reputations depend on their 'win and loss' records, they find it more difficult to persuade the leading consultants to work for them."[32] Youthful, handsome, male candidates with pretty wives and all-American-looking children are preferred. Short, bald, divorced, and older candidates are a burden to the media consultant in the era of visual media campaigning. "Hot" candidates are a dying breed. Television is the "cool" medium.

Less substance in campaigns seems to be yet another result. Campaigns have rarely been great instruments for education and enlightenment, but the extensive use of thirty- and sixty-second promotional spots has vastly expanded the importance of image and style at the expense of substance. Joseph Napolitan makes a strong case for television spots that strike a responsive chord in the mind of the viewer: "Triggering responses from stored material not only is more effective than giving the voter a mass of new material to learn (because learning is one of the most difficult of the brain's jobs while remembering is one of the easiest), but also is less expensive."[33] The brevity of these appeals to voters makes certain that if issues are discussed at all, they will be handled in the most simplified terms.

30. Sabato, *The Rise of Political Consultants*, 357–58.
31. Dan Nimmo, *The Political Persuaders: The Techniques of Modern Election Campaigns* (Englewood Cliffs, 1970), 42–45.
32. Salmore and Salmore, *Campaigns, Parties, and Candidates*, 89.
33. Joseph Napolitan, *The Election Game and How to Win It* (Garden City, 1972), 29.

New campaign techniques probably have been beneficial to the Republican party in the South. At the beginning of the 1960s, southern Republicans had no governors, no United States senators, and only seven United States congressmen. After the 1984 elections, they had two governors, ten United States senators, and forty-three United States congressmen. This is rather remarkable success to be achieved in two decades. The new campaigning style, with its candidate-centered approach, has placed diminished emphasis upon party. Its focus on personality and style has likely played an important role in the Republican party's success.[34] However, in state legislative races and local campaigns where organization and old-style handshaking are still used extensively, the new technology is of no help to Republicans, and they have fared poorly.

A final consequence of the changes in campaigning is that the new techniques have the potential of making political campaigning a spectator sport. In pretelevision days, a successful campaign required volunteers to do door-to-door canvassing, stuff letters, put up posters, and join in efforts to get voters out to the polls on election day. Modern campaigns orchestrated by professional consultants, financed by PACs and direct mail, and conducted through computers and mass media allow a candidate to run without seeing or touching a voter. Tina Rosenberg makes the point quite well: "Direct mail adds yet another barrier between the candidate and the public simply by making it less necessary to go out into the rough and tumble of the real world. Much political accountability has already been eroded by television commercials in which a candidate speaks with the assurance that he won't also have to listen. Similarly, in a direct mail letter a candidate hides behind his letterhead, not having to worry about tough questions like, 'Can you win?' and 'Where do you stand?' "[35]

According to Iris Kelso, a perceptive New Orleans journalist who has observed Louisiana politics for two decades, in that state modern, media-oriented "political campaigns are a form of entertainment, not instruction."[36] That is precisely the nature of the old politics of demagoguery, and it is a tragic indictment of the new politics.

---

34. As Sabato explains in *The Rise of Political Consultants*, 290–97.
35. Tina Rosenburg, "Diminishing Returns: The False Promise of Direct Mail," *Washington Monthly*, XV (June, 1983), 38.
36. Iris Kelso, "The Image Makers," New Orleans *Times-Picayune/States Item*, September 11, 1979.

CONCLUSIONS

In the past two decades the South, once a distinct region with a colorful tradition of flamboyant campaigning from the stump, has joined — for better or for worse — the national mainstream of media-based campaigning. This form of campaigning is largely directed by professional consultants on a fee-for-service basis. Consultants come from within the region and from outside.

Modern statewide campaigns are now carefully planned efforts based upon information about voters obtained through polling. Whereas candidates once appealed in person to voters' beliefs, biases, emotions, fears, and passions from the stump with lengthy speeches, they now make those appeals via television, in living color, with thirty- and sixty-second promotional spots, and through carefully written and targeted letters produced by electronic word processors. The old-style campaigners had to guess at the feelings of the voters, whereas today's campaigners, thanks to polling, can discern them scientifically.

Progressive southerners once longed for the day when the South would shed its idiosyncrasies and join the national mainstream. In campaigning, that day has arrived. Now progressives might well ask themselves if the present is a significant improvement upon the past. But regardless of the good or evil inherent in modern campaign techniques, they are now as much a part of the South as black-eyed peas and corn bread. There will be no turning back in Dixie.

Government and PART THREE
Leadership

In the 1890s the Solid South system was built on Jim Crow, one-party politics, malapportionment, formal and informal disfranchisement of the masses, plus regional autonomy from national politics and policies. From then until the transformations of the 1960s the South's governing institutions, political leadership, and public policies were virtually frozen in time. The dramatic, wide-ranging political development experienced by the industrialized and democratic world in this three-quarters of a century bypassed the South. Thus, Key's sad lament in 1949 that the region lacked the political organization and leadership requisite to dealing with its manifold problems.

The pattern of governance established in the 1890s included the most powerful regional bloc of senators and congressmen to be found in Washington. The southern delegations amassed seniority through the one-party system, using their positions to represent essentially elite interests and to veto unwanted federal intervention in racial, social, and economic matters in Dixie. By contrast, the region's governors were the weakest in the country, usually little more than showmen who "entertained and inflamed" the masses with demagogic rhetoric and neo-Populist symbolism and did little else. The South's legislatures were such caricatures of representative democratic bodies that a 1969 study found them to be the worst in the nation. State and local judiciaries were little more than legal appendages of wealth and sanctioned virtually any violations of constitutional protections deemed necessary to protect the segregated society. And a bureaucratic structure evolved in a chaotic, haphazard manner mainly to serve well-placed interests and provide jobs for the faction in power at a given time. Leadership in all these institutions was very much drawn from a traditional elite. Although some rabble-rousers would occasionally attain office, women, blacks, racially moderate whites, and—for the most part—Republicans were excluded. It was a one-dimensional, closed, and inflexible system, which was why it finally shattered.

The changing economics, demographics, and attitudes described in

Part One and the sweeping political transformations analyzed in Part Two produced significant governmental reform and new leadership in the South. The institutional changes have made different public policies possible, and contemporary leaders have altered—at least to some degree—the South's public policies. It is as if a logjam were broken in the 1960s and the pent-up impetus for change suddenly released. The result has been sweeping reforms in the system of governance and the recruitment pattern of officials. The five essays in this section document this transformation.

In Charles Bullock's description and assessment of the power and policy orientations of southern congressional delegations, he first explains the bases of the South's historically exaggerated legislative influence and the policy commitments of the traditional elite who were sent to Capitol Hill from Dixie. He then explores the several reasons for the decline in the region's power in the 1970s and the replacement of the Solid South generation of congressional elders. Bullock also compares and contrasts the policy preferences of southern Democrats and Republicans now in Congress with each other and with their predecessors in the areas of civil rights and the economy.

The next essay focuses on that group of recent southern governors dubbed by the national media and political commentators as the "New South" class. Larry Sabato identifies and describes these leaders and locates them in the transformed political environment. He explains how they have led significant reform movements in state governments and concludes by commenting on the ideological orientations of the New South types, examining Reubin Askew as an illustrative example and speculating on their role in the changing federal system.

The types of legislators currently being elected to office, the many reforms professionalizing legislative institutions across the South, and patterns of legislative behavior are examined by Patricia Freeman, Lee Bernick, and David Olson. They explain how reapportionment, urbanization, black enfranchisement, and partisan trends have altered the traditional recruitment pattern, bringing a younger and more diversified group into the state legislature. The current membership of the Tennessee legislature is contrasted with that of the 1930s as a case in point. They also describe the many reforms creating a more professional body, focusing on a key area—sunset legislation. Finally, the changing workload and role of the legislatures across the South are explored.

The least-studied political institutions in the South have been the judiciary and the bureaucracy. Ronald Marquardt comments on the lack of attention paid to the southern judiciary and endeavors to clarify the politics of this branch of government. He first describes and assesses how judges are chosen through the curiously apolitical partisan selection process used in all but a few states of the Old Confederacy, and he gives a detailed account of the career backgrounds and personal characteristics of the judges recruited through this process. Last, Marquardt analyzes the serious flaws in the selection process and points to needed reforms and areas for further study.

Edward Wheat concludes the section on governing institutions and leadership by endeavoring to shed light on the burgeoning bureaucracy. He describes the traditional fragmentation of the South's administrative agencies, explains the major reorganization efforts and civil service reforms, and looks at the political consequences of these changes. Wheat offers comments on such specific innovations as Jimmy Carter's implementation of zero-based budgeting in Georgia in 1971. He closes with an assessment of the new incoherence these "reforms" have created in the administrative branch of southern state governments.

The South in Congress: Power and Policy

CHARLES S. BULLOCK III

*Historically, Congress is where southern politics
have exerted greatest national influence.*
　　　　　　　—Jack Bass and Walter DeVries,
　　　　　　　*The Transformation of Southern
　　　　　　　Politics* (1976)

During most of the last century the White House was off limits to southerners because of their opposition to civil rights for blacks. The South has not dominated the Supreme Court or the bureaucracy either, and thus, as Bass and DeVries, Key, and virtually all other commentators have noted, the region's major power has resided in Congress. Indeed, around mid-century the Senate was known as "the old Southern home." The southern role in Congress is best understood by looking at two key dimensions: the power of southern congressional delegations and the policies they pursue.

In Congress southerners have traditionally constituted approximately 25 percent of the House and a slightly smaller share of the Senate. Despite being a minority, they have succeeded many times in controlling congressional decisions on those issues most salient to the region's leaders. Although during the last twenty years there has been a decline in the South's congressional power, southern delegations still remain a force to contend with. This essay briefly reviews the traditional bases for southern congressional influence and discusses the region's declining power due to congressional reforms, loss of senior members, and the rise of southern Republicanism.

Turning to policy objectives, one finds that for the most part southern legislative efforts historically have been directed essentially but not exclusively toward conservative goals. This was due in part to the power exercised over the delegations by black-belt elites and business interests. (An exception to this pattern was the support for Roosevelt's New Deal generated by the terrible deprivation of the Depression.) In the 1930s the South blocked enactment of antilynching legislation. During the 1950s the southern delegations delayed and watered down the terms of civil rights bills and numerous welfare proposals. When domestic aid programs have been approved, southerners in Congress frequently have ensured that their region receives a disproportionate share of the benefits whether the program be one designed to help farmers or to rejuvenate urban areas. Beginning with the Eisenhower presidency, the South has opposed foreign aid but has supported a strong national defense. In the early days of the Reagan administration, the South played an essential part in what many have characterized as the most significant change in policy direction since the New Deal, with the passage of social welfare reforms, tax cuts, and Reagan's overall budget proposals.

The changes that have reduced the South's congressional influence have also brought about some reorientation in the policy preferences of southern legislators. Increased black influence, a major new element in southern politics, has also altered policy preferences and is discussed in the essay's third section. The last section will assess changes in Democratic and Republican southern legislators' policy positions as a consequence of congressional reforms, the decline in senior Democrats, the rise of southern Republicanism, and black politics.

BASES OF SOUTHERN CONGRESSIONAL INFLUENCE

There have traditionally been several important factors enhancing the South's power. The very nature of the American Congress has been a boon to southern legislators. The bicameral, committee-dominated legislative process provides numerous opportunities to defeat proposals. Whereas enactment of legislative change requires a victory at every step of the way, southern conservatives need triumph only once in order to maintain the status quo.

In mobilizing obstructionist forces at key points in the complex labyrinth of the legislative process, the South has enjoyed several advantages. Chief among these during the 1950s was the House Rules Committee. In combination with conservative Republicans, southern Democrats on Rules bottled up civil rights, social welfare, and education bills for years. One such instance, occurring in the late 1950s, concerned a civil rights bill languishing in Rules. When Speaker of the House Sam Rayburn, a Texas Democrat, called the office of the committee chairman, "Judge" Howard Smith of Virginia, an aide informed him that the chairman was out of town. When asked why, the aide replied that Smith had gone home to check on a barn that had burned on his farm and he wouldn't be back for several weeks. The Speaker later remarked that this was the first time he'd known a congressman to resort to arson in order to kill a bill!

In the Senate southerners exploited the filibuster. Until 1964 no southern filibuster on a civil rights bill had ever been cut off. In the 1970s when southerners found themselves increasingly unable to prevent cloture, James Allen (D-Ala.) devised the post-filibuster filibuster. This technique delayed a vote even after cloture by calling up hundreds of previously introduced amendments. (This loophole proved to be short-lived, since Senate rules were changed in 1979 to prohibit this.)

A final element in building the citadel from which southerners operated was the seniority system. For almost three-quarters of a century, congressional committee chairs have been, with few exceptions, members of the majority party who had the longest continuous service on the committees. Until recently, few southerners faced serious Republican challenges. In contrast, the Republican sweeps of 1946 and 1952 ousted many senior members from the North. For two decades after the mid-1950s, southerners constituted a disproportionate share of the senior Democrats.

In the 88th Congress (1963–1964), southern Democrats filled 62.5 percent of the Senate committee chairs, although they constituted only 31 percent of all Senate Democrats. From the 86th (1959–1960) through the 93rd (1973–1974) Congresses, southern Democrats held, on average, 57 percent of the committee chairs. A similar pattern existed in the House from the 84th (1955–1956) through the 90th (1967–1968) Congresses. During this period southern Democrats held, on average, 59 percent of the committee chairs while averaging 37 percent of House Democrats. During much of this period southern Democrats filled the most important committee chairs in both chambers (George Mahon [D-Tex.] on Appropriations, Howard Smith [D-Va.] and William Colmer [D-Miss.] on Rules, and Wilbur Mills [D-Ark.] on Ways and Means in the House and Russell Long [D-La.] on Finance and William Fulbright [D-Ark.] on Foreign Relations in the Senate).

Southern congressional influence has been built on factors other than the seniority system and the ability of the region's legislators to exploit the structural features that tilt the institution toward inaction. Of great importance have been the parliamentary skills of some southern leaders. Examples include onetime Senate Majority Leader Lyndon Johnson's legendary persuasive abilities; the thorough knowledge of congressional rules by such men as the late Senators Richard Russell (D-Ga.) and James Allen; the bargaining power of leaders like former Congressman Howard Smith or Congressman Charles Stenholm (D-Tex.) who could deliver the votes of southerners in order to block legislation viewed as too liberal.[1]

Until quite recently another ability for which frustrated opponents thought southerners had a unique aptitude was in predicting what action Congress was likely to take at a particular time. Since fewer southerners than northerners represented districts from which serious electoral challenges were likely to come, southerners could spend more time observing congressional deliberations and less time engaging in campaign-related activities. From watching Congress in action, southerners not only learned parliamentary maneuvering, but the most astute also developed a keen understanding which enabled them to anticipate what Congress was likely to do when handling important legislation. This frequently made them the institution's chief strategists. One of the best at predicting how the House was likely to react to a legislative proposal was longtime Speaker Sam Rayburn. In describing his ability, Robert Caro writes that "he had what one observer was to call an 'indefinable knack for sensing the mood of the House'; he seemed to know by some instinct for the legislative process, 'just how far it could be pushed,' what the vote on a crucial bill would be if the vote were taken immediately, and what it would be if the vote were delayed a week. Asked decades later about this knack, he would reply: 'If you can't feel things that you can't see or hear, you don't belong here.' "[2]

A final component of southern influence has been the ideological positioning of most southern Democrats. Southern leaders could extract concessions because on many issues southern Democrats' preferences fell between those of northern Democrats on the left and Republicans on the right. Except when there is a Republican majority or an extraordinarily large and cohesive set of northern Democrats (1965–1966, for example), southern Democrats, if united, will hold the balance of power.

It is not surprising, then, that although northern Democrats have out-

1. Doris Kearns, *Lyndon Johnson and the American Dream* (New York, 1976), 120–26. Allen was such a master of Senate rules that he was often said to have "swallowed the rule book."

2. Robert A. Caro, "The Years of Lyndon Johnson," *Atlantic*, CCXLVIII (November, 1981), 52.

numbered southern Democrats in the House since 1949, southerners have been on the winning side of House roll calls more frequently than have northerners.[3] Like so much of southern politics, however, this is changing as the South's congressional influence declines.

DECLINING SOUTHERN INFLUENCE

The 1970s saw a diminution in southern influence in Congress. This change resulted from reforms approved by Congress, generational replacement, and partisan turnover.

Pressures from liberal, junior members prompted a number of congressional reforms. These were designed to decentralize and redistribute power which was taken from the committee chairs and passed out to those who chaired subcommittees. The beneficiaries of this redistributive effort tended to be less senior, less conservative, and less southern than the committee chairs who had formed a ruling oligarchy in the House since 1910.

One of the reforms limited the number of committee and subcommittee chairs an individual can hold. In the House a member can chair only 1 of the 22 committees and approximately 140 subcommittees. The smaller Senate is less restrictive, allowing each member to chair a maximum of 4 committees and subcommittees—a drop from the 10 one senator chaired in the 94th Congress (1975–1976). (The Senate has 16 standing committees divided into 100 subcommittees.) The House also reduced the committee chairs' influence over the staff. Whereas in the past the chair of the full committee made all personnel decisions, now both the subcommittee chairs and the minority party can hire and fire some staff members. These two decentralizing reforms made subcommittees and their chairs more autonomous and were intended, in part, to weaken the influence of the conservative southerners who had disproportionately held committee and subcommittee chairs.[4]

Even more important than decentralizing committee influence was the 1974 uprising in the House Democratic Caucus. The horde of northern freshmen swept into Congress by the Watergate backlash voted to unseat the senior southerners who chaired the Agriculture (Bob Poage, Tex.), Armed Services (Edward Hebert, La.), and Banking and Currency

---

3. Barbara D. Sinclair, "Who Wins in the House of Representatives: The Effect of Declining Party Cohesion on Policy Outputs, 1959–1970," *Social Science Quarterly*, CVIII (June, 1977), 125.

4. On the rise and consequences of subcommittee government, see Lawrence C. Dodd and Richard L. Schott, *Congress and the Administrative State* (New York, 1979).

(Wright Patman, Tex.) committees. As a consequence of this deviation from the seniority rule, other chairs became more solicitous of the opinions of rank and file members—more than two-thirds of whom were typically from the North. Gone are the autocratic chairs who could single-handedly bottle up legislation in their committee or, like former Ways and Means Chair Wilbur Mills (D-Ark.), could strike a bargain with the president and then deliver the agreed-upon legislation.

Even had the power of committee chairs not been pruned back, southern influence would have diminished during the 1970s. The ranks of senior Democratic southerners, some of whom had come to Congress when Franklin Roosevelt occupied the White House, were depleted by death, defeat, and a more generous retirement program. By 1987, there were eighteen southerners in the House and three in the Senate who had twenty or more years of seniority. Of the senior southern senators, one was a Republican (Strom Thurmond, S.C.), and John Stennis (Miss.) and Ernest Hollings (S.C.) were Democrats. Southerners constituted 30 percent of the senior senators and 37 percent of the senior congressmen. By contrast, in 1966 the twenty-two House southerners who had served two decades constituted 46 percent of the senior members, and southerners accounted for 46 percent of the most senior senators.

Below the layer of senior southerners who dominated the Congress of a generation ago was a cohort which included northerners as well as southerners. After the mid-1950s, many northern urban districts were as electorally secure for Democrats as the one-party South had been since the 1890s. Northerners, therefore, could acquire seniority rivaling that of southerners, and they profited greatly in the 1970s from the depletion of the senior ranks of southerners. In the 89th Congress (1965–1966) southerners held 13 of 20 House committee chairs and 9 of the 16 chairs in the Senate. By the 100th Congress (1987–1988), southerners chaired only 7 of 22 House committees, and southern Democrats chaired 7 of 16 Senate committees.

The rising strength of the Republican party has further eroded the position of southern Democrats. Growth in Republican congressional strength has been closely linked to the party's fortunes in presidential elections. Republicans have enlarged on the beachhead established in 1952, when Dwight Eisenhower carried four southern states and helped four new Republicans win seats in the House of Representatives.

Republican fortunes were advanced as well by Barry Goldwater's 1964 quest for the White House. In contrast to the negative consequences of the Goldwater candidacy for Republicans in most of the coun-

TABLE 1

Southern Senators Serving Since 1960 with More than Twenty Years Seniority

Name	Tenure	Seniority in Years	Major Committee(s)
John Stennis (D-Miss.)	1947–	40 +	Armed Services,* Appropriations*
Richard Russell (D-Ga.)	1933–71	38	Armed Services,* Appropriations*
Russell Long (D-La.)	1949–87	38	Finance*
John McClellan (D-Ark.)	1943–79	36	Appropriations,* Government Affairs*
James Eastland (D-Miss.)	1943–79	36	Judiciary*
Allen Ellender (D-La.)	1937–72	35	Appropriations,* Agriculture*
Harry F. Byrd, Sr. (D-Va.)	1933–65	32	Finance*
John Sparkman (D-Ala.)	1946–79	32	Foreign Relations,* Banking and Currency*
Lister Hill (D-Ala.)	1938–69	31	Labor and Public Welfare*
William Fulbright (D-Ark.)	1945–75	30	Foreign Relations*
Strom Thurmond (D, R-S.C.)	1957–	30 +	Judiciary*
Spessard Holland (D-Fla.)	1946–71	25	Appropriations
Herman Talmadge (D-Ga.)	1957–81	24	Agriculture*
John Tower (R-Tex.)	1961–85	24 +	Armed Services*
Sam Ervin (D-N.C.)	1954–75	21	Judiciary
A. Willis Robertson (D-Va.)	1946–67	21	Banking and Currency*
Ernest Hollings (D-S.C.)	1966–	21 +	Budget

*The senator at some time chaired the committee or was the ranking minority member.

try (the Republican party suffered a net loss of one Senate and thirty-seven House seats), whites in the Deep South flocked to the banner of this conservative, one of the few Senate Republicans to vote against the 1964 Civil Rights Act. Goldwater followers were the first Republicans since Reconstruction to be elected to the House from Alabama, Georgia, and Mississippi. Also as a result of Goldwater's candidacy, Republicans picked up a Senate and a House seat in South Carolina when Senator Strom Thurmond and Congressman Albert Watson defected from the Democratic party rather than support Lyndon Johnson.

Table 2 shows that other major impetuses for Republican congressional strength were provided by Richard Nixon's 1972 landslide and

TABLE 2

Southern Republican Strength in Congress, by State, 1961–1987

State	Republican Senate Seats														House Republicans 1987
	1961	1963	1965	1967	1969	1971	1973	1975	1977	1979	1981	1983	1985	1987	1987
Texas	1	1	1	1	1	1	1	1	1	1	1	1	1	1	10
South Carolina			1	1	1	1	1	1	1	1	1	1	1	1	2
Tennessee				1	1	2	2	2	1	1	1	1			3
Florida					1	1	1				1	1	1		7
North Carolina							1	1	1	1	2	2	2	1	3
Virginia							1	1	1	1	1	2	2	2	6
Mississippi										1	1	1	1	1	1
Alabama											1	1	1		2
Georgia											1	1	1		2
Arkansas															1
Louisiana															3
Southern Republicans in the House	7	11	17	24	24	25	34	28	28	30	39	34	43	40	

President Reagan's 1980 and 1984 sweeps. In 1980 Republicans picked up four Senate seats including the first Republican senators popularly elected from Alabama (Jeremiah Denton) and Georgia (Mack Mattingly). They also added nine House seats. Half of the South's twenty-two senators were Republicans in 1983, including both the senators from North Carolina and Virginia. Only Arkansas and Louisiana did not have a Republican senator. This was quite a change from 1961, when John Tower, in something of a fluke, won a special election to fill the Texas Senate seat vacated by Lyndon Johnson and became the South's first Republican senator. Republican strength in southern House delegations reached an all-time high of forty-three in 1985.

The mid-term election of 1986 was not kind to Republican members of Congress. The GOP lost all four Senate seats they had added in 1980 and failed to win an open seat in Louisiana. The contests in Alabama and Georgia were very close, so that even in losing, the GOP displayed greater strength than had been usual in the past.

The rise of southern Republicanism reduced southern Democrats' congressional power by cutting short the careers of some through reelection defeats, thereby lowering seniority in the region. Furthermore, the depleted ranks of southern Democrats have at times been insufficient to fill as many important positions as they held a generation ago. A solidly Democratic South would also have more influence within the Democratic party since it would constitute a larger share of the party's membership.[5]

We can better understand the relative role of the South among Democratic senators if we compare the 99th Congress (1985–1986) with the 83rd (1953–1954), an earlier time when Republicans controlled the Senate. In 1985 twelve southerners constituted 26 percent of the Democratic party's senators. In 1953 the twenty-two southerners held 47 percent of their party's forty-seven Senate seats. In mid-1987, with Democrats back in control, southerners accounted for 30 percent of the majority party.

It is not only congressional reforms, generational replacement, and partisan turnover that have altered the traditional pattern of the South's congressional politics. Of equal if not greater significance has been the dramatic rise in black political participation.

SOUTHERN LEGISLATORS' POLICY PREFERENCES ON CIVIL RIGHTS

Barriers to black registration were so effective that only a quarter of the South's voting-age blacks were on the voter lists in the late 1950s. Dis-

5. See, for example, Julius Turner, *Party and Constituency: Pressures on Congress* (Baltimore, 1951) and the revised edition by Edward V. Schneier, Jr. (Baltimore, 1970).

crimination was fiercest in communities where blacks were concentrated and where the consequences of their exercising influence through the ballot were thus most threatening. With the implementation of legislation and court orders aimed at assuring equal access to the voting booth for all races, black registration rose rapidly beginning in the 1960s. In 1984 the Bureau of the Census estimated that 66 percent of all southern blacks were registered and 33 percent actually voted. These levels of participation, almost as high as those for whites, have brought to blacks an important role in the politics of many southern communities.[6]

Black votes have come to carry more weight as larger numbers of blacks have registered and many whites have supported Republican candidates. These two features have caused southern Democratic legislators to become distinctly more supportive of policies favored by blacks than are southern Republicans. With black votes now needed by hard-pressed Democrats, the fears that appealing for black votes would set off a fatal backlash among white voters have been overcome. In the past, as V. O. Key pointed out in 1949, legislators whose districts had large concentrations of blacks were the least supportive of the policy preferences of their black constituents — a pattern that changed in the 1970s.[7]

The changes in southern legislators' voting records directly attributable to black political activity are most visible on civil rights issues. A good illustration is provided by the responses southern House members have given to voting-rights legislation over the years, as Richard Engstrom's essay in this volume explains and as Table 3 indicates. Most white Democrats have supported the last two renewals of the Voting Rights Act, and in 1981 the overwhelming majority of Democrats were joined by a majority of southern Republicans in supporting final passage.

As southern Democrats have responded to their black constituents and have supported civil rights legislation, the two regional wings of the Democratic party have begun to draw together on this issue. Although still much more conservative than their northern colleagues, southern Democrats have been moved to the center. At the same time, northern Democrats also have shifted toward the center by becoming somewhat less liberal than in the late 1960s and early 1970s. During the first Eisen-

6. See the discussion in the essay by Parker in this volume; see also Harrell R. Rodgers, Jr., and Charles S. Bullock, III, *Law and Social Change* (New York, 1972), 15–54, and U.S. Department of Commerce, Bureau of the Census, *Voting and Registration in the Election of November 1984* Series P-20, No. 397 (Washington, D.C., 1985), 1, 3.

7. V. O. Key, Jr., *Southern Politics in State and Nation* (New York, 1949), 670, and Charles S. Bullock, III, "Congressional Voting and the Mobilization of a Black Electorate in the South," *Journal of Politics*, XLIII (August, 1981), 669.

TABLE 3
Percentages of Southern House Members Who
Supported Final Passage of Voting Rights Acts, 1957–1981

	Democrats	Republicans	Total
1957	14.3	13.3	13.3
1960	7.2	28.6	8.7
1965	32.9	23.5	31.4
1970	33.8	11.5	28.3
1975	72.7	33.3	62.5
1981	90.9	63.9	81.3

SOURCES: Merle Black, "Racial Composition of Congressional Districts and Support for Federal Voting Rights Legislation in the American South," *Social Science Quarterly*, LIX (December, 1978), 442; *Congressional Quarterly Weekly Report*, XXXIX (October 10, 1981), 1982.

hower administration (1953–1956), northern Democrats supported civil rights and civil liberties legislation 98 percent of the time whereas southerners voted for these bills less than 1 percent of the time. In the first two years of the Carter administration, northern Democratic support had slipped to 77 percent, and southern Democratic backing had increased to 37 percent.[8] Indeed, southern Democrats scored slightly higher in 1977–1978 than did the more liberal wing of the Republican party. A quarter of a century earlier, liberal Republicans had a record similar to that of the northern Democrats.

The southern congressional response to voting-rights legislation illustrates the impact of black political activity. When a network of discriminatory techniques kept blacks from voting, white legislators ignored black policy preferences and catered exclusively to the desires of the whites who could vote. Often the tone of the legislative response was set by those who most strongly endorsed the tenets of white supremacy. Once blacks became a sizable share of the electorate in some districts, taking stands in opposition to black preferences had a cost factor. The costs were especially high for Democrats, who found white-collar voters gravitating to the Republican party. As many whites of higher socioeconomic status abandoned the Democratic party, blacks assumed larger roles in determining the outcomes of both Democratic primaries and gen-

8. Barbara Sinclair, "Agenda and Alignment Change: The House of Representatives, 1925–1978," in Lawrence C. Dodd and Bruce I. Oppenheimer (eds.), *Congress Reconsidered* (Rev. ed.; Washington, D.C., 1981), 234, 241.

eral elections. Black support became the key to winning the Democratic nomination in many districts, and black votes, though rarely a majority, were often essential for Democrats to defeat Republicans in general elections. An excellent example of the new relationship between black voters and white Democratic legislators comes from a 1981 special election in Mississippi.

Republicans won Mississippi's 4th Congressional District from 1972 through 1980. In 1980 the potential Democratic vote split when Leslie McLemore, black chairman of the political science department at Jackson State University, polled 31 percent of the vote running as an independent. He ran in part to protest the state Democratic party elite's unwillingness to support black leader Henry Kirksey for the Democratic nomination. The Democratic nominee, Britt Singletary, won 30 percent of the vote, which allowed incumbent Jon Hinson, the Republican, to win reelection with only 39 percent of the vote. Hinson was later arrested in a congressional office-building bathroom for engaging in homosexual acts and resigned.

In the subsequent special election, Republican Liles Williams led the field of eight candidates with 45 percent of the vote. White Democrat Wayne Dowdy was second with 25 percent. Since no one received a majority, these two candidates entered a runoff. Williams was endorsed by President Reagan and was much better financed than his opponent. However, Democratic hopefuls had learned by 1981 that where black voters are numerous (blacks constituted 37 percent of the district's voting-age population in 1980), their support is essential. Dowdy overcame Williams' substantial first-primary lead and won 51 percent of the vote. Dowdy sought black support by promising that if elected he would support the Voting Rights Act extension—a promise that would have been suicidal only a few years earlier. (Although Dowdy was the strongest supporter of the Voting Rights Act, the other serious Democratic candidates displayed no antiblack tendencies.) Dowdy also pledged to select a black for a major staff position.

Black voters contributed to the Dowdy victory in two ways. He ran extremely well among blacks, winning as much as 99 percent of the vote in some black precincts.[9] (Republican Williams did not seek black support.) A much higher black turnout in the runoff than in the first primary was a second consideration in Dowdy's triumph. The increased participation among Dowdy's black supporters was not mirrored in urban white precincts, where Williams ran well.

9. Cliff Treyens, "Surge in Black, Rural Turnout Put Dowdy over Top," Jackson Clarion Ledger, July 8, 1981, Sec. B, p. 1.

Dowdy could not have won exclusively with black votes. He was able to attract black support without alienating rural whites, who are no longer always inveterate Democrats. To appreciate the significance of Dowdy's ability to resurrect the New Deal coalition that included some urban blue-collar workers, remember that since 1968 white Mississippians have overwhelmingly rejected Democratic presidential nominees.[10]

Dowdy has been reelected three times. He kept his pledges to the black community, and blacks have provided vital support. The differentiation between Dowdy and Williams on the race issue was clear and decisive. This cleavage on civil rights is a recent phenomenon and does not carry over to all policy domains, particularly economic ones.

SOUTHERN LEGISLATORS' POLICY PREFERENCES ON ECONOMIC REGULATION

On many issues the pattern has been for southern Democrats to vote with Republicans and against northern Democrats. This pattern, referred to as the Conservative Coalition, has been visible on congressional roll calls since 1937. Although the press, as well as political scientists and historians, have made much of the Conservative Coalition, in fact southern and northern Democrats more frequently unite in opposition to Republicans.

The Conservative Coalition (CC) has attracted attention because it is often able to thwart liberal policy initiatives. In both the House and Senate, when conservative southern Democrats have been too few to prevent the adoption of liberal policy proposals, they have turned to Republicans.

Government regulation of the economy, the item on which Democrats formerly were most cohesive, is now one on which the two wings of the party diverge widely, as southerners vote with Republicans.[11] The CC has also often emerged to oppose foreign aid and some civil rights issues, particularly busing to promote school desegregation. Southern Democrats have drifted away from their northern colleagues on issues reflecting the higher priority southerners assigned to the preferences of their constitutents and the desire for unfettered economic development in the region at the expense of party loyalty.[12] A change in the kinds of issues subsumed under governmental management of the economy helps ac-

10. Loretta Pendergrast, "Dowdy Wins Despite Delay of Help and Taint of Washington Liberals," Jackson *Clarion Ledger*, July 8, 1981, Sec. B, p. 3.

11. Aage R. Clausen, *How Congressmen Decide* (New York, 1973), 94.

12. Barbara Sinclair Deckard, "Political Upheaval and Congressional Voting: The Effects of the 1960s on Voting Patterns in the House of Representatives," *Journal of Politics*, XXXVIII (May, 1976), 326–45.

count in part for the changes in alignments.[13] As consumer protection and the balancing of energy development against environmental protection have come to the fore, regional differences have assumed greater importance. A number of southern Democrats have sided with business interests and developers in opposing the limitations favored by northern Democrats. Rising Democratic disagreement has made it difficult for the party's leaders to enact liberal regulatory programs, which helps account for the failures experienced by Jimmy Carter, a Democrat in office at a time when his party held a huge majority in the House.

Democratic defectors, popularly referred to as "Boll Weevils," held the balance of power in 1981 on the issues at the heart of President Reagan's economic recovery program. At the time these bills were debated, Democrats held a 50-vote majority in the House. The president triumphed when conservative Democrats voted with a solid phalanx of Republicans to cut taxes and funding for a variety of domestic programs. Democratic defections allowed President Reagan to command an ideological — even if not a partisan — majority in the House. Declines in President Reagan's popularity after 1981 weakened his influence with southern Democrats, thereby impairing his ability to lead.

The CC, critical to President Reagan's fortunes, in the House mobilizes on 15 percent of the roll calls. When active, it has triumphed 70 percent of the time in the House since 1970. The success rate in the Senate since 1970 has averaged 73 percent.[14] The success level in recent years has been lower than during the coalition's first generation of activity. From 1939 to 1956 the CC won 92 percent of the House roll call votes on which it was active, including six years in which it never lost.

The success of the CC is most strongly influenced by the size of its membership. When northern Democrats were numerous following the electoral avalanches that buried many Republicans in 1958 and 1964, CC success levels fell to their lowest points. The coalition's effectiveness also dropped in 1974, as a new class of Democrats replaced those Republicans pulled down by the undertow of Watergate. Conversely, when there is a Republican majority, the CC infrequently loses.

The pattern identified as the Conservative Coalition has never taken on the trappings of a formal organization, with state leaders, a staff, or offices. This is in no small part due to the unwillingness of legislators to

13. Sinclair, "Agenda and Alignment Change," 239–40.
14. Calculated from figures in Steven Blakely, "Conservatives: A Rise in Unity but not Victories," *Congressional Quarterly Weekly Report,* XLIV (November 15, 1986), 2908.

formalize behavior that contradicts the norms of party loyalty.[15] The CC has instead been a voting bloc based on shared policy interests.

Toward the end of the Carter presidency, conservative House Democrats formed the Conservative Democratic Forum (CDF). Of the forty-seven congressmen who had affiliated with the forum by mid-1981, thirty-nine were southerners.[16] This constituted approximately 55 percent of all southern Democrats in the House. In 1982 the CDF, under the leadership of Texan Charles Stenholm, took steps to qualify as a political action committee so that it could raise and distribute campaign funds to candidates who shared its principles. In the Senate, all but two southern Democrats belong to and constitute the bulk of a fourteen-member conservative caucus.

With organization has come the coordinated efforts that produced payoffs at the beginning of the 97th Congress (1981). After CDF leaders met with House Speaker Tip O'Neill (D-Mass.), O'Neill named several CDF members to the powerful Steering and Policy Committee, and others were named assistant party whips. Other CDF members received assignments to highly sought after standing committees. These gains did not continue into the 98th Congress, for the Democratic House leaders interpreted Republican losses suffered in 1982 as evidence of growing public disillusionment with Reagan's economic policy. With the allure of the president's program declining, the Democratic Caucus did not fill the requests of CDF members who sought improved assignments. In a rare example of party disciplining, Phil Gramm (Tex.) was expelled from the Budget Committee, where he had been the president's leading Democratic supporter. (He then resigned from Congress, ran and won overwhelmingly as a Republican in the special election to fill the seat.)

CONCLUSIONS

In the last quarter century, several major themes have characterized the role of the South in Congress. First, the institutional bases for the region's influence have seriously eroded, especially as a result of the liberal-initiated reforms of the 1970s. Contributing to a weakening of southern

---

15. David W. Brady and Charles S. Bullock III, "Coalition Politics in the House of Representatives," in Lawrence C. Dodd and Bruce I. Oppenheimer (eds.), *Congress Reconsidered* (Rev. ed.; Washington, D.C., 1981), 189; James T. Patterson, *Congressional Conservatism and the New Deal* (Lexington, 1967), 250–87.

16. Irwin B. Arieff, "Conservative Southerners Are Enjoying Their Wooing as Key to Tax Bill Success," *Congressional Quarterly Weekly Report*, XXXIX (June 13, 1981), 1026.

Democratic influence has been the departure of the region's senior cadre at a time when a generation of northern Democrats was acquiring extensive seniority.

Second, the Republican party has become a significant factor. In 1987 it held more than a third of the South's House seats and had a majority in the Virginia delegation. Among southern senators, Democrats, who held all the seats as recently as 1960, held sixteen of twenty-two in 1987, an increase of four over 1985. The rise of Republicanism, which some observers had thought would simply give the South a second conservative party, has instead provided alternatives to many southern voters. Particularly on civil rights issues, southern Democrats and Republicans in Congress have responded quite differently, the Democrats moving to the left and the Republicans staking out a position well to the right.[17]

The moderation of southern Democrats on civil rights matters can be traced in part to a third major change. Increased political participation by blacks, who have voted predominantly Democratic, has forced many Democratic legislators to be attentive to black policy interests. White Democrats who remain adamantly opposed to black interests tend not to remain in Congress but to either lose the nomination to more tolerant opponents or lose the general election when black voters support a black independent or sit out the election.

Fourth, over the last quarter century there have been substantial changes in the voting alignments of southern Democrats in Congress. Although southern Democrats have edged closer to the northerners in their party on civil rights, a wider gap has opened over issues of government regulation. The Conservative Coalition continues to appear about as frequently as in the past. In 1981, in a Congress with fewer northern Democrats, conservative southern Democrats provided the margin of victory for President Reagan's economic reforms.

During 1982, disillusioned with Reaganomics, southern Democrats moved back toward the northern wing of their party. The initial Boll Weevil defections and the swing away from apostasy were both due to the same factor—responsiveness to perceived constituency preferences. As southern Democrats have come face-to-face with Republican challengers, they have become more responsive to their constituents and less attentive to party leaders. This has produced support for conservative economic programs, a prodevelopment stance, and hesitancy about con-

17. Bullock, "Congressional Voting and the Mobilization of a Black Electorate in the South," 673.

sumer protection. When the issue is one that may promote the advancement of southern economic interests, the region's two parties often take similar stands, although Republicans as a whole are to the right of the Democrats since the former lack the latter's leavening of liberalism.

The growing divergence of the parties on civil rights also has its basis in constituency responsiveness. The wholesale movement of blacks into the Democratic party has created a constituency that supports civil rights and social welfare. On these issues southern Democratic legislators have moved toward their northern colleagues. As a result, the issue of race, which has dominated the politics of the South, is receding, and the economic issues which have divided Republicans and Democrats in the rest of the country are assuming heightened significance. To the extent that southern Democratic legislators can retain the allegiance of some of the conservative whites who were once the party's backbone, southerners in Congress will remain less liberal than their fellow partisans from the North.

New South Governors and the Governorship

LARRY SABATO

*The state capitols are over their heads in problems
and up to their knees in midgets.*
—James Reston,
New York *Times* (1962)
*There may have been, a decade ago, stronger individual governors
in the Big Five States, but never, in this reporter's experience, a group of 50
governors—from New England to Dixie—as capable as the current crop.*
—David Broder,
Washington *Post* (1976)

The gubernatorial changes that have occurred over the last several decades have been just as significant as the juxtaposition of Reston's and
Broder's comments imply.[1] Most observers of the American governorship agree that we have seen the development of a new breed of more
professional and energetic state chief executives in that time. The South
has been no exception. Indeed, it appears likely that in no other region
has the change in the kind and quality of governor been more dramatic.

Many southern governors who have served throughout this century
have been variously described as "flowery old courthouse politicians,"
"machine dupes," "political pipsqueaks," and "good-time Charlies."
These titles do not fairly describe all past southern governors by any
means; some in the first half of the century, such as Florida's Napolean
Broward, Louisiana's Huey Long, or Virginia's Colgate Darden, could
rival any of today's number. Still, it is reasonably clear that fewer southern governors today are like Louisiana's Jimmie Davis, whose main public accomplishment seemed to be composing and singing "You Are My
Sunshine." Rather, the southern governor today is better represented by

1. Reston quoted in Andrew M. Scott and Earl Wallace, *Politics USA: Cases on the American Democratic Process* (Rev. ed.; New York, 1974), 90, Broder in Washington *Post*, June 12, 1976, p. 90.

the likes of Jim Martin of North Carolina, Bob Martinez of Florida, and Bill Clinton of Arkansas—all youthful, vigorous chief executives (even if they cannot sing).

Although the trend to more capable governors is clear, the reasons for the change are not so obvious. This essay will examine the chief executives over more than three and a half decades of great change (1950–1987), looking first at their personal characteristics, backgrounds, and occupations and noting the changes that have occurred. The patterns of electioneering and party competition will then be explored as crucial elements in the recent transformation of the southern governor. Next, a description of the changing contours of the state executive branch in the South will show how the structure and operation of his division of government can influence a governor's effectiveness. A fourth section will examine the most commonly shared ideological leanings of the New South governors and the policy agenda they have pursued, and finally, the southern governor's new relationship with the federal government will be characterized.

RECENT SOUTHERN GOVERNORS

Table 1 lists the ninety-two southern governors who served in the thirty-seven-year period between 1950 and 1987. Since the Democratic party almost completely dominated southern politics until recently, seventy-seven Democrats comprise the lion's share of the list. The sixteen Republican governors in the table were all elected after 1965. There is one "Republocrat," Mills E. Godwin of Virginia, who served as a Democrat during his first gubernatorial term (1966–1970) and as a Republican during his second term (1974–1978). No Independents won election as governor during this period, although one, Henry E. Howell, Jr., of Virginia, came very close in 1973, winning 49.3 percent of the vote in losing to Republican Godwin. (The absence of a Democratic nominee for governor was partially because of that party's weakness in the wake of the McGovern debacle of 1972.)

Democrats won 108 of the 127 separate elections for governor in the three and a half decades.[2] In reviewing the results, and those for other offices, an observer is struck by the frequency with which famous family

2. Throughout this essay the 1966 Georgia gubernatorial election is counted as a Democratic victory. This is because Democrat Lester Maddox was selected governor by the state legislature, even after trailing Republican Howard "Bo" Callaway in the vote count. The heavily Democratic legislature selected the governor because neither candidate secured an absolute majority of the vote as required under Georgia law.

TABLE 1
Governors of the Southern States, 1950–1987

States and Governors	Party	Years of Service
ALABAMA		
James E. Folsom	D	1947–1951, 1955–1959
Gordon Persons	D	1951–1955
John Patterson	D	1959–1963
George C. Wallace[c]	D	1963–1967, 1971–1979, 1983–1987
Lurleen B. Wallace	D	1967–1968
Albert P. Brewer[a]	D	1968–1971
Fob James	D	1979–1983
Guy Hunt	R	1987–
ARKANSAS		
Sid S. McMath	D	1949–1953
Francis Cherry	D	1953–1955
Orval E. Faubus	D	1955–1967
*Winthrop Rockefeller	R	1967–1971
*Dale Bumpers	D	1971–1975
*David Pryor	D	1975–1979
*Bill Clinton	D	1979–1981, 1983–
Frank White	R	1981–1983
FLORIDA		
Fuller Warren	D	1949–1953
Dan McCarty	D	1953
Charley E. Johns[a]	D	1953–1955
LeRoy Collins[b]	D	1955–1961
Farris Bryant	D	1961–1965
Haydon Burns	D	1965–1967
Claude R. Kirk, Jr.	R	1967–1971
*Reubin O. D. Askew	D	1971–1979
*Robert Graham	D	1979–1987
Bob Martinez	R	1987–
GEORGIA		
Herman Talmadge[b]	D	1949–1955
S. Marvin Griffin	D	1955–1959
S. Ernest Vandiver	D	1959–1963
Carl E. Sanders	D	1963–1967
Lester G. Maddox	D	1967–1971

TABLE 1—*continued*
Governors of the Southern States, 1950–1987

States and Governors	Party	Years of Service
*Jimmy Carter	D	1971–1975
*George Busbee	D	1975–1983
Joe Frank Harris	D	1983–
LOUISIANA		
Earl K. Long[c]	D	1948–1952, 1956–1960
Robert F. Kennon	D	1952–1956
Jimmie H. Davis[c]	D	1960–1964
John J. McKeithen	D	1964–1972
Edwin W. Edwards	D	1972–1980, 1984–1988
*David Treen	R	1980–1984
MISSISSIPPI		
Fielding L. Wright[a]	D	1946–1952
Hugh White[c]	D	1952–1956
James P. Coleman	D	1956–1960
Ross R. Barnett	D	1960–1964
Paul B. Johnson	D	1964–1968
John Bell Williams	D	1968–1972
William L. Waller	D	1972–1976
Cliff Finch	D	1976–1980
*William Winter	D	1980–1984
Bill Allain	D	1984–1988
NORTH CAROLINA		
W. Kerr Scott	D	1949–1953
William B. Umstead	D	1953–1954
Luther H. Hodges, Sr.[a]	D	1954–1961
Terry Sanford	D	1961–1965
Dan K. Moore	D	1965–1969
Robert W. Scott	D	1969–1973
*James E. Holshouser, Jr.	R	1973–1977
*Jim Hunt	D	1977–1985
*Jim Martin	R	1985–
SOUTH CAROLINA		
J. Strom Thurmond	D	1947–1951
James F. Byrnes	D	1951–1955
George Bell Timmerman, Jr.	D	1955–1959

TABLE 1—*continued*
Governors of the Southern States, 1950–1987

States and Governors	Party	Years of Service
Ernest F. Hollings	D	1959–1963
Donald S. Russell	D	1963–1965
Robert E. McNair[a]	D	1965–1971
*John C. West	D	1971–1975
James B. Edwards	R	1975–1979
*Richard Riley	D	1979–1987
*Carroll A. Campbell, Jr.	R	1987–
TENNESSEE		
Gordon Browning[c]	D	1949–1953
Frank G. Clement	D	1953–1959, 1963–1967
Buford Ellington	D	1959–1963, 1967–1971
*Winfield Dunn	R	1971–1975
Ray Blanton	D	1975–1979
*Lamar Alexander	R	1979–1987
Ned R. McWherter	D	1987–
TEXAS		
Allan Shivers[a]	D	1949–1957
Price Daniel	D	1957–1963
John B. Connally	D	1963–1969
Preston Smith	D	1969–1973
Dolph Briscoe	D	1973–1979
William Clements	R	1979–1983, 1987–
*Mark White	D	1983–1987
VIRGINIA		
John S. Battle	D	1950–1954
Thomas B. Stanley	D	1954–1958
J. Lindsay Almond, Jr.	D	1958–1962
Albertis S. Harrison, Jr.	D	1962–1966
Mills E. Godwin, Jr.[d]	D, R	1966–1970, 1974–1978
*Linwood Holton	R	1970–1974
John N. Dalton	R	1978–1982
*Charles S. Robb	D	1982–1986
*Gerald L. Baliles	D	1986–

SOURCES: Compiled from various issues of *Book of the States* (Chicago, 1942–1987).

TABLE 1—*continued*

NOTES: If the term of an incumbent began before 1950, the full dates of tenure are nonetheless listed. "Interim governors," those who held office for just a few days or weeks between a change of administrations, are not included in this study. Usually the cause of succession was the election of the incumbent governor to the U.S. Senate, whose members take the oath of office shortly after New Year's Day. Since most state gubernatorial terms do not officially commence until the second week of January, the incumbent governor (and senator-elect) is forced to resign shortly before the end of his term. The lieutenant governor or other designated officer then becomes governor until the newly elected administration legally takes office.

*A "New South" governor. Naturally, the "New South" designation is a subjective one, for which the author is solely responsible. Judgments about currently serving governors are especially tentative.

aSucceeded to the governorship after the death, resignation, or disability of the incumbent.

bInitially elected to the governorship by the state legislature or the people in midterm after the death, resignation, or disability of the term's original incumbent.

cHad also served part or all of a previous term as governor before 1950.

dGodwin ran and was elected as a Democrat for his first term and as a Republican for his second term.

eWallace's career certainly symbolizes the transformation in southern politics. First elected governor as a diehard segregationist in 1962, he won a second, nonconsecutive term in 1970, again using racist appeals. In his third campaign, in 1974, the race issue was more muted. By 1982, when Wallace achieved yet another political comeback, blacks were a major part of his neo-Populist electoral coalition, and Wallace's decisive victory over a far right-wing GOP gubernatorial candidate was due in no small measure to blacks. Although black support was given grudgingly in some quarters, Wallace aggressively and openly sought black votes and campaigned as a "changed man" on the issue of race. He declined to run again in 1986, because of failing health, and finally left the governorship in January, 1987.

names appear and reappear: the Longs of Louisiana, the Scotts of North Carolina, the Talmadges of Georgia, the Byrds and Battles and Daltons of Virginia. Although family connections work wonders outside the South as well—one has only to think of the Kennedys or the Browns or the Rockefellers—politics in some southern states has been closely identified with family, elites, and oligarchy.[3] Partially because of tradition, partially because of the lack of strong two-party competition, and partially because the issue of race so dominated the politics of the South and blinded southerners to other concerns, a large number of relative incompetents and, sadly, even buffoons were elected to fill the governorships in many southern states. "Farmer Jim" Ferguson of Texas, who was impeached and removed from office on account of corruption, and "Uncle Earl" Long of Louisiana, who gained national notoriety by escaping in his pajamas from the Houston mental institution his wife had put him in

3. Even a cursory reading of V. O. Key's *Southern Politics in State and Nation* (New York, 1949) reveals as much.

(then attempting to remove from the state payroll all who had assisted her!), are pathetic illustrations. (In all fairness, prior to this incident Long's administration had witnessed some notable accomplishments.)

Gradually, however, southern politics has opened up, and generally better candidates have won office. This trend accelerated in the mid-1960s with the abolition of the poll tax, the passage of the Voting Rights Act, the subsequent creation of a broad-based mass electorate, and the court-ordered reapportionments and redistrictings of state and federal legislatures. All of this tumult in the electoral system created new majority coalitions in many southern states and permitted the rise of fresh faces in gubernatorial politics.

The new majority coalitions are more progressive mainly because blacks are an important component, and racism has thus become a far less overt theme in southern politics. It should be noted, however, that the "progressivism" of New South governors is often restricted to racial moderation and structural reform of state government. On economic issues, particularly social welfare, they can be quite conservative and even niggardly, reflecting both the antitax mood of the electorate and hard economic times, as well as severe reductions in federal aid to states. The irony here is substantial, of course: the modern southern governors are in some respects far less progressive on economic policy than many of the populist, segregationist governors of earlier times who combined racism with programs for their poor white constituents (which blacks, of course, shared in).

As for the "fresh faced" southern chief executives themselves, as a group they are younger, better educated, and more thoroughly trained for the job of governor—and they compare favorably with governors from any other region in the country. For example, southern governors elected in the 1970s had an average age at inauguration of about forty-five, the youngest of any region and about two years below the national average. They had about 18.6 years of formal educational training, the highest of any region and about a year more than the national average. About 65 percent of recent southern governors have had prior office experience in the state legislature or in a major statewide elective office (or both), the two jobs considered to offer the most appropriate and helpful training for governors-to-be.[4]

Most importantly, these new southern governors' vistas and agendas

4. See Larry Sabato, *Goodbye to Good-Time Charlie: The American Governorship Transformed* (Rev. ed.; Washington, D.C., 1983), 31–33, 27–28, and 33–45.

extended far beyond the issue of race. The list of southern governors elected before 1966 is dominated by segregationists of limited vision — men like John Patterson of Alabama, Orval Faubus of Arkansas, and Ross Barnett of Mississippi. Although some moderate and capable southern governors could certainly be found before 1966 — LeRoy Collins of Florida, Ernest Hollings of South Carolina, and Luther Hodges and Terry Sanford of North Carolina, for instance — it was only after the political reforms noted above that moderates became predominant in the southern states. In some cases the Republican party was the vehicle for moderation, with New South candidates like Winthrop Rockefeller of Arkansas and Linwood Holton of Virginia riding the crest of reform into office. In other states, the Democratic party first adjusted to the tides of change, allowing moderates like Reubin Askew of Florida and John C. West of South Carolina to secure gubernatorial nominations and capture their statehouses. Even in states such as Alabama, where the change is less perceptible and dramatic, old-time segregationist governors like George Wallace have responded to new political realities, abandoning overt antiblack rhetoric and substituting broad-based campaign appeals that sometimes have attracted both black and white citizens. Overall, with the possible exception of Alabama because of Wallace's long reign, every southern state has had at least one progressive New South governor since 1970, and most have had two or more. (The New South governors are identified in Table 1.)

Although the general trend in southern governors is encouraging, the picture is not an entirely rosy one. These chief executives, even if more forward-looking and capable, remain an undiversified group. Except for two women who succeeded their gubernatorial husbands — Miriam "Ma" Ferguson of Texas in 1924 and Lurleen Burns Wallace of Alabama in 1966 — no woman has served as governor in any southern state. Both women were used as surrogate officeholders by their husbands, Lurleen because George Wallace was constitutionally ineligible to succeed himself, and "Ma" by "Farmer Jim" Ferguson because he had been forbidden to ever hold office again after he was impeached and convicted.[5] But even

5. One woman, Lieutenant Governor Evelyn Gandy of Mississippi, came reasonably close to being elected in 1979 in her own right, but she was defeated for the Democratic gubernatorial nomination in a runoff primary by William Winter, who went on to win in the general election. Gandy lost the Democratic gubernatorial nomination yet again in a 1983 runoff primary, won by state Attorney General Bill Allain.

Ferguson, under the banner of "two governors for the price of one," ran his wife five times, and she was elected twice for terms of two years apiece in 1924 and 1932. Lurleen Burns Wallace died of cancer midway through her term on May 7, 1968.

though no southern woman has yet been elected governor in her own right, a distinction first achieved nationally by the late Ella Grasso of Connecticut in 1974 and Dixy Lee Ray of Washington state in 1976, it is true that women have served as lieutenant governors in South Carolina (Nancy Stevenson) and Mississippi (Evelyn Gandy), and women are serving in all southern state legislatures. A woman (Mary Sue Terry) was also elected state attorney general in Virginia in 1985. Since legislative and statewide offices are the primary escalators to the governorship, perhaps the time is not far off when the gubernatorial sex barrier will fall. A hopeful sign occurred in one of the South's border states in 1983 when Lieutenant Governor Martha Layne Collins succeeded in her bid to become chief executive of Kentucky.

An observer would have far more difficulty predicting the election of a southern black governor any time soon, even though the black proportion of the electorate is greater in the South than in any other region. Race has faded as a dominant issue in gubernatorial elections, but racial prejudice — and not just in the South — still lurks just below the surface. Only Virginia, which narrowly elected a black, L. Douglas Wilder, as its lieutenant governor in 1985, has even matched Colorado and California, which elected black lieutenant governors in the 1970s (neither of whom is still in office). Perhaps as more blacks are elected to southern state legislatures, the opportunities for them to advance to statewide office will increase. This hope is tempered by the fact that no black man or woman has ever been popularly elected governor of any state in the history of the American Republic.[6] On the other hand, Wilder's improbable 1985 election in Virginia — engineered by a clever campaign and aided by weak opposition — suggests that circumstances sometimes create unusual electoral opportunities. And racial prejudice was not enough to prevent an Hispanic, Bob Martinez, from winning the Florida governorship handily in 1986.

The group of southern governors is undiversified in other respects. Over the thirty-seven years surveyed for this study, virtually all of them were Protestants (primarily Baptists, Methodists, and Presbyterians). The South, a region where Protestant fundamentalism is deeply rooted, has recorded but three Catholics and no Jew on its list of most recent governors. By contrast, more than a fifth of governors from other regions have been Catholic, and about 2 percent have been Jewish.[7] Yet another

6. One black man, however, did briefly serve as Louisiana's governor during Reconstruction, but he was not popularly elected.

7. See Sabato, *Goodbye to Good-Time Charlie*, 28–30, 25–27.

area where southern governors have been less diversified than the national corps of chief executives is pregubernatorial occupation. Fully 92 percent of recent southern governors have been either lawyers or businessmen (compared with about 82 percent nationally), and only a handful were drawn from any other professions or trades.[8]

SOUTHERN GOVERNORS IN A CHANGING ELECTORAL ENVIRONMENT

Since governors are political creatures, they inevitably must conform to the electoral environment in their states. This includes public attitudes, campaign styles, socialization patterns, and many of the factors explored by the various essays in this volume. And the degree of success governors achieve during their terms is determined in no small measure by their ability to succeed themselves, the climate of party competition, and the voting habits of their constituents. As it happens, significant changes in these elements of the election systems have occurred in most states over the past few decades, and the changes have clearly helped to produce a more capable corps of southern chief executives.

Of great importance to each governor is the length of his term. From the beginning of the nation, elites and—to a lesser extent—citizens have argued fiercely about the proper length of an executive term of office. By now nearly all state government experts agree that a four-year gubernatorial term is far more desirable than a two-year term, the longer term giving the governor a better chance to gain control of the government and develop a real program and record of accomplishment.[9] Historically, the South was more inclined than other regions to set the governor's term at four years rather than two. In 1950, for example, only nineteen of thirty-seven nonsouthern states gave their governors a term of four years, whereas eight of eleven southern states did so.[10] Gradually, other regions came to see the wisdom of granting the chief executive a longer, more stable tenure, and by 1987 only three nonsouthern states (New Hampshire, Rhode Island, and Vermont) retained the two-year term, and no southern state did so.

One reason southern states were more inclined toward the four-year term, though, was that their governors were severely limited in their abil-

8. Included in this small number were a few farmers and educators, two dentists (Winfield Dunn of Tennessee and James Edwards of South Carolina), a housewife (Lurleen Wallace), and a country singer (Louisiana's Jimmie Davis).

9. These arguments are discussed at length in Sabato, *Goodbye to Good-Time Charlie*, 97–105.

10. The three southern states with two-year gubernatorial terms in 1950 were Arkansas, Tennessee, and Texas.

ity to succeed themselves consecutively. The deeply rooted, historical distrust of executive power manifested itself in the South by a prohibition against a governor serving two consecutive terms in each of the eight southern states that had a four-year gubernatorial term in 1950. By contrast, almost all nonsouthern states either permitted the governor to succeed himself once or placed no limitation whatsoever on the number of consecutive terms he could serve. The succession limits weakened the governorship in the South, reducing the chances for a progressive or populist movement to attain significant policy changes. They also strengthened the state legislatures and served the interests of dominant political factions by giving machine leaders the opportunity to "reward" more stalwarts with the governorship and quickly to remove the occasional antimachine governor.[11] It is yet another sign of a strengthened governorship in the South that seven states (Alabama, Florida, Georgia, Louisiana, Mississippi, North Carolina, and South Carolina) have abandoned the one-term limitation just since 1965, with only Virginia persisting in the prohibition of consecutive gubernatorial terms.[12] Southern governors have generally capitalized on the political potential inherent in the right of succession. Of the fifteen instances (as of mid-1987) in which a four-year chief executive in the South has been eligible to run for immediate reelection and has done so, ten have won whereas five have been denied an extended tenure.

The spread of two-party politics has also contributed to the emergence of the New South governors of recent times.[13] For a century after the Civil War, the essential element of competition was missing from southern politics, and states developed, to varying degrees, the malaise of one-partyism. A one-party system is undesirable because it can easily result in second-rate government. If a party is assured of victory regardless of whom it nominates for governor, it is likely to treat the governorship more as a gold watch given for dedicated service to the party than as a public trust where the best qualified men and women should be placed. On the other hand, if a strong, competitive party system exists, a party will logically seek the strongest and ablest candidate available, whether

11. See Sabato, *Goodbye to Good-Time Charlie,* 100.
12. Other southern states have also made term changes for the better since 1950. Texas has changed from the two-year to the four-year term and allows its governor unlimited consecutive reelection. Tennessee abandoned its unusual system of a two-year term coupled with a requirement that no person could serve as governor more than six terms (12 years) or for more than six of any consecutive eight years. Presently Tennessee permits its governor to serve two consecutive four-year terms.
13. See Sabato, *Goodbye to Good-Time Charlie,* 116–48.

he or she be in or out of the party. Better governors and superior state governments result. (At least this is the theory. Alas, it does not always work so neatly.)

Fortunately, after decades of one-party rule, most states in the South appear to be gradually moving toward two-party democracy in gubernatorial and most other *statewide* (but not local) elections. The movement is uneven and occasionally halts, but it is clearly perceptible. From 1930 to 1965, not a single Republican was elected to a southern governorship, whereas from 1965 to 1986 Republicans won nineteen of seventy gubernatorial elections (about 27 percent of the total). Arkansas, Florida, North Carolina, South Carolina, and Tennessee have each elected a pair of Republicans, and Virginia has had three GOP state administrations. After the 1986 elections, Republicans controlled nearly half the southern statehouses (Alabama, Florida, North Carolina, South Carolina, and Texas), and only Georgia and Mississippi have yet to elect a Republican governor in the modern era. Furthermore, the Democratic percentage of the major party vote for governor has declined in every single southern state; even where Republicans continue to lose, their losses are by smaller margins.[14]

Additional evidence of the increase in two-party democracy is provided by the changes that have taken place in the venerable old institution of Confederate democracy, the primary.[15] Even though the primary is still almost universal as the Democratic party's gubernatorial nomination method, it has sharply declined in importance in most southern states. As the Republican party has become more competitive statewide and has either threatened Democratic hegemony or won the governorship outright, voter interest in the primary has waned. The primary is, rightly, no longer perceived as the point of final electoral decision. The general election now deserves that status, and unlike in the Solid South era, citizens now vote in large numbers in November because it really matters. Coupled with this change has been the nationwide loosening of party ties and the growing independence of the electorate that made voters less inclined to take part in a strictly party affair.

Thus, the vote in gubernatorial primaries as a proportion of the general election vote has shrunk considerably. Whereas the southern Democratic primary vote from 1930 to 1950 was ten times the general election total, the electoral pattern in recent years has been quite different. In ev-

14. *Ibid.*, 119, 124–25.
15. *Ibid.*

ery southern state, voter interest in the primary has dwindled compared with the general election, and in many cases the decline has been drastic. In gubernatorial elections since 1971, general election turnouts have exceeded primary turnouts in all southern states except Mississippi. Just as the South is no longer "solid," the primary is no longer paramount and no longer tantamount to election—yet another signpost of changing gubernatorial politics in the Old Confederacy.[16]

REFORM AND REVOLUTION IN STATE GOVERNMENT

The competitive politics of the New South, then, has produced a group of generally able chief executives who are permitted to serve in office longer and develop their administrations more fully. Yet many intelligent and capable governors through the years have been stopped dead in their tracks by the institutional obstacles and bureaucratic barriers that seemed to dominate state governments for decades. Not coincidentally, however, many of these institutional barriers have been dislodged and swept away in recent times, a development that has permitted the new governors to use their appreciable talents and to work relatively unhindered.

Foremost among the conditions that encumbered governors were antiquated state constitutions. "The constitutions of the States are their greatest shame" moaned Robert S. Allen in 1949, and he was surely correct. They were, for the most part, voluminous tomes, sometimes undemocratic in character, which prescribed toothless executives and nightmarish administrative structures for state governments. Many of these archaic and even outrageous features were truly "grotesque parodies on modern government."[17]

The era about which Allen wrote has fortunately passed into history. Whereas only five states rewrote their constitutions from 1902 to 1963, eleven states adopted completely new constitutions in the twelve years from 1964 to 1976, and five of the eleven were in the South: Georgia, Florida, Louisiana, North Carolina, and Virginia.[18]

The constitutional revisions and executive branch reorganizations also resulted in greater gubernatorial appointive powers at the highest levels of state government, strengthened budgetary and managerial authority,

16. See Larry Sabato, *The Democratic Party Primary in Virginia: Tantamount to Election No Longer* (Charlottesville, 1977).

17. Robert S. Allen, *Our Sovereign States* (New York, 1949), xv. See pp. xv–xx for a description of the inadequacies of state constitutions existing at the time.

18. Two other southern states, Texas and Arkansas, also drafted new constitutions, but they were rejected in the ratification process.

and augmented staff and salary.[19] The virtual explosion of reform in state government, then, has had a significant effect on the governorship. In most of the states of the South (and in other regions), the governor has come closer to being the master of his own house, not just the father figure—though the bureaucracy and professionalism of state government inevitably limits a governor's authority (as Edward M. Wheat suggests in his essay in this book).

The reform of state government in the South has not stopped with the governor, of course. If there is a new breed of governor, for example, a new breed of legislator emerges as well, and state legislatures have yielded some of the finest recent state chief executives, such as Florida's Reubin Askew and Georgia's George Busbee. There can be little doubt that recent political reforms like court-ordered reapportionment—the redrawing of electoral districts to insure that every legislator represents approximately the same number of people and that each person's vote is thus about equal in weight—are largely responsible for the legislative transformation.

This strengthening of the legislature, which has made it more prestigious and representative, has not been wholly advantageous to governors; some of the changes have come at the expense of their prerogatives. As the legislatures have become more professional in various areas, they have requested a correspondingly greater voice in state government. For instance, the governor now has to work more closely on financial matters with the legislature, since virtually all legislatures now have full-time, year-round staffing of their appropriation committees.

Yet the gains for the governor far outweigh the losses. On taking office today, southern governors generally find more well-informed, independent, representative, and accountable legislatures that by and large work far more closely and are vastly more in tune with the chief executives than those of only a decade ago. Former governor Reubin Askew of Florida, who listed the rise of state legislatures as one of the three primary causes for a strengthened governorship, expressed the view of many governors when he claimed that legislative reform "has not adversely affected the governor; it's resulted in the strengthening of the whole system."[20]

At least in the American experience, the best government seems to be a

19. For details of these developments, see Sabato, *Goodbye to Good-Time Charlie*, 57–96; see also Thad L. Beyle and Lynn Muchmore, *Being Governor: The View from the Office* (Durham, 1983).

20. Interview with the author, September 8, 1976, Tallahassee, Florida.

properly balanced one, in which neither the executive nor the legislative branch is weak and debilitated and in which each has the authority and the resources to fulfill its responsibilities. The emergence of both governor and legislature in this mold is a new and propitious phenomenon in state government in the South and elsewhere.

IDEOLOGICAL PREFERENCES AND POLICY
AGENDAS OF NEW SOUTH GOVERNORS

The issue of reorganization and governmental reform is but one of a number of consistent and recurrent themes in the administrations of most New South governors. Racial moderation, fiscal conservatism leavened with some mild tax reform, environmental protection, and educational innovation are other notable elements.

The campaigns and administrations of Governor Reubin Askew of Florida, one of the most outstanding of the new breed of southern chief executive, provides an illustration.[21] First of all, Askew's background and training are in many ways typical of his modern gubernatorial peers. The son of a carpenter, Askew is a well-educated lawyer by profession. He is a nondrinker and nonsmoker, as well as being a very religious former Sunday school teacher whose integrity is judged rocklike. Before running for governor, he served two terms in the Florida House of Representatives (1959–1963) and then two terms in the state senate (1963–1970) as the representative from Pensacola in the largely rural northwestern panhandle of Florida. His leadership was recognized in the senate by his election to the post of president pro tempore, and he was generally considered a persuasive and effective legislator.

Despite his accomplishments, he announced for governor in 1970 as a virtual unknown statewide and was considered far behind three other Democratic primary contenders. Yet his attractive personal qualities, which projected well on television, and a dramatically different platform that broke away from the traditional noncontroversial issues, soon helped him attract support. Askew promised to work for establishment of a corporate income tax, to open up state government to groups shut out in the past (such as blacks and young people), and to enact severe penalties for businesses that polluted. Even more than his specific issues, Askew's refreshing candor and unquestioned rectitude seemed especially

21. For a thorough review of Askew's career (and those of other Florida governors), see David R. Colburn and Richard K. Scher, *Florida's Gubernatorial Politics in the Twentieth Century* (Tallahassee, 1980). See also Michael Barone, Grant Ujifusa, and Douglas Matthews, *The Almanac of American Politics, 1978* (New York, 1977), 158–63.

welcome to Florida voters tired of corruption and stale leadership. In the end, Askew finished second in the initial Democratic primary and then easily defeated the front-runner, former state attorney general Earl Faircloth, in the runoff. The general election yielded a runaway victory for Askew as well. Incumbent Governor Claude Kirk, the first modern Republican chief executive of Florida, was running for a second term, but his tenure had been regarded as corrupt and his personal behavior as embarrassingly flamboyant. Askew won 57 percent of the vote and became governor at the age of forty-two.

Once in office, Askew managed to secure passage of virtually all major planks of his election platform. Both the legislature and the voters approved a constitutional amendment to establish the corporate income tax, and Askew also was able to obtain legislative assent for Florida's first mineral severance tax (on phosphate mined in the state). Yet despite his achieving a generally more progressive tax system, Askew remained a staunch fiscal conservative, opposing the establishment of a personal income tax and any increase in the sales tax while supporting a reduction in county property taxes.

With the revenues from the corporate and severance taxes, Askew was able to propose and secure modest social welfare reforms. Workmen's compensation benefits were increased, as was state aid for family assistance programs. A fairer and more generous system of educational finance was also developed.

Environmental concerns that captured the public's imagination in the early 1970s also played a role in the Askew administration. Askew was not "antigrowth"; that is, he did not want to restrict migration to Florida. Rather he sought to protect the environment in the face of growth. The governor received legislative assent for the first statewide land-use plan, and the voters gave their backing in November, 1972, to a $200 million allocation for the purchase of environmentally endangered lands.

As with most of the management-oriented New South governors who inherited antiquated and poorly organized state governments, Askew concentrated much of his energy on governmental reform. Among many accomplishments in this category, he reduced the number of "spoils system" appointments and divested himself of much of his judicial appointment power, placing the decisions in the hands of a nonpartisan judicial commission. He also secured a "Government in the Sunshine" law (a kind of state Freedom of Information Act), established a state "Federal Trade Commission" to control deceptive trade practices, created a statewide grand jury, and modernized the state election code.

Again, like most of the New South governors, it is in the area of race relations that Askew will probably be best remembered. His racial moderation was a clear break with Florida's past. Except for LeRoy Collins (who served from 1955 to 1961), no other true racial progressive had managed to win the governorship in modern times. Askew's predecessor, Claude Kirk, had actually closed the schools in one Florida county to prevent school busing. Previous Florida governors' stances on race had varied somewhat, ranging from sheer demagoguery to more courtly and studied opposition to school integration; their antiblack racial views, however, were consistent.

Askew's inauguration marked the beginning of a new era of race relations, and he called for "equal rights for all" in his inaugural address. Shortly after taking office, he commissioned a survey of state employees that revealed that fully 89 percent of black workers were receiving wages below poverty level. As a result, the governor initiated a major affirmative action plan that concentrated more minorities in better-paying jobs and doubled the number of blacks in state government by 1972. Simultaneously, Askew greatly increased the number of blacks serving on important part-time state boards and commissions, and he appointed Joseph Hatchett to the Florida Supreme Court, the first black on the highest state court since Reconstruction. Remarkably, Askew even supported busing to achieve racial balance in the school system. Calling busing "a necessary element in achieving" integrated schools, he actively urged voters to reject an antibusing referendum in 1972. Although the referendum passed by a massive 3-to-1 margin, Askew's standing with the voters seemed to increase because of his forthrightness and courage.

The 1974 election returns certainly confirmed Askew's political stature, as the governor won the primary and general elections in landslides. Placing a hundred-dollar limit on his campaign contributions in "The Year of Watergate," Askew trounced his sole Democratic challenger (the incumbent lieutenant governor) and went on to bury Democrat-turned-Republican Jerry Thomas, a former state senate president, in November. Still immensely popular upon leaving office in 1978 – Askew was constitutionally prohibited from seeking a third consecutive term – he accepted a post in the Carter administration as special trade representative in 1979–1980. With Carter's 1980 reelection defeat, Askew unsuccessfully sought the presidency himself in 1984. His bid for the Democratic nomination never caught fire, and he was forced to drop out of the race shortly after the New Hampshire primary.[22]

22. Ironically, Askew might well have been able to secure the Democratic nomination

Askew's gubernatorial career was clearly a remarkable one, yet there are many parallels with other New South governors. Like Askew, young, professional, and legislatively trained individuals have sought and won the highest state executive office and have been able to serve consecutive terms. Although almost uniformly fiscally conservative and anything but extravagant on social welfare spending, such southern governors have often been able to achieve limited, progressive tax reforms. In keeping with their "good government" and management-oriented nature, these governors have also concentrated great effort in the field of governmental reform, efficiency, and reorganization. Perhaps most significantly, though, they have all moved in the same new direction on the fundamental issue of southern politics: race. The moderation and progressivism on racial matters exhibited by the New South governors, produced by both sincere conviction and electoral pragmatism in a region with a large black vote, is certainly their most distinguishing, and historically important, feature.

BEYOND STATES' RIGHTS:
THE SOUTHERN GOVERNOR IN THE FEDERAL SYSTEM

Just as the new southern governors have begun to put the issue of race behind them, so too have they started to look beyond the narrow confines of "states' rights" to a broader view of their states' proper role in the federal system.

The national income tax, the Great Depression, and foreign crises were all partially responsible for the decline of the states in this century. In essence, however, nothing was as pivotal as the states' own lack of will and resources to meet challenges. The states complained that the national government had "preempted" them in the tax field, but no evidence suggests that most or even any southern states would have adopted the income tax if Washington had not in 1913. The charge that the national government had encroached upon the prerogatives of the states in policy and functional fields also reverberated from shore to shore from the New Deal onward, but again the implication was that the states would have taken action themselves, or could have afforded to, in the same policy fields. More likely, little or nothing would have been done in most states even had the national government "returned" the "stolen" fields to the states.

It is not unfair to say that state inaction, either because of limited resources or vision, plus wrongdoing, as in segregation policies, led to

---

in 1976, when Carter did, but he refused to run then. In 1972 Askew had turned down George McGovern's offer of the Democratic vice-presidential nomination.

much of the national government's growth in this century. The states had themselves to blame for a good number of their federal troubles. As Adlai Stevenson once remarked, "There would be less talk about states' rights if there had been fewer states' wrongs."

Fortunately, the recent transformation of state government—the result of a stronger governorship, a reapportioned legislature, widespread constitutional revision, large-scale reorganization, and the spread of two-party competition, among other factors—has energized the states and enabled them to compete for authority and responsibility with the national government. In the disillusioning aftermath of many Great Society programs, the limitations of the national government were exposed. Many well-intentioned policies had met failure not because they were intrinsically misdirected but because their standards had been nationalized. Decentralization—community control—was often the missing element. With the realization that the states and their localities would probably be more successful in administering the same programs, and with the knowledge that the transformed states and their leaders were more capable and willing than ever before to undertake new programs and duties, the national government gradually began to reverse the power flow with innovations like revenue sharing (now defunct) and block grants.

Southern governors have been quick to take advantage of changing intergovernmental conditions. Three of the recent New South governors, Reubin Askew of Florida, George Busbee of Georgia, and Bill Clinton of Arkansas, rose to become chairmen of the National Governors' Association, each serving with distinction while taking the lead in attempting to forge a new partnership between the states and the national government. Governors in seven southern states (Arkansas, Florida, North Carolina, South Carolina, Tennessee, Texas, and Virginia) established Washington offices to enable their states to participate more fully in the federal system and to lobby directly for congressional and presidential actions benefiting their states. Moreover, virtually all recent southern governors have established a staff position of "federal-state coordinator" within their own offices to monitor and direct intergovernmental developments. And, of course, one New South governor, Jimmy Carter of Georgia, insured that he was heard in the nation's capital by becoming the first Deep South candidate since 1848 to be elected president.

Carter's election as president, in a real sense, signaled the reemergence of the southern governor on an equal footing with his counterpart in other regions of the country. The acceptance that he found around the nation highlighted the significant changes that had transformed southern governors from the "good-time Charlies" of old to the competent and creative corps of more recent times. Carter's reelection loss need not damage this development.

CONCLUSIONS

In their personal characteristics, by the changing politics that produced them, and in the structure of state governments and intergovernmental relations they preside over, the new southern chief executives differ dramatically from their predecessors. They are younger, better educated, and better trained for their responsibilities, though, as yet, not more demographically representative. They are the product of new political trends which have spread throughout most of the states of the South in the last two decades. And they have reorganized their state governments thoroughly and conducted their relations with the federal government more cooperatively, in keeping with the South's reemergence into the national mainstream. Moreover, in moving beyond race and beyond states' rights for the most part, the modern group of governors in the South has helped to transform the country's conception of their region and, more importantly, to remold their own citizens' conceptions of their states.

Southern State Legislatures: Recruitment and Reform

E. LEE BERNICK
PATRICIA K. FREEMAN
DAVID M. OLSON

For our part, and we think many citizens will share our view, the sooner the Legislature closes the safer the state's population will feel. While every legislative body does some good and necessary things, the public welfare usually takes a good many beatings before any session is concluded.
—Knoxville Journal
(February 24, 1949)

State legislatures today have emerged from obscurity into the spotlight of professional and public attention.
—Malcolm Jewell (1968)

Although many southern governors and U.S. senators have been famous individually, the southern state legislator—and sheriff—most fully embody the traditional image of the southern politician. That stereotype is the white male country lawyer with a secretary on one knee and a jug on the other, ranting against Yankees and spouting racial slurs while personally profiting from office. In the 1970s and 1980s, however, such an image, whatever its validity in the past, is far from accurate.

In spite of this and other stereotypes, southern legislators and legislatures have always been quite diverse. For example, if during the Solid South era the Virginia legislature was at one extreme of gubernatorial domination, the South Carolina legislature was at the other. And though all were predominately Democratic in partisan composition, the factional structure of that party ranged from Louisiana's strong central leadership to the often chaotic "friends and neighbors" pattern of Florida's multifactionalism.

Southern legislatures and their individual members are today quite different from those of the 1930s and the 1940s and have become much

*Bernick and Olson acknowledge the support of the Graduate Research Council of the University of North Carolina at Greensboro and thank their research assistant, John Kilgore.

more similar to legislatures in the rest of the country. The significant changes in the economy of the South have contributed to this phenomenon. For example, the region is characterized by an increasing level of wealth and industrialization, factors associated with greater government activity. Industrialization generates more problems which demand attention, whereas enhanced wealth enables the state to increase the level and quality of public services. Politics and public policy have also been altered by the emergence of professional organizations such as the National Conference of State Legislatures. This and similar bodies facilitate communications and policies transcending traditional parochial concerns, as do the many federal agencies active in the region. Also, substantial inmigration appears to be having a major impact on support for changes in state government and public policies.[1]

The impact of these trends on the political institutions and processes of the states has been the subject of much speculation but little empirical analysis.[2] This essay examines two broad types of change in southern legislatures: first, changes in the type of person recruited to legislative office and second, the increased professionalism of the institution. Specifically, we will first trace the evolving partisan composition and social characteristics of southern legislatures over the past three decades. Second, since legislators' behavior is shaped by the characteristics of the institution in which they must operate, an analysis of several key legislative features is deemed essential to an understanding of the hows and whys of southern politics.[3] Thus, we will explore the extensive number of institutional reforms enacted in recent years, the nature of the legislative structure (including leadership functions and committees), work load and executive-legislative relations, plus legislative oversight of the state bureaucracy.

Unfortunately, neither reliable nor consistent evidence is available on all of the relevant topics. State legislatures as a whole are not well documented, and the evidence that exists for one state is rarely found uniformly for others. Moreover, the classic and comprehensive studies of southern politics have paid scant attention to the legislatures.

1. William Lyons and Robert F. Durant, "Assessing the Impact of Inmigration on a State Political System," *Social Science Quarterly*, LXI (December, 1980), 473–84.
2. See Malcolm Jewell, "The State of the U.S. State Legislative Research," *Legislative Studies Quarterly*, VI (February, 1981), 6.
3. Malcolm E. Jewell and Samuel C. Patterson, *The Legislative Process in the United States* (Rev. ed.; New York, 1977), 3–59; Samuel C. Patterson, "Legislators and Legislatures in the American States," in Virginia Gray, Herbert Jacob, and Kenneth N. Vines (eds.), *Politics in the American States* (Rev. ed.; Boston, 1983), 160.

PARTISANSHIP AND SOCIAL CHARACTERISTICS

Today, as in the past, the most distinctive feature of southern legislatures is their overwhelmingly Democratic partisan makeup. Democratic party dominance of subnational elections in the South is well documented.[4] Figure 1's charting of Democratic percentages in legislatures from 1953 to 1983 at multiple time periods reveals the variations that have occurred over a thirty-year period and highlights significant developments within this era. In addition, partisan patterns in both upper and lower houses of the southern region (which for the purposes of our study, includes the eleven states of the Confederacy plus Oklahoma and Kentucky[5]) are analyzed.

Turning to social characteristics of southern state legislators, one finds much change since the Solid South era. In the traditional political culture of that time the role of government was to secure the continued maintenance of the existing social order. To do so, political power went to a relatively small and self-perpetuating group drawn from the established elite who often inherited their "right" to govern through family ties or social position.[6] As the traditionalist political culture has eroded, different types of people are being recruited. In the absence of data from across the entire South, this phenomenon is explored through an analysis of the backgrounds of state legislators in one state, Tennessee, during selected intervals from 1930 to 1983.

Partisan Composition

Figure 1 depicts the percentage of seats held by Democrats in the upper and lower chambers of the legislatures of the South and non-South from 1953 to 1983. Democrats have experienced a small but nonetheless slow and steady decline in the South's legislatures. In 1953 they occupied 96 percent of the senate seats and 93 percent of the house slots across the region's thirteen states; by 1983 they had dropped to 84 percent and 81 percent respectively.

The South's upper chambers have consistently been slightly more Democratic than the lower houses, a difference most likely due to the

---

4. Malcolm E. Jewell, *The State Legislature: Politics and Practice* (Rev. ed.; New York, 1969); John F. Bibby, Cornelius P. Cotter, James L. Gibson, and Robert J. Huckshorn, "Parties in State Politics," in Gray, Jacob, and Vines (eds.), *Politics in the American States*, 65–67.

5. This definition corresponds to the one used by *Congressional Quarterly.*

6. Daniel J. Elazar, *American Federalism: A View from the States* (Rev. ed.; New York, 1972), 99.

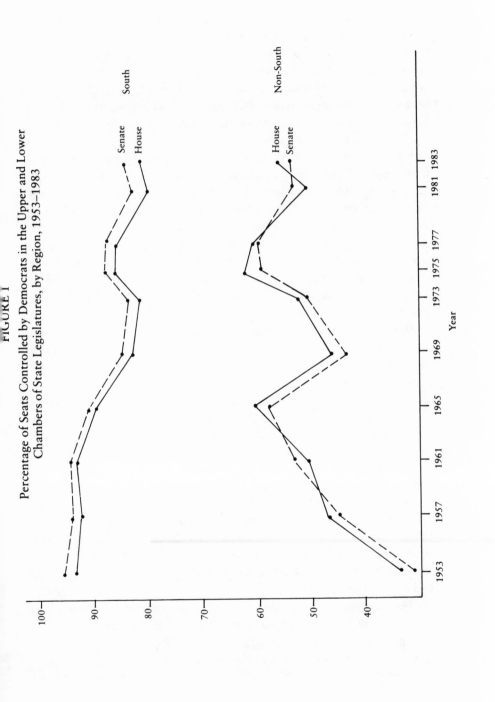

FIGURE 1

Percentage of Seats Controlled by Democrats in the Upper and Lower
Chambers of State Legislatures, by Region, 1953–1983

smaller house districts, which allow small pockets of Republican voters a greater opportunity to put one of their own in office. Over the thirty-year period Democratic fortunes have significantly improved in legislatures of the non-South. In 1953, whereas Democrats were in almost complete control of southern legislatures, they held only 31 percent and 34 percent of the senate and house seats outside the South. However, by 1983 Democrats in nonsouthern legislatures had 54 percent of the senate seats and 57 percent of the house posts.

Figure 1 clearly shows that party fortunes in state legislatures are not immune to national elections and trends. Nixon's victories in 1968 and 1972 brought Democrats in both southern and nonsouthern legislatures to their lowest totals. Their decline was halted by the 1974 post-Watergate Democratic resurgence. In the South this gain continued with the 1976 election of a native son as president, although Democrats lost seats elsewhere that year. The Republicans' double victory in taking the U.S. Senate and the presidency in the 1980 elections was paralleled by an increase in their numbers in legislatures of both the South and the non-South. Finally, it would appear that the 1982 referendum on the Reagan presidency and Republican policies—which brought Democrats twenty-six additional seats in the U.S. House—affected state races, resulting in a slight increase in Democratic legislators throughout the country.[7] The trend is toward convergence of partisan patterns in South and non-South. Still, in 1983 the South's legislatures were some 50 percent more Democratic than those outside the region.

Looking from aggregate analysis of southern legislatures to an assessment of the individual states, one finds important variations within the region, as illustrated in Figures 2 and 3 and Table 1. At one pole are Alabama, Arkansas, Louisiana, and Mississippi, where the Democrats have never held less than 90 percent of either senate or house. At the other pole are Kentucky and Tennessee, where Democrats have rarely held 80 percent of the seats in either chamber and Republicans have always had a strong base of support in the states' eastern sections.[8] Indeed, in these two states Democratic control was seriously challenged in the first Nixon term. Oklahoma, though somewhat more subject to Democratic control, also has been consistently below the Democratic average of the thirteen states.

In terms of their change over time Virginia and Florida are the most

7. John F. Bibby, "State House Elections at Midterm," in Thomas E. Mann and Norman J. Ornstein (eds.), *The American Elections of 1982* (Washington, D.C., 1981), 121–26.
8. Malcolm E. Jewell, *Legislative Representation in the Contemporary South* (Durham, 1967).

FIGURE 2

Percentage of Democrats in Southern Legislatures, 1953–1983: State Houses of Representatives

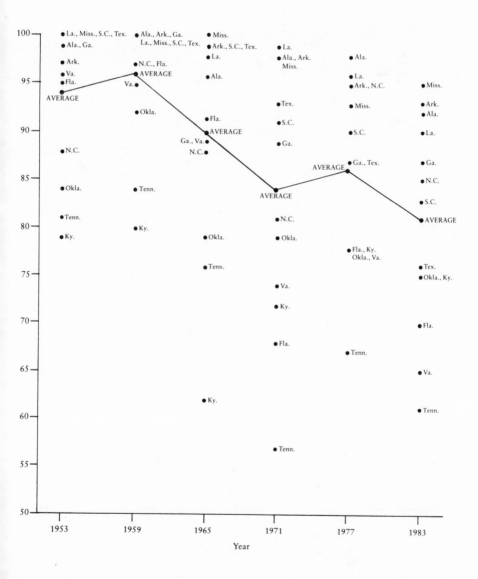

FIGURE 3

Percentage of Democrats in Southern Legislatures, 1953–1983: State Senates

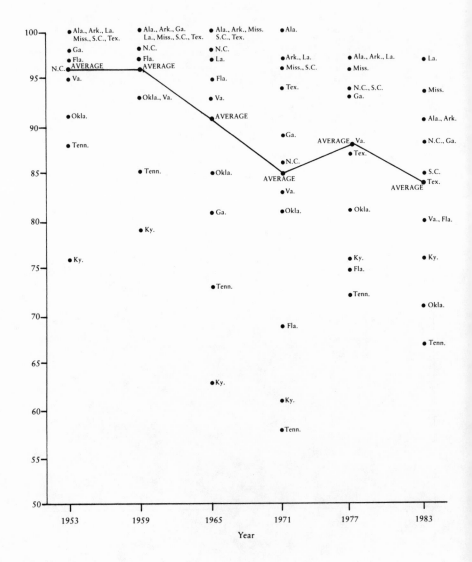

Year

TABLE 1
Percentage of Seats Controlled by Democrats in Southern Legislatures, by Chamber, 1953–1983

UPPER HOUSE

State	Highest Percentage	Lowest Percentage	Year of Lowest Percentage	Mean Percentage	Number of Times Democratic Percentage Over	
					90%	80%
Alabama	100	91	1983	99	16	
Louisiana	100	97	1965	99	16	
Arkansas	100	91	1983	98	16	
Mississippi	100	94	1983	97	16	
South Carolina	100	85	1983	96	13	3
Texas	100	74	1981	93	12	3
Georgia	100	81	1965	92	10	6
North Carolina	98	70	1973	90	10	4
Virginia	95	78	1979	88	7	7
Oklahoma	91	71	1983	84	4	8
Florida	97	58	1967	81	7	1
Kentucky	79	61	1971	74		
Tennessee	88	58	1971	72		6

TABLE 1 – *continued*
Percentage of Seats Controlled by Democrats in Southern Legislatures, by Chamber, 1953–1983

LOWER HOUSE

State	Highest Percentage	Lowest Percentage	Year of Lowest Percentage	Mean Percentage	Number of Times Democratic Percentage Over	
					90%	80%
Alabama	100	92	1983	98	16	
Mississippi	100	93	1977	98	16	
Arkansas	100	93	1983	97	16	
Louisiana	100	90	1983	97	16	
South Carolina	100	83	1973	94	10	6
Texas	100	76	1981	93	10	4
Georgia	100	83	1973	92	7	9
North Carolina	97	71	1973	86	4	8
Virginia	96	65	1983	84	6	3
Florida	97	65	1969	80	6	1
Oklahoma	92	72	1981	79	1	4
Kentucky	80	57	1969	74	3	
Tennessee	84	50	1969	68		4

SOURCE: Compiled from various volumes of *Book of the States* and from *Congressional Quarterly*, XL (November 13, 1982), 2848–49.

interesting. Both states' legislatures were once almost completely dominated by the Democratic party. As late as 1965 Democrats had over 90
percent of the seats in Florida's two chambers, but after reapportionment, the election of a Republican governor in 1966, Nixon's wins, and
Reagan's wins, that state is today most competitive and consistently has
a lower percentage of Democrats in the two chambers than the southern
average. In Virginia, Democratic fortunes also have changed dramatically, especially in the lower house, where the Democrats held "only" 65
percent of the seats in 1983.

Partisan changes in the remaining four states, South Carolina, Texas,
Georgia, and North Carolina, are either inconsistent or less dramatic.
For example, North Carolina has always had a few Republicans in the
legislature, and the Democrats' lowest percentages came in 1973, when
they held 70 percent and 71 percent of the senate and house seats.[9] In
both Georgia and South Carolina the Democrats' dominance declined,
but they controlled over 80 percent of the seats during the sixteen time
points examined. Of these four states Texas changed the most, for although the Texas legislature was once completely Democratic, enough
Republicans now occupy seats in both chambers to raise the specter of
partisanship.[10]

Clearly, the South's legislative chambers are something less than a single homogeneous entity, yet what the partisian composition will be in
the future is unclear. However, recent research findings on state legislative elections in the South indicate that "a very high proportion of legislative districts are safe," an ill omen for Republicans. The study found that
75 to 100 percent of the legislative elections in nine of the southern states
examined were won by comfortable margins—more than 60 percent of
the votes. In another two states over half of the seats were found to be
safe. (Two states, Arkansas and South Carolina, were not analyzed.)[11]
Although southern states have elected Republicans as governors and U.S.
senators and have supported Republican presidential candidates, Republicanism has not trickled down as much into the essentially local district
elections for state legislators. Thus, there would appear to be very little
prospect for any sudden or drastic change in the partisan composition of
state legislatures.

9. *Ibid.* Moreover, Republicans have had some success in electing a governor, U.S. senators, and members of the U.S. House of Representatives.
10. Robert Harmel and Keith Hamm, "Development of a Party Role in a No-Party Legislature," paper presented to Citadel Symposium on Southern Politics, Charleston, 1984.
11. Patterson, "Legislators and Legislatures," in Gray, Jacob, and Vines (eds.), *Politics
in the American States*, 149.

TABLE 2

Proportion of Lower Chamber Districts with Contested Primaries,
1976 and 1978, by Party, Urbanism, and Region: Selected States

Party and Urbanism	Non-South	South
DEMOCRATIC		
Metropolitan	60.34	45.76
Rural	29.63	52.13
REPUBLICAN		
Metropolitan	26.31	10.26
Rural	24.24	6.03

SOURCE: Calculated from Craig H. Grau, "Competition in State Legislative Primaries,"
Legislative Studies Quarterly, VI (February, 1981), 46.
Each figure represents the percentage of districts that were contested in the specified category.

Another problem southern Republicans continue to confront is in attracting able candidates to legislative races. The competition for the Republican nomination is minimal in the South, as illustrated by the low incidence of contested Republican legislative primaries there (see Table 2). In contrast, a much higher proportion of the Republicans' nonsouthern legislative primaries were contested, at least for selected states in the years 1976 and 1978, and Democratic primaries, on the whole, were more contested than Republican in both regions.[12]

Somewhat offsetting these two Republican minuses of safe Democratic seats and scarce legislative aspirants is the growing number of suburban districts. This outgrowth of reapportionment generally favors Republicans and is likely to be of increasing significance.

Social Characteristics: The Case of Tennessee

Social characteristics are at least as important as partisanship in determining the makeup of southern legislatures, and legislators in Tennessee will serve as a case in point. Table 3 shows support for the traditional description of the southern officeholder as closely tied to politics through family. In 1930 almost half of all legislators had a parent who had held at least one local office, and slightly over half had a close relative who had held a state or national office. Election to the state legislature followed other types of political service for 61 percent of the legislators and almost two-thirds were lawyers.

No women served until the 1950s, and no blacks until the mid-1960s.

12. Craig H. Grau, "Competitive in State Legislative Primaries," *Legislative Studies Quarterly,* VI (February, 1981), 35–54.

TABLE 3
Background Characteristics of Tennessee State Legislators

	1930	1950	1964	1978	1984
Female	0%	2%	3%	2%	4%
Black	0%	0%	0%	7%	5%
College graduate	54%	62%	72%	94%	93%
Lawyer	66%	56%	47%	26%	20%
Previously held elected office	61%	63%	54%	24%	16%
Close relative held state or national political office*	28%	18%	10%	4%	**
Parent held local office	48%	36%	25%	22%	**
Democratic party	78%	86%	80%	66%	59%

*"Close relative" means a parent, grandparent, aunt, or uncle.
**Data not available

Thus in 1930 the legislature in Tennessee was a very homogeneous body, with a significant number of its members connected to politics through their families.

However, the significant changes that have occurred in the type of person recruited to the state legislature have eroded considerably the "insider's club" nature of the southern state legislature. A greater diversity of people has been elected, as traditional recruitment patterns are gradually being transformed. The rate of college graduates serving in the legislature has increased from 54 percent in 1930 to 93 percent in 1984, a predictable increase, given the overall increase in educational levels in the state during this period. More surprising are the sharp declines in the percentage of legislators who are lawyers and the number with an elected position prior to service in the legislature. The proportion of attorney legislators fell from 66 percent in 1930 to 20 percent in 1984, and the number who held an elected political office before going to the statehouse shows a drop from a high of 63 percent in 1950 to 16 percent in 1984.

Finally, legislators serving during the late 1970s were much less likely to have a close relative who had served in a state or national office or a parent with legislative experience at the local level. Political recruitment, at least to the state legislature, has opened up. The traditional southern political culture, which held that officeholding is reserved for those from the elite who have family connections in politics, seems to have undergone a significant change.

These altered recruitment patterns can be attributed, among other factors, to reapportionment and black enfranchisement, demographic and partisan changes, and increased legislative professionalism. Federal decisions on reapportionment and voting rights have facilitated participation in legislative politics by urban citizens and blacks. One example of the old system is Florida, where until the late 1960s, because of malapportionment, the five most populous counties had only 14 percent of the seats in the state senate while accounting for more than half the state's population. Urban and suburban representation increased substantially as a result of reapportionment, as did the number of ethnic lawmakers and blacks. In Tennessee, the first black since Reconstruction was elected to the legislature in 1964, and five were elected in 1966, which represents the largest number entering the legislature at any one time. As Table 3 shows, the percentage of blacks has increased gradually since then, with 8 percent of the state legislature in 1982 comprised of black representatives.

Across the South the number of black state legislators tripled from 1971 to 1982, whereas in the rest of the country the increase was less than one-half. In 1971, of all black legislators in the country, 24 percent sat in southern capitals; by 1982, that proportion had risen to almost 41 percent. The average southern state legislature in 1971 had two black members, but by 1982 the number had grown to six—compared with only three in other states. Now legislatures which once fostered Jim Crow laws have greater numbers of black representatives than any other region in the country. Female membership, however, still remains lower in the South than elsewhere. In 1980, of the eight states with less than 4 percent women legislators, five were in the South; no southern state legislature was more than 15 percent female. This lack of women members may explain why these southern legislatures proved the burial ground of the Equal Rights Amendment, which passed only in Texas and Tennessee (and the latter tried to rescind its ratification).

Also contributing to political change in the South are increased urbanization, industrialization, wealth, and educational levels—factors that not only expand political understanding but also produce higher levels of political efficacy. When combined with new communications systems which disseminate greater information about political life, these factors can have important political consequences and contribute to an "opening up" of politics beyond the traditional elite.

LEGISLATIVE REFORM IN THE SOUTH

State legislatures across the nation have long been regarded as outmoded institutions unable to respond to any significant political problem. For decades the press and many private organizations have called for "reforms" and "professionalization"; the goals of these groups can be summarized as follows:

1. The length of legislative sessions, their frequency, or the subjects to be discussed should not be restricted.

2. Legislative compensation should be high enough to attract qualified people from all social and income levels.

3. The legislature should provide itself with a professional staff that can meet information needs on a continuing basis. Working conditions should reflect the serious business being conducted (legislators, for example, should have individual offices).

4. The number of committees should be reduced so that members can gain expertise in a particular area or areas.

5. The legislature should play a more active role in the areas that have been largely left to the executive, such as the appropriation of public funds and the evaluation of policy. To this end, legislative oversight needs to be improved.[13]

All legislatures were judged to need improvement, and extensive changes were called for in states where legislative service was a part-time activity, legislatures met infrequently, salaries were low, and little staff assistance was available. The southern states were regarded as being particularly in need of reform. In 1969 the Citizens Conference on State Legislatures conducted an evaluation of state legislatures, and although criticism of their methodology has left some question regarding the exact scale score of individual states, their general ranking has generated little debate. The South ranked lower than any other region, with its legislatures (except Florida's) characterized as the least capable.[14] Some were caricatures of effective democratic assemblies. For instance, one legislator from Mississippi described constituents' impressions of the state's law-making body in these terms: "Whenever I talk to any of my people who have been to Jackson and seen the legislature, it seems the first thing they question is how disgusting it was to watch members breaking peanut shells and throwing them on the floor or reading newspapers or jabbering with lobbyists while the House is in session and conducting business."[15]

13. See Jesse Unrah and Donald G. Herzberg, "Legislative Reform: An Overview," in Donald G. Herzberg and Jesse Unrah, *Essays on the State Legislative Process* (New York, 1970), 105–106.

14. Citizens Conference on State Legislatures, *State Legislatures: An Evaluation of Their Effectiveness* (New York, 1971).

15. David B. Ogle, *Strengthening the Mississippi Legislature: An Eagleton Study and Report* (New Brunswick, 1971), 41.

Virtually all southern legislatures have changed substantially and for the better during the past two decades. Florida, described as making "dramatic progress in the past fifteen years," was one of the first states to add interim sessions, which have been very productive.[16] South Carolina and—in the border area—Kentucky have also instituted such sessions, and their impact can be substantial. A Kentucky legislator, for example, said that the laws developed during the state's initial interim sessions were "significant and complex, and probably could not have been passed if they had been introduced in the sixty-day regular session."[17] Most American legislatures in the 1950s met only in biennial sessions, though more southern legislatures met biennially than northern (90 percent to 40 percent). By 1983, 80 percent in both the North and South met in annual sessions, an essential shift toward making legislatures more active and informed participants in the formation of state policy.

Since much of the work of legislatures is conducted in committees, a frequent target for reform has been the committee structure, and one suggestion has been to reduce committee numbers.[18] As can be seen in Table 4, the southern legislature of the 1950s averaged about thirteen more committees than a nonsouthern legislature in both chambers—although lower houses across the country usually had more committees. Southern state legislatures, even in 1983, still had more committees than some of their northern counterparts, but the number per legislature in both regions has been reduced by over a third; in the process, the disparity between the two regions has lessened.

Increases in frequency of sessions and reductions in the number of committees were vigorously advanced in the 1960s and 1970s as essential reforms to increase the capacity of legislatures to act. Both trends have been as fully felt in the South as nationally.

The role of leadership is another major component of state legislatures, but because of the paucity of relevant information, one can only speculate on the internal structure of leadership, and followership, within the chambers of the fifty states.[19] Historically, the region's weak governors, factional politics, and low degree of party organization meant that longtime leaders within the state legislatures were immensely power-

16. Alan Rosenthal, *Legislative Performance in the States* (New York, 1974).

17. Alan Rosenthal, *Legislative Life: People, Process, and Performance in the States* (New York, 1981), 202.

18. Citizens Conferences on State Legislatures, *The Sometimes Government* (Kansas City, Mo., 1973).

19. Jewell, "State of U.S. State Legislative Research," 8; Malcolm E. Jewell, "Survey on Selection of State Legislative Leaders," *Comparative State Politics Newsletter*, I (1980), 7–21.

TABLE 4
Average Number of Committees by Chamber, Region, and Years

Years	House		Senate	
	South	Non-South	South	Non-South
1952–1953	42.15	29.50	36.08	23.40
1962–1963	35.23	22.78	29.00	18.29
1982–1983	23.46	18.35	16.46	13.89

SOURCES: *Book of the States, 1952–1953*, p. 100; *Book of the States, 1962–1963*, p. 49; *Book of the States, 1982–1983*, p. 217.

ful. Southern states still appear to have more factionalism within their political parties than is true elsewhere. However, the election of Republican officeholders in the South may bring increased unity to southern Democrats, and this, combined with the emergence of stronger governors, is destined to reduce the personal power of key legislative leaders.

Membership stability is frequently cited as a key ingredient to institutional development, and legislatures with frequent turnover are thought to be less developed and to have a diminished ability to act.[20] The membership turnover of legislatures, both South and North, has decreased since the 1960s, though the rate of change has differed slightly. Southern legislatures in the late 1970s had a slightly lower rate of membership turnover than did northern legislatures, though they had about the same rate in the 1963–1972 period.[21] The fact that state legislatures are increasingly confronting significant public issues induces the participation of individuals who have traditionally not been active in state politics, those, for example, desiring to make a career of public service and those motivated by policy concerns.

The higher salaries of today's state legislators make it possible for individuals to serve who wish to make the legislature a career (though one still will not prosper financially on a state legislator's salary). When legislative salaries were low, particularly in relation to the time involved, participation was limited to the well-to-do and to those in such occupations as law and large-scale farming with sufficient flexibility to allow time away in the state capital.

More recent improvements are computerization, increased staff, and improved facilities, including the expansion of office space. The utilization

20. Jewell and Patterson, *Legislative Process in the United States*, 34.
21. Rosenthal, *Legislative Life*, 136–38.

TABLE 5
Average Percentage of New Members by Time Period, Chamber, and Region

Period and Chamber	Region	
	Non-South	South
1963–1972		
Senate	30.05%	31.52%
House	35.39%	35.48%
1973–1978		
Senate	27.14%	24.71%
House	32.96%	30.82%

SOURCE: Alan Rosenthal, *Legislative Life: People, Process, and Performance in the States* (New York, 1981), 136–37.

of computers means that statutes are instantly available for legislative evaluation. Most budget systems are now on computer, increasing greatly the amount of information readily available to legislators. In Mississippi, for example, print-outs on a television screen are used to clarify the presentation of data in appropriations hearings. And Florida has impact analysis built into the fiscal/budgetary and educational finance system.

During the 1970s most states made staffs available to some committees and to legislative leaders, and intern programs have also provided staff assistance at relatively low cost. An example of the staffing increase taking place in many states is found in Kentucky, where in the past ten years the Legislative Research Committee, which provides professional staff for members, has grown from approximately seventy-five employees to over two hundred, 80 percent of whom are professionals.

A big improvement in facilities for southern legislatures has meant that in the last few years individual offices for members were made available for the first time in Tennessee, Arkansas, Mississippi and Kentucky. And two new office buildings nearing completion in Georgia will increase legislators' facilities there.

Southern states have also adopted a few "innovative" changes which have proved successful. In 1975, for example, a Kentucky Public Information Office was created with the goal of improving the public's awareness of legislative activities. Constituents now are able to call and find out the status of a particular bill.

A final measure of institutional development is the amount of money

TABLE 6
Professional Staff, 1979: Number of States by Region

Number of Staff	Non-South		South		Total	
	N	%	N	%	N	%
Low (1–75)	16	43.3	5	38.5	21	42
Moderate (76–200)	11	29.7	5	38.5	16	32
High (201–800)	10	27.0	3	23.1	13	26
Totals	37	100.0	13	100.1	50	100

SOURCE: Alan Rosenthal, *Legislative Life: People, Process, and Performance in the States* (New York, 1981), 207.

TABLE 7
Staff Assistance to Individual Legislators in at Least One Chamber, 1979:
Number of States by Region

Type of Staff	Non-South		South		Total	
	N	%	N	%	N	%
Some Professional	11	29.7	3	23.1	14	28.0
Nonprofessional	18	48.6	7	53.8	25	50.0
Secretarial Pool	18	48.6	5	38.5	23	46.0

SOURCE: Alan Rosenthal, *Legislative Life: People, Process, and Performance in the States* (New York, 1981), Table 10.2, p. 211.

NOTE: Since the categories are not mutually exclusive and states may thus be counted in more than one category, percentages will not equal 100.

spent by the state on its legislature. Presumably, those legislatures which are more highly institutionalized and professional will have higher levels of expenditures.[22] Table 8 presents a rank ordering of the state legislatures based upon the per-legislator expenditure relative to the national average. Unlike in the various Citizens Conference evaluations, when most southern legislatures ranked in the bottom third, the region's states no longer group together.[23] In fact, three southern states rank in the top

22. Expenditure levels "loaded" very highly in Grumm's measure of professionalism. John Grum, "The Effects of Legislative Structure on Legislative Performance," in Richard I. Hofferbert and Ira Sharkansky (eds.), *State and Urban Politics* (Boston, 1971).
23. Citizens Conferences, *The Sometimes Government*, 48–54.

TABLE 8
Ranking of States by Expenditures for State Legislatures, 1982

	State	Expenditures (in Thousands of $)	Per Legislator	Ratio to National Average
1	California	103,139	854.49	7.843
2	New York	86,545	412.12	3.761
3	Alaska	22,694	378.23	3.451
4	Michigan	41,430	279.99	2.555
5	Illinois	41,617	235.12	2.146
6	Pennsylvania	50,429	199.36	1.819
7	Florida	30,706	191.91	1.751
8	Louisiana	25,616	177.89	1.623
9	New Jersey	19,160	159.67	1.457
10	Texas	27,502	151.94	1.386
11	Massachusetts	28,402	142.02	1.296
12	Washington	20,179	137.27	1.253
13	Wisconsin	17,566	133.08	1.214
14	Hawaii	9,525	125.33	1.144
15	Oregon	9,689	107.66	.982
16	Ohio	13,972	105.85	.966
17	Minnesota	20,756	103.26	.942
18	Arizona	8,074	89.71	.871
19	Nebraska	4,385	89.49	.817
{ 20	Kentucky	11,545	83.66	.763
{ 20	Virginia	11,701	83.58	.763
22	South Carolina	12,501	73.54	.761
23	Oklahoma	10,582	71.02	.648
24	Colorado	6,867	68.67	.627
25	Nevada	4,023	67.05	.612
26	Maryland	12,392	65.91	.601
27	Missouri	12,447	63.18	.577
28	Indiana	8,388	55.92	.510
29	Georgia	12,853	54.46	.497
30	West Virginia	7,100	52.99	.484
31	Connecticut	9,903	52.96	.483
32	Alabama	7,084	50.60	.462

TABLE 8 — continued
Ranking of States by Expenditures for State Legislatures, 1982

State	Expenditures (in Thousands of $)	Per Legislator	Ratio to National Average
33 Iowa	7,577	50.51	.461
34 Kansas	8,011	48.55	.443
35 Tennessee	6,389	48.40	.442
36 Delaware	2,739	44.18	.403
37 North Carolina	6,782	39.89	.364
38 New Mexico	4,218	37.66	.344
39 Rhode Island	5,601	37.34	.341
40 Mississippi	6,071	34.89	.318
41 Montana	4,956	33.46	.305
42 Utah	3,119	29.99	.274
43 Arkansas	3,751	27.79	.254
44 Maine	4,230	22.99	.210
45 Idaho	2,344	22.32	.204
46 South Dakota	2,141	20.39	.192
47 North Dakota	2,763	18.42	.168
48 Wyoming	1,412	15.35	.140
49 Vermont	2,630	14.61	.133
50 New Hampshire	4,185	9.87	.090
Average		109.59	

SOURCE: Government Finances, *State Government Finances in 1982* (Washington, D.C., 1983), 39–51.

ten, and seven of the thirteen are in the top one-half of the rankings. Only Mississippi and Arkansas rank among the bottom ten. Thus, on this measure of institutional capacity southern legislatures compare quite favorably with those in the rest of the country.

In sum, although a few of the southern states have made only a limited number of changes and provide few of the resources necessary for a thorough, systematic analysis of the issues confronting the state, most of the legislatures improved substantially during the 1960s and 1970s. Indeed, the South as a region would no longer be classified as lagging behind the rest of the nation in legislative professionalism.[24]

WORK LOAD

The political changes discussed above—reapportionment, industrialization, urbanization, changing recruitment patterns, and the professionalization of state legislatures—have significant policy consequences. Research has shown that reapportionment affects the way state funds are allocated, although the state's budget does not necessarily increase. As expected, more money is granted to urban areas and to urban-related policies such as education and public health. And although the reasons are not entirely clear, the professionalism of state legislatures creates more responsiveness to lower-income groups.[25] This might be a reflection of the different type of person recruited to the legislature and/or the increased capacity of the legislature to make decisions. Both legislative professionalism and legislative reapportionment are associated with the adoption of innovative public policies or policies that have not been widely enacted in other states.[26]

The greater heterogeneity in membership has led to legislative consideration of a greater variety of issues. Since losing a bid for reelection is of greater consequence when legislative service is viewed as practically a full-time activity, members are more concerned about representing and pleasing their constituents. Furthermore, not having an automatic "in" to political service through family ties, those who do run have a greater commitment to upholding the political preferences of their constituents.

The number and variety of demands on the legislature will continue to increase as the South experiences greater industrialization and growth. State legislatures, particularly now with program development and implementation shifting from the federal government to the states, will find

24. This discussion of the changes occurring in southern state legislatures has drawn on the following sources: Robert L. Chartrand and Jane Bortnick, *State Legislative Use of Information Technology* (Westport, Conn., 1978); Council of State Government, *American State Legislatures: Their Structures and Procedures* (Lexington, 1971 and 1977); Malcolm Jewell and Lee S. Greene, *The Kentucky and Tennessee Legislatures* (Lexington, 1967); Rosenthal, *Legislative Performance* and *Legislative Life*; Lucinda S. Simon, *A Citizen's Guide to Staffing Patterns* (Denver, 1979); and Ogle, *Strengthening the Mississippi Legislature.*

Telephone interviews were conducted with a staff member in each of four states: Tennessee, Alabama, Georgia, and Kentucky. They were asked to describe the changes that have occurred in legislative professionalization in their state within the past fifteen years.

25. See Rosenthal, *Legislative Life*, 30.

26. Edward G. Carmines, "The Mediating Influence of State Legislatures on the Linkage Between Interparty Competition and Welfare Policies," *American Political Science Review*, LXVIII (September, 1984), 1118–24.

TABLE 9

Average Number of Bills Introduced and Enacted
in Two Time Periods, South and Non-South Legislatures

	South		Non-South	
	1970–71	*1979–80*	*1970–71*	*1979–80*
Bills Introduced	3,093	3,425	3,629	3,636
Bills Enacted	1,205	1,133	780	737
Percentage Enacted	38.9	33.1	21.5	20.3

SOURCES: *Book of the States, 1972–1973*, pp. 74–75; *Book of the States, 1982–1983*, pp. 206–207.

it necessary to accelerate their changing procedures in order to deal adequately with this societal transformation. It seems quite likely that within the next two decades many state legislatures in the South will be in the forefront in adopting legislative reforms and in terms of sheer work load. The flow of work and activity by state legislatures can be measured — if only roughly — by several indicators, including the number of bills, review of federal funds, and oversight of the executive branch.

Bills

On the average, southern state legislatures receive fewer bills per biennium than other legislatures but enact a larger number of them. The enactment rate is thus about 15 percent higher for southern state legislatures than for those outside the South, a difference perhaps due to the local and private bills in the South's legislatures. The disparity has declined slightly over the 1970s, though the enactment rate itself has declined in both regions.

The tendency of southern legislatures to enact legislation is even more marked if the number of bills is related to the socioeconomic circumstances of the state's population. Based upon characteristics of population size, industrialization, and urbanization, southern legislators enact much more legislation than do nonsouthern legislators. On the average, from 1963 to 1974 southern legislatures enacted almost 250 bills more than would be expected by those population characteristics, whereas the average nonsouthern state enacted only 87 bills more than expected.[27]

Although the above measure excluded "resolutions," the category of "bills" is highly diverse among the states. Since we have no reliable means of systematically developing a uniform subgrouping within the larger

27. Rosenthal, *Legislative Life*, 258–64.

"bills" category, and since we examine here the averages among legislatures grouped by region, some of the variations of specific states are perhaps reduced in the aggregate figures.

Federal Funds

One test of the convergence of southern legislatures with their counterparts is the response to new sets of circumstances that affect all states simultaneously. The alterations in federal funding of many programs vital to the states, wrought by the Reagan administration, is such a circumstance. How are the various state legislatures responding? Are they by default permitting state decisions to be made by the governor, or are they taking stronger measures—through appropriations and oversight—to make those decisions themselves?

Southern legislatures do not differ from nonsouthern ones in their response to this new situation. About 40 percent of both regional sets of legislatures are responding strongly and vigorously, whereas a quarter of each set are leaving such decisions to the governor. An important element of this legislative response is oversight.[28]

Legislative Review and Oversight

Southern legislatures, more frequently than others, have an array of oversight mechanisms and procedures. For example, a higher proportion of southern legislatures than nonsouthern ones (85 percent to 62 percent), have the power to *review* all administrative regulations. But there is no regional difference in their power to *repeal* administrative regulations, with the same proportion of southern as nonsouthern (33 percent) legislatures having this authority. That is, although southern legislatures more often have the power to review, their power to take decisive action is no greater than that of northern legislatures.

Oversight is an important component of legislative professionalization, and some regard sunset laws as the most significant oversight approach. The goals of sunset legislation are to enforce accountability of administrative agencies to the legislature, to curtail unnecessary bureaucratic activity, and to formalize long-neglected oversight activity. Southern states have been particularly active in the adoption and implementation of sunset laws to enhance legislative oversight, being among the first

28. See Winnefred Austermann, *A Legislator's Guide to Oversight of Federal Funds* (Denver, 1980) and Patricia K. Freeman and E. Fletcher McClellan, *The Consequences of Increased Legislative Oversight of Federal Funds: The Case of Tennessee* (Knoxville, 1981).

TABLE 10
Legislative Review of Administrative Agency Regulations, by Region

	South		Non-South		Total	
	N	%	N	%	N	%
A. ALL RULES REVIEWABLE						
Yes	11	84.6	23	62.2	34	68
No	2	15.4	14	37.8	16	32
Totals	13	100.0	37	100.0	50	100
B. RULES REPEALABLE						
Yes	4	33.3	12	33.3	16	33.3
No	8	66.7	24	66.7	32	66.7
Totals	12	100.0	36	100.0	48*	100.0

*Data are missing for two states.
SOURCE: *Book of the States, 1982–83*, pp. 225–27.

in the nation to enact such legislation. All but Virginia have adopted some type of sunset law, and an examination of Tennessee's version will show the potentially positive impact these laws have.

Under Tennessee's comprehensive sunset law all agencies created by the legislature are reviewed. Common Cause, and most observers, recommend against sunset laws with so wide a scope, suggesting that states begin with regulatory agencies, at least until they become familiar with the review process. Tennessee, however, has managed to schedule the many reviews prudently. The state relies on a "limited program audit," with the number of hours assigned for review of an entity depending on the agency's significance. For example, less than fifty hours were allotted to the review of four agriculture boards, whereas almost four thousand hours were expended on the Department of Insurance. The report of review findings makes apparent the major recommendations, and sunset has resulted in a substantial number of changes in Tennessee.

In order to ascertain and assess the frequency of different types of changes, each of the fifty-three entities evaluated in 1978, 1979, and 1980 was assigned to one of four categories indicating the final action taken: termination, significant legislative action, significant administrative action, or no action. Termination obviously means that the legislature voted to discontinue the operations of the entity. Any changes in

TABLE 11
Sunset and Legislative Oversight

Type of Review	Non-South		South	
	N	%	N	%
SUNSET SCOPE				
Comprehensive	5	14	7	53
Regulatory	13	35	4	31
Other forms	14	38	1	8
None	5	14	1	8
Totals	37	101*	13	100
PRELIMINARY EVALUATION MEANS				
Committee	14	38	9	69
Other	11	30	2	15
None	12	32	2	15
Totals	37	100	13	99*
OTHER LEGISLATIVE REVIEW MEANS				
Yes	16	43	4	31
No	21	57	9	69
Totals	37	100	13	100
OTHER OVERSIGHT PROCEDURES				
Yes	16	43	10	77
No	21	57	3	23
Totals	37	100	13	100

*Rounding errors
SOURCE: Book of the States, 1982–1983, pp. 226–27.

structure, major alterations in procedures, or substantial funding revisions constituted a significant change. If the action was taken in the legislature, it was designated a legislative change; otherwise it was considered
an administrative change.

Analysis of the three-year period shows that a considerable number of
the reports invoked some type of response—termination, significant legislative action, or a major administrative change. Table 12 shows a cur-
vilinear pattern for the number of entities terminated: in 1978 27 percent

TABLE 12
Action Taken Subsequent to Sunset Report, by Year, in Tennessee

	Percentage of Entities Evaluated		
	1978	*1979*	*1980*
Terminated	27	36	15
Significant Legislative Action	15	0	30
Significant Administrative Action	11	22	23
No Significant Action	47	42	30
	n = 26	n = 14	n = 13

were terminated as compared with 36 percent in 1979, but only 15 percent in 1980. The trend toward fewer terminations should not be taken as an indication that sunset evaluations are less stringent or that the reviews are taken less seriously, but rather that the type of entity under evaluation changed. The major departments and agencies predominate in the reviews conducted during the third year are obviously less likely to be terminated than the smaller entities. And the incidence of other types of changes increased, with the legislature in particular becoming more active in mandating shifts. No cases in 1979 led to significant legislative action in response to a sunset report; in 1980 almost one-third of the reports invoked a legislative response. The number of sunset reports resulting in a significant administrative response has increased as well, from 11 percent in 1978 to double that in 1979 and 1980.

Considerable attention in the sunset evaluations was devoted to issues usually regarded as measuring the entity's "responsiveness." The degree to which agencies, especially regulatory bodies, observed due process in dealing with the public was evaluated, as were personnel procedures and compliance with affirmative action requests in particular. Of the significant number of changes produced, some were a result of legislative mandate but most came from voluntary action in anticipation of criticism. In many instances the alterations in agency structure and procedure were made prior to the evaluation, a frequent occurrence which means that the actual impact of sunset is greater than such studies as the one above indicate.

CONCLUSIONS

Southern legislatures, in the midst of change, have grown relatively less Democratic and substantially less homogeneous. Black and female representation has increased, many more occupations are represented, and members are less likely to come from politically active families. This profile indicates the declining influence of the traditional elite that has long dominated southern politics. Four factors primarily account for these changes in recruitment patterns: reapportionment and black enfranchisement, growing party competition, demographic and economic changes, and the professionalism of state legislatures.

The dominant "Traditionalistic" political culture in the South is slowly eroding. Higher levels of urbanization, industrialization, and education, improved communications, and higher per capita income are making citizens of the South increasingly concerned with public policy and are stimulating demand for a professional public service and an expansion of the political elite. Thus, the political culture of the South is blending with that in other regions. Although the South is not the only region of the country experiencing changes, for most observers the cultural alterations taking place there seem more dramatic, partly because the South was isolated for an extended period. Moreover, due to demographic and institutional changes and to substantial immigration, the cultural reorientation seems to be occurring with great speed, giving the appearance of a virtual transformation in the South's political culture.

Southern political institutions will continue to change in order to meet the demands of an increasingly complex society. A vast number of societal forces push southern state legislators into more involvement with what was only recently very much a part-time role. The federal initiative is strong and the message clear: if the states do not legislate and act appropriately in areas from highways to health care, the federal government will not provide funding. Increased legislative staffs lead to more laws, as writing legislation is what many staffers are hired to do. And faced with more attentive constituents, legislators are increasingly under pressure to pass bills for interest groups and others who request them. To complicate matters further, laws beget more laws, as additional legislation is usually necessary to implement and further clarify a public policy initiative.

Thus, the legislators serving now face more issues and must be willing to deal substantively with many public topics. And the professionalization of the legislature has given them the tools to do so in a more effective manner. The fact that most southern states have undertaken legislative oversight and conduct the reviews in a fairly comprehensive manner is one indication of this trend.

The growth in legislative oversight reflects a commitment among state legislators to devote a certain amount of time and staff resources to an activity that receives little attention among the public and thus provides few rewards for individuals in terms of recognition from their constituents. Even so, legislators appear to be not only willing to confront some of the more significant problems in the states but also to increasingly engage in program implementation and evaluation. This increased policy role reflects the process of professionalization and the change in the type of person recruited.

The adoption of sunset legislation has affected southern state governments in many ways. One pragmatic consequence is that states sometimes report substantial savings resulting from the reviews, which reinforces the evaluation process and perhaps facilitates additional activity. For example, Tennessee reports a savings resulting from sunset of over $4,500,000. Such savings, along with the changes made in various programs, are immediate, instrumental policy changes.[29] Another major benefit of evaluation is "knowledge building," the accumulated information provided by evaluations which over time will improve understanding of the policy process.[30]

We observe in these trends a nationwide common institutional development among the state legislatures. Regional differences are decreasing. National problems are producing a common response, though each state responds out of its own past and in its own accents.

29. Carol H. Weiss, "Where Politics and Evaluation Research Meet," *Evaluation*, I (1973), 37–43.

30. See Nathan Caplan *et al.*, *The Use of Social Science Knowledge in Policy Decisions at a National Level* (Ann Arbor, 1975), and Robert F. Rich, "Use of Social Science Information by Federal Bureaucrats," in Carol H. Weiss (ed.), *Using Social Research in Public Policymaking* (Lexington, 1977).

Judicial Politics in the South: Robed Elites and Recruitment

RONALD G. MARQUARDT

As the courts have come to be involved more and more in public questions that focus attention on their procedures and decisions, their position in our society is more open to question and subject to challenge.
—Paul Nejelski,
State Court Journal (1977)

The first fact one encounters in studying judicial politics in the South is that so few scholars have addressed the subject. The two academic disciplines most likely to serve as wellsprings for such analysis, political science and law, have focused their attention elsewhere. Historically, political scientists have been enamored with studying the output of the United States Supreme Court, much to the detriment of state and lower federal courts. This seems to be a permanent love affair. And the behavioral movement in the discipline failed to produce many studies concerning state or regional judicial politics. Scholars on judicial politics, unlike those in other areas of the discipline (voting behavior, for example), are handicapped by the difficulty of piercing the purple curtain which more or less surrounds all courts. This may explain the paucity of data, as Malcolm Jewell noted in his presidential address to the 1981 Southern Political Science Association convention. Bemoaning "the neglected world of state politics," Jewell said: "At the state judicial level, we lack comparative data on contested judicial elections and the frequency of incumbent defeat. Very few efforts have been made to collect biographical information on state appellate court judges, and consequently we lack comprehensive data on the attributes of judges, such as partisan and public office holding or even previous judicial positions. State appellate court decisions have not been collected or codified adequately for the fifty states."[1]

This neglect is not new. One finds that the seminal works on southern politics, for example, have all but ignored the state judiciary. Key, Havard, and Bass and DeVries pay little attention, if any, to the role of courts in state politics, perhaps because state courts in the South were weak sisters in relation to the other branches.[2] Studying the region's judicial politics paled in comparison with the more exciting subjects of partisan and factional politics, with their Byzantine intrigues and cast of colorful characters. Neglected by scholars, the state courts have quietly taken care of business, civil and criminal, fitting rather cozily into the economic and political scheme of things.

The legal profession has contributed little to the literature on southern judicial politics, perhaps because the audience of legal publications is interested more in learning the techniques of how to win cases for clients than in analyzing the system. Or maybe it's due to lawyers' fondness for pretending the judicial branch is outside of politics. In any event law journals are often highly technical and are compartmentalized jurisdictionally.

The South is a good place to study judicial politics because, as Jewell notes, "Southern politics is still in the process of change, and we can learn much about political institutions during a period of evolution."[3] It is also true that the South is catching up to the rest of the country in producing lawyers and embracing legalism, and the region's courts thus will play greater policy-making roles in the future than they did say, in Key's time. For example, groups such as the Moral Majority increasingly look to the state courts as appropriate and accessible avenues through which to seek their political goals.

Given the increased role of the courts and the sparse attention paid to judicial politics, it is time we do as Jewell advises and reverse the neglect of this and other important areas of subnational politics. A logical place to begin in reference to the judiciary of any region like the South is to look more closely at who the judges are, how they are selected, the

---

1. Malcolm Jewell, "The Neglected World of State Politics," *Journal of Politics*, XLIV (August, 1982), 646. The lone exception appears to be Lee S. Greene's "The Southern State Judiciary," in Taylor Cole and John H. Hallowell (eds.), *The Southern Political Scene, 1938–1948* (Gainesville, 1948).

2. V. O. Key, Jr., *Southern Politics in State and Nation* (New York, 1949), William Havard (ed.), *The Changing Politics of the South* (Baton Rouge, 1972), and Jack Bass and Walter DeVries, *The Transformation of Southern Politics: Social Change and Political Consequence Since 1945* (New York, 1976).

3. Jewell, "The Neglected World of State Politics," 654.

changes occurring in the recruitment process, plus the implications of judicial selection and the judges' social and background characteristics. These are the subjects of this essay.

SYSTEMS OF JUDICIAL RECRUITMENT, STRUCTURE, AND STAFFING

A majority of southern states still rely on the voters to select judges, although this pattern eroded somewhat in the 1970s. Seven states use the partisan primary scheme, and Louisiana has an open primary selection system. Thus, 73 percent of all the South's supreme court and intermediate appellate judges are chosen by the voters. At the trial level reliance upon the electorate for judicial selection is even more common, with 89 percent of the South's trial judges on courts of general jurisdiction being elected by voters.[4] The figures for courts of limited jurisdiction, such as justice of the peace or municipal courts, though unavailable, are undoubtedly even higher.

At first blush, reliance upon the populace to select the judiciary seems incongruent in a traditional culture wherein politics has historically been dominated by elites. There are, however, countervailing tendencies to elitism in the region which explain the adherence to the electoral mode of judicial selection. The South was a bastion of Jacksonian democracy before the Civil War, with the long ballot being particularly popular. In 1832 Mississippi became the first state to create an entirely elected judiciary.[5] All but two of the southern states soon followed suit. After the war and Reconstruction, in the 1880s and 1890s, Populism had a great effect on the legal profession, the judiciary, and virtually everything else. For example, during the Populist era Kentucky debated a constitutional amendment to bar the existence of lawyers in that state.[6]

Today only Virginia and South Carolina choose their judges by legislative selection, as they have done since colonial times. In 1976 Florida opted for the merit selection system for appellate judges. Also in 1976 Louisiana Democrats attempted to reduce the mushrooming costs of political campaigns for all offices by changing to an open primary system and thereby avoiding the second or runoff primary. Tables 1, 2, and 3 present a capsule summary of the selection system (with salaries).

4. The above figures are calculated from Tables 1, 2, and 3 of the National Center for State Courts' *National Court Statistics Project, State Courts Organization, 1980* (Washington, D.C., 1981).

5. Philip L. Dubois, *From Ballot to Bench* (Austin, 1980), 3.

6. David Riley, "The Mystique of Lawyers," in *Verdicts on Lawyers*, eds. Ralph Nader and Mark Green (New York, 1976), 83.

TABLE 1
Southern State Supreme Courts, 1980

State	No. of Justices	Method of Selection	Term in Years	Salary	Method of Selection of Chief Justice	Salary of Chief Justice
Alabama	9	Partisan Election	6	$42,265	Partisan Election	$42,800
Arkansas	7	Partisan Election	8	42,399	Partisan Election	46,253
Florida	7	Merit Plan[1]	6	48,525	Court Rotation	48,525
Georgia	7	Partisan Election	6	48,530	Court Election	48,530
Louisiana	7	Nonpartisan[1]	10	61,635	Seniority of Service	61,635
Mississippi	9	Partisan Election	8	46,000	Seniority of Service	47,000
North Carolina	7	Partisan Election	8	54,288	Partisan Election	55,440
South Carolina	5	Elected by Legislature	10	55,088	Elected by Legislature	62,177
Tennessee	5	Partisan Election	8	57,799	Court Rotation	62,616
Texas	9	Partisan Election	6	56,700	Partisan Election	57,200
Virginia	7	Elected by Legislature	12	54,000	Seniority of Service	56,500

SOURCE: National Center for State Courts, *National Court Statistics Project, State Courts Organization, 1980* (Washington, D.C., 1981), Tables 1 and 2.

[1]Changed from partisan election in 1976

TABLE 2
Southern Intermediate Appellate Courts, 1980

State	No. of Judges	Method of Selection	Term in Years	Salary
Alabama	8	Partisan Election	6	$40,660
Arkansas	6	Partisan Election	8	39,803
Florida	39	Merit Plan	6	46,063
Georgia	9	Partisan Election	6	48,842
Louisiana	33	Nonpartisan Election	10	58,673
Mississippi*				
North Carolina	12	Partisan Election	8	51,396
South Carolina	5	Elected by Legislature	6	Not established
Tennessee	21	Partisan Election	8	52,983
Texas	51	Partisan Election	6	48,200
Virginia*				

SOURCE: National Center for State Courts, *National Court Statistics Project, State Courts Organization, 1980* (Washington, D.C., 1981), Table 3.
*Did not have intermediate appellate courts in 1980

TABLE 3
Southern State Trial Courts of General Jurisdiction, 1980

State	No. of Judges	Population Per Judge	Method of Selection	Term in Years	Salary
Alabama	113	34,400	Partisan Election	6	$34,000
Arkansas*	63	30,200	Partisan Election	6	39,441
Florida	302	32,300	Nonpartisan Election	6	43,704
Georgia	110	49,700	Partisan Election	4	41,328
Louisiana	161	26,100	Nonpartisan Election	6	55,712
Mississippi*	65	38,800	Partisan Election	4	41,000
North Carolina	66	89,000	Partisan Election	8	45,636
South Carolina	31	100,680	Legislative Election	6	55,088
Tennessee	58	39,900	Partisan Election	8	48,166
Texas	310	45,900	Partisan Election	4	40,500
Virginia	111	48,200	Legislative Election	8	47,000

SOURCE: National Center for State Courts, *National Court Statistics Project, State Courts Organization, 1980* (Washington, D.C., 1981), Tables 4, 9, 10.
*Includes Circuit and Chancery Court Judges

TABLE 4
The Bureaucratization of the Southern Judiciary, 1980

State	Date of Establishment of Judicial Disciplinary Commission	Date of Establishment of Judicial Compensation Commission	Date of Establishment of State Court Administrative Office	State Level Court Administration Personnel	Support Personnel—State Supreme Court	Support Personnel—Other Appellate	Support Personnel—Courts of General Jurisdiction[a]	Total Support Personnel[a]
Alabama	1973	1975	1971	40	47	26	820	933
Arkansas	1977	None	1965	10	22	22	76	130
Florida	1966	1972	1972	13	76	186	359	634
Georgia	1972	1971	1973	19	40	4	1,020	1,146
Louisiana	1968	1975	1954	7.8	56	94	877	1,034.8
Mississippi	1979	None	1974	5	34	N.A.	N.A.	—
North Carolina	1973	None	1965	46	26	43	1,923[b]	2,038
South Carolina	1976	None	1973	11	32	N.A.	56	99
Tennessee	1979	None	1963	16	30	41	N.A.	—
Texas	1965	None	1977	7	37	165	N.A.	—
Virginia	1971	None	1952	19.5	33	N.A.	N.A.	—

N.A. = Not available

SOURCE: National Center for State Courts, *National Court Statistics Project, State Courts Organization, 1980* (Washington, D.C., 1981), Tables 14, 15, 18, 19.

aIncludes clerk of court personnel but not court reporters, law clerks, or judges

bIncludes district attorneys, public defenders, and clerical staff

A second important item about the contemporary southern judiciary, revealed by the data in Table 4, is its espousal of the concept that efficient operation of a judiciary necessitates the establishment of a court bureaucracy. Legal and judicial professionalism and court bureaucratization have developed slowly in the southern states. A study published in 1973 ranked Alabama, Arkansas, and Mississippi forty-eighth, forty-ninth, and fiftieth respectively on a legal professionalism scale. Only North Carolina finished in the top one-third (in fifteenth place), and the majority of the remaining southern states fell in the bottom one-third of the rankings.[7] As Table 4 indicates, the creation of judicial disciplinary commissions, the centralization of state court administration, and the formation of judicial compensation commissions did, for the most part, occur throughout the region in the 1970s. As the number of attorneys proliferates at a near geometric rate and as the rush to the courthouse continues, enhanced legal professionalism and the bureaucratization of the southern judiciary are trends certain to accelerate.

Changing economic and social conditions are leading the southern states slowly to emulate the reforms that have previously taken place in the more heavily industrialized and populated states, which may doom the historically dominant mode of electoral selection. For social and economic development simply brings about a greater need for laws, litigation, and lawyers. And as lawyers are the participants trained in the rules of the legal-judicial game, attorneys and their interest groups play a powerful role in shaping state judicial politics. They lobby for such agencies as judicial disciplinary commissions and state court administrators and usually favor the merit selection system for judges.

As traditional Jacksonian and neo-Populist influences are mitigated by the acceptance of new standards of judicial politics promulgated by the dominant professional group, major reform pressures will focus on those states that still use the partisan election system for selection of their judges and have yet to adopt the full range of bureaucratic innovations. The next decade should see major changes in the selection process, structure, and staffing of the southern judiciary.

SOCIAL CHARACTERISTICS AND
CAREER PATTERNS OF SOUTHERN JUDGES

The few existing studies on the social and background characteristics of the state judiciary in the South reinforce what everyone familiar with the topic already knows: it is a stronghold of white, male, Democratic, Prot-

7. Henry Glick and Kenneth Vines, *State Court Systems* (Englewood Cliffs, 1973), 12.

estant judges who have close ties in the state in which they serve. This is particularly true where partisan election is used. In 1972 Bradley Canon found only three Catholics (and no Jews) out of 100 supreme court justices elected on a partisan ballot in the southern states. The same study reported that all but 5 of the total 135 justices in the South were affiliated with the Democratic party. Another study published in *Judicature* in 1973 found no blacks serving on state supreme courts and only 17 black judges serving on lower trial courts in the eleven southern states. Yet another study, published in 1980, concluded, "Though blacks in the south have been able to secure some political offices, the trial bench does not seem to be one of them." The same conclusion applies to the appellate courts. Although blacks have made progress at the federal level, thanks to the appointive system, the opportunity for them to serve on the state and local bench in the South is quite limited.[8]

When the opportunity comes for a black to reach the highest state court bench, it usually arises through gubernatorial appointment to an unexpired term. Such was the case of Justices Reuben Anderson (Mississippi), George Brown (Tennessee), and Oscar Adams (Arkansas), who were appointed between the years 1980 and 1985 to fill unexpired terms. The number and distribution of black judges in several state judicial systems is depicted in Table 5.

Women have not fared much better in obtaining judicial positions in the South. As recently as 1977 only three women served on state supreme courts (in Alabama, Arkansas, and North Carolina), and four served on state intermediate appellate courts (in Florida, North Carolina, Tennessee, and Texas).[9] Table 6 indicates that several southern states lag behind the national average for female judges at both the trial and appellate level. Florida is the only southern state that significantly exceeds the national average for women in the judiciary, and four states—Georgia, Mississippi, Louisiana, and South Carolina—are woefully deficient. This may be because in the region's traditionalist culture women have only recently begun to enter the legal profession in any numbers. The partisan election system may also be at fault.[10]

8. Bradley C. Canon, "The Impact of Formal Selection Processes on the Characteristics of Judges—Reconsidered," in *Judicial Administration: Text and Readings*, eds. Russell R. Wheeler and Howard R. Whitcomb (Englewood Cliffs, 1977), 130; Allen Ashmen, "The Black Judge in America: A Statistical Profile," *Judicature*, CVII (June–July, 1973), 20; John Paul Ryan *et al., American Trial Judges* (New York, 1980), 128.

9. Beverly Blair Cook, "Women Judges: The End of Tokenism," in *Women in the Courts*, eds. Winifred L. Hepperle and Laura Crites (Williamsburg, 1978), 100–103.

10. Almost 50 percent of over three hundred female judges surveyed had initially received their appointment by gubernatorial selection. Only 17 percent of the judges had been ini-

TABLE 5
Number and Distribution of Black Judges, 1982

State	Appellate Court	General Jurisdiction	Limited Jurisdiction	Total Black State Judges
Alabama			4	4
Arizona			1	1
Arkansas				
California	1	28	34	63
Colorado		3	1	4
Connecticut		6	2	8
Delaware				
District of Columbia	2	12		14
Florida		7	4	11
Georgia		2	3	5
Illinois		35		35
Indiana		3		3
Iowa		1	2	3
Kansas		1		1
Kentucky		2	3	5
Louisiana		4	3	7
Maryland		5	6	11
Massachusetts		2	8	10
Michigan		20	10	30
Minnesota		2		2
Mississippi			1	1
Missouri		2	4	6
Nebraska				
Nevada		1		1
New Hampshire				
New Jersey		2	1	3
New York				
North Carolina		2	9	11
Ohio		5		5
Oklahoma		1		1
Oregon		1	1	2
Pennsylvania		21	4	25
South Carolina		1		1
Tennessee		5	1	6

TABLE 5—*continued*
Number and Distribution of Black Judges, 1982

State	Appellate Court	General Jurisdiction	Limited Jurisdiction	Total Black State Judges
Texas		4		4
Virginia		1	7	8
Washington		1	2	3
Virgin Islands				
West Virginia		5		5
Wisconsin		2		2
Totals	3	187	111	301

SOURCE: Harry A. Poloski and James Williams (eds.), *The AFRO-American* (New York, 1983), 351.

With the exception of the major metropolitan areas in the United States, most minorities and women receive their judicial posts through some type of appointive means. A good example of such an appointment was the 1981 selection of Justice Lenore Prather to be the first female to serve on the Mississippi Supreme Court. Although Mississippi is a partisan election state, Justice Prather was nominated by the governor to fill an interim vacancy. Should additional states in the South embrace the merit system, opportunities for minorities and women to serve on the bench may accelerate.

Whether male or female, black or white, southern judges seem to possess extraordinarily strong ties to their communities and states. One indication of this was Canon's finding that a greater percentage of judges in the South than in any other region received both an in-state undergraduate education (84 percent) and an in-state legal education (80 percent). Whether this pattern can be attributed to regional culture or to the heavy reliance on partisan selection systems is difficult to distinguish. It may be the latter. Herbert Jacob, for instance, discovered much the same degree of localism in a study of partisan election states outside the South.[11]

---

tially selected by partisan ballot. See Susan Carbon, Pauline Houldren, and Larry Berkson, "Women on the State Bench: Their Characteristics and Attitudes About Judicial Selection," *Judicature*, CXV (December–January, 1982), 299.

11. Canon, "The Impact of Formal Selection Processes," 129; Herbert Jacob, "The Effect of Institutional Differences in the Recruitment Process: The Case of State Judges," *Journal of Public Law*, XIII (1964), 104.

TABLE 6
Women Serving on State Appellate and Trial Courts, 1980

State	Appellate Court Judges			Trial Court Judges			Total Trial and Appellate Courts		
	Total Men & Women	Women	Percent Women	Total Men & Women	Women	Percent Women	Total Men & Women	Women	Percent Judges Women
Alabama	17	1	5.9	483	10	2.1	500	11	2.2
Arkansas	13	1	7.7	317	8	2.5	3,300	9	2.7
Florida	46	4	8.7	500	26	5.2	546	30	5.5
Georgia	16			2,428	7	.3	2,444	7	.3
Louisiana	40			872	6	.7	912	6	.7
Mississippi	9			656	5	.8	665	5	.8
North Carolina	19	2	10.5	202	3	1.5	221	5	2.3
South Carolina	10			703	1	.1	713	1	.1
Tennessee	26	1	3.8	478	5	1.0	504	6	1.2
Texas	79	1	1.3	2,505	27	1.1	2,574	28	1.1
Virginia	5	0		71	1	1.4	76	1	1.3
Southern States	280	10	3.5	9,215	99	1.1	9,495	109	1.1
All States	926	47	5.1	25,724	520	2.0	26,650	567	2.1

SOURCE: Cynthia Epstein, *Women in Law* (New York, 1981), Table 13.1.

Turning to entry positions for judges, one finds that no clear-cut differences are detectable between judges in the South and other regions. One 1980 study of the professional and career patterns of the South's trial judges categorized the states in the following manner:[12]

District attorney or public official (typically high)	*Private practice dominant*
Alabama	Arkansas
Georgia	Louisiana
South Carolina	Mississippi
	North Carolina
	Tennessee
	Virginia

Private practice substantial and lower courts significant	*Private practice and lower courts (balanced)*
Texas	Florida

Given the prominent role of the district attorney in many southern states, it is surprising that more judges did not have prosecutorial experience immediately prior to reaching the bench. Both the Midwest and the West possess a greater percentage of supreme court justices with prosecutorial experience.[13] One possible explanation for the predominance of the private practice classification may be that until recently lawyers could not advertise.[14] All the states in that category, except for Virginia, use the partisan election system, and running for a judicial office—whether one succeeded or not—often provided name recognition and other resources crucial for building a private practice. Also surprising was the finding that supreme court justices in the South tended to have greater legislative experience than their counterparts in all other regions of the country. Not surprising, given the extensive reliance on the partisan election system, was that the South ranked third among the four regions in justices having prior judicial experience before taking a seat on their state's highest appellate court.[15] Rather than moving up through the court

12. Ryan *et al., American Trial Judges,* 126.
13. Canon, "The Impact of Formal Selection Processes," 129.
14. Even following *Bates* v. *State Bar of Arizona,* 433 U.S. 350 (1977), many southern states through their codes of professional responsibility severely restricted advertising by lawyers, particularly in the electronic media.
15. Canon, "The Impact of Formal Selection Processes," 129.

system, as is the pattern where appointive systems prevail, judicial candidates are free to run for whichever court they wish. Although trends can be identified, none of the studies reported great variations between the regions as to occupational career paths for either trial or appellate judges.

One of the most interesting analyses of judicial background and recruitment is Atkins' and Glick's 1974 study examining state supreme court decision-making in relation to the method of judicial selection.[16] Although the small number of cases used in the study taints the findings, and the near uniformity of the electoral selection process in the South restricted the opportunity for comparing the relationship of selection system and decision-making, the study has value. It is one of the very few efforts to categorize state supreme court output. Briefly stated, the four hypotheses of the study are:

1. Judges chosen by governors and legislatures would have a tendency to support state appellants.

2. Judges chosen by partisan and nonpartisan methods would display lower support for criminal defendants.

3. Corporation and superior economic litigants would find the greatest support among judges selected by state legislatures.

4. Judges in partisan election states would give greater support to inferior economic litigants.

None of the findings was statistically significant, but analysis of the data contained in Table 7 does reveal some interesting variations.[17] South Carolina and Virginia, where the judges are selected by the legislature, did show substantial support for appellants who were classified as superior economic litigants. And several states utilizing the partisan election method—Alabama, Louisiana, Georgia, and Texas—have very low support levels for criminal defendants and a very high rate of support for inferior economic litigants. Other findings were diametrically opposite the stated hypotheses (perhaps because of the low number of cases from several states).

Much more descriptive and analytical study of southern judicial politics than the few studies cited above is needed. Electorates need to be probed, decision-making categorized, campaign expenditures scruti-

16. Burton M. Atkins and Henry R. Glick, "Formal Judicial Recruitment and State Supreme Court Decisions," *American Politics Quarterly*, II (October, 1974), 427.
17. Atkins and Glick concluded that formal judicial recruitment methods have little impact upon state supreme court decision-making. *Ibid.*, 447.

TABLE 7
Percentage of Support for Appellants in Selected Cases:
State Supreme Courts, 1966

State	State or State Agency	Criminal Defendant	Corporation	Superior Economic Litigant	Inferior Economic Litigant
National Mean	44.11	22.11	34.54	40.73	30.81
Alabama	37.5	6.3	40.0	40.0	40.0
Arkansas	54.5	41.7	57.1	50.0	28.6
Florida	66.7	20.0	60.0	80.0	85.7
Georgia	28.6	11.1	33.3	60.0	33.3
Louisiana	37.5	7.8	20.0	100.0	67.7
Mississippi	50.0	35.7	41.2	25.0	33.3
North Carolina	33.3	31.6	14.3	33.3	36.4
South Carolina	50.0	23.5	16.7	63.6	16.7
Tennessee	40.0	68.0	43.8	29.7	25.0
Texas	64.3	16.5	59.3	60.0	76.5
Virginia	50.0	44.4	52.9	88.9	50.9

SOURCE: Burton M. Atkins and Henry R. Glick, "Formal Judicial Recruitment and State Supreme Court Decisions," *American Politics Quarterly*, II (October, 1974), 438.

nized, and minority and women judges identified. Such research would help move the arguments for change from the polemical realm and provide some basis for rational choices.

PROSPECTS FOR CHANGE AND REFORM IN THE FUTURE

As previously mentioned, the growing impetus for reform will be generated by higher economic and political stakes being brought before the courts. An increase in the volume and value of litigation will result in a movement toward greater bureaucratization, some structural reform (for example, the probable creation of intermediate appellate courts in Virginia and Mississippi, which are the only two southern states that currently lack such courts), and an emphasis on tightening and streamlining the rules of the judicial game. All such changes will be accomplished in the name of efficiency but will also have the effect of enhancing the role of the professional in southern judicial politics.

It is likely that judicial reform will follow the path established in the 1970s. That is, it will be incremental and brought about by professional elites. Recent examples are Alabama's abolition of its justice of the peace courts and replacement of them with legally trained district court judges in 1973 and Mississippi's agonizing process to adopt new rules of civil procedure in 1982. Such changes were fought for by the legal profession either through their organizations or—as in Alabama—through participation in broadly based blue-ribbon committees formed especially to achieve reforms.[18]

The one possible exception to the incremental pattern of reform could be in the manner in which judges are selected. As we have seen, an overwhelming percentage of judges in the South are ostensibly selected on a partisan election basis. The continued widespread use of this method is increasingly challenged by supporters of the merit plan in which the voters' role is significantly reduced. The history of judicial reform movements in the United States indicates the merit plan devotees will likely win.

Partisan election systems are certainly vulnerable to attack on many points, the most common accusations being that they produce judges of lesser quality, impair judicial independence, and lack accountability.[19] All three criticisms are applicable to varying degrees in the South, but the lack of empirical research makes it difficult to ascertain with precision the exact situation.

The quality argument usually states that because of the rigors of running a campaign, many successful lawyers refrain from seeking judicial office. A pool of high-quality legal talent, therefore, may be unavailable, whereas less-qualified lawyers who happen to have a propensity for shaking hands in malls and parking lots may be elected. In a recent poll of twelve Wyoming supreme court justices selected under the merit plan, eight of them stated that they would not have sought office under the elective system used until recently in that state.[20] Polling such a small sample is obviously weak evidence, but it does give some credence to the argument. Also, one can argue that it is difficult to identify any recent southern state judge chosen by election who has contributed significantly enough to jurisprudential thinking to receive widespread public acclaim. It is more likely that real judicial achievement has been attained by the southerners on the federal bench, who received their office through the appointment process.

This charge is mitigated by both the difficulty of identifying characteristics of a quality judge and the problems of isolating the reasons why

18. A brief description of Alabama's reform effort is contained in M. Roland Nachman, "Alabama's Breakthrough for Reform," *Judicature*, CVI (October, 1972), 112.

19. Dubois, *From Ballot to Bench*, 6–35.

20. R. Stanly Lowe, "Merit Selection in the Equality State," *Judicature*, CIX (February, 1976), 336.

persons do not seek elective judicial office. A brilliant practitioner, for example, might see the parade of cases and often bumbling advocates coming before the trial bench as essentially boring and opt out. Low salary and prestige, heavy work loads, and lack of administrative and political support are just a few of the many reasons that could explain a potential candidate's reluctance to run for office. Although the reduction in quality criticism receives widespread acceptance at an intuitive level, more studies need to be completed before the partisan election system is seriously called into question or eliminated on the basis of this charge.

The second major indictment of the partisan election system is that it impairs judicial independence. An elected judge, it is feared, will bow to the collective wishes of the community (his constituency) in meting out "justice," much to the detriment of the individual plaintiff or defendant, not to mention the law. Southern state judges, who are so much a product of the local culture, are no doubt sensitive to the political community.[21] Many civil rights activists accused of violating state laws were victims of this communal pressure, and when courts forced states to reform major institutions such as schools, mental hospitals, and prisons, it was the appointed federal judges who initiated the needed changes.[22] Even though state court judges are also responsible for enforcement of the federal Constitution, litigants most often prefer to argue their cases before the more insulated federal bench. Stories abound concerning criminal cases, particularly involving heinous acts, in which the state trial judge decides the case or sentences a defendant while looking over his shoulder.[23] It is admittedly difficult to identify the controlling variable in a judicial ruling, but the impairment problem is ripe for case studies.

The most substantial argument against popular election of state judges

21. For several case studies detailing the sensitivity of southern judges to the body politic see Leon Friedman (ed.), *Southern Justice* (New York, 1965). Discussions of civil rights lawyers' attempts to remove cases from southern state courts to federal courts are contained in Jack Bass, *Unlikely Heroes* (New York, 1981), 215–16, and Edward Heck and Joseph Stewart, "Ensuring Access to Justice: The Role of Interest Group Lawyers in the 60s Campaign for Civil Rights," *Judicature*, CXVI (August, 1982), 84.

22. Not only judges were influenced by local pressure, but members of the legal profession also succumbed to economic and social pressure. See Jack Oppenheim, "The Abdication of the Southern Bar," in Friedman (ed.), *Southern Justice*, 127–35. A good discussion of federal court reform in a southern state is found in Jethro Lieberman's, *The Litigious Society* (New York, 1981).

23. Unfortunately, many of these stories, although widely discussed among members of the bar, remain undocumented. Only the most outrageous trial court injustices, such as the Leo Frank case in Georgia or the Alabama Scottsboro case, receive scholarly attention. Some case studies of trial judge timidity are contained in Lovis Goldberg and Eleanore Levenson, *Lawless Judges* (New York, 1956), 67, and Howard James, *Crises in the Courts* (New York, 1977).

is that this creates a lack of accountability. Although this seems contradictory on its face, it appears to be largely true for a host of reasons. Existing studies of southern judicial elections suggest very low voter participation. Those who do vote often face virtually insurmountable problems in making rational choices, since the competition vital to clarifying a voter's options is largely missing from judicial elections. Indeed, sitting judges often run unopposed or with little real competition. As Atkins and Glick point out, it is a dramatic "exception to the rule" for an incumbent judge to lose an election.[24]

Compounding the problem is that in many states judicial candidates running for office are restrained by the Code of Judicial Conduct from addressing the issues in a campaign. This results in two campaign strategies, neither of which is particularly helpful to voters. The candidates may take the high road and focus campaigns on innocuous issues such as years in legal practice, bar memberships, or family ties in the community. Or they may resort to hyperbole to impress their name upon the public, producing a negative type of campaign usually filled with vague assertions and innuendo. For example, a candidate in 1982 for a trial judge post in Mississippi effectively used the slogan "Victims Have Rights Too," giving the subtle but clear message that the incumbent had been soft on criminals, whereas the new judge would be tough. The candidate defeated the incumbent judge, a rare accomplishment, but lost somewhere in the campaign was the reality that the incumbent had been a "law and order" judge when meting out criminal sentences. Thanks to professionally imposed constraints and such campaign hijinks, numerous scholars have concluded that judicial elections are "insufficiently salient" to the voting public.[25]

Another deficiency of the partisan election in the South is that it can effectively disfranchise a segment of the voting public. Many southern states have closed primary systems with the real judicial contest settled long before the general election. In a closed primary, voters must identify

24. Paul Nejelski, "The Tension of Popular Participation," *State Court Journal*, I (Fall, 1977), 29; Atkins and Glick, "Formal Judicial Recruitment and State Supreme Court Decisions," 447.

25. Charles A. Johnson, Roger C. Shaefer, and R. Neal McNight, "The Salience of Judicial Candidates and Elections," *Social Science Quarterly*, LIX (September, 1978), 371–78. See also Charles Sheldon and Nicholas P. Lourich, "Voters in Contested, Non-Partisan Judicial Elections: A Responsible Electorate or a Problematic Public?" paper presented at the Western Political Science Association, San Diego, March 26, 1982. The problem of constraints was first raised twenty-five years ago in John Wood, "State Judicial Selection: Realities vs. Legalities," *State Government*, XXXI (January, 1958), 17–19.

their party preference to receive either a Democratic or Republican primary ballot. Republican voters, therefore, are excluded from voting in the Democratic primary, which, for all practical purposes, is when state and local judges are chosen.

Lack of voters, issueless campaigns, and voter exclusion through closed primaries are not atypical in American politics. But what makes the judicial partisan election procedure particularly fraudulent is that a system of statutory measures and professional constraints has been imposed by legal associations, judicial commissions, and lawyers in the state legislatures so that the process can never really work effectively.[26] The major professional constraint imposed under the partisan election system is Canon 7 of the Code of Judicial Conduct, which forbids a candidate to issue any "pledge or promise of conduct in office" and, more importantly, prohibits statements concerning any "disputed legal or political issues."[27] One study of Florida judges on the implications of this restraint produced these findings: 92.6 percent of the judges felt it was inappropriate to take a stand on issues, 84.8 percent felt it was inappropriate to criticize the conduct of an opponent, and only 43.5 percent stated that it was acceptable for judicial candidates to speak at political rallies.[28] Canon 7 certainly makes it difficult to conduct a typical partisan election contest for the judiciary. And courts do enforce the code, as do legal and judicial associations.[29] In fact, the closer a state comes to approximating a true partisan election system, with real competition, debate on salient issues, and greater politicization, the greater the demand by legal and judicial professionals to change to a merit or nonpartisan selection procces.

Thus the constraints on the partisan selection system in the South do tend to substantiate the critics' charge of a lack of accountability. All southern states utilizing the partisan election have some means of replacing a judge who leaves the bench before his term expires. This process usually involves appointment by the governor and may entail legislative approval. Several studies have found that approximately one-half of all

26. Wood, "State Judicial Selection," 17–19.

27. Almost all states have now adopted the code either by legislative or state supreme court action. The proscriptions quoted here are found at Canon 7B(1)(c). For the complete code, see *American Jurisprudence 2d Desk Book* (Rochester, 1979), Item 90.

28. Burton M. Atkins, "Judicial Elections," *Florida Bar Journal*, L (March, 1976), 152.

29. For an analysis of recent cases see Clyde W. Curtis, "Judicial Ethics: Removal from Office for Political Activity," *Missouri Law Review*, XLVI (1981), 676; J. Scott Grey, "Ethical Conduct in a Judicial Campaign: Is Campaigning an Ethical Activity?" *Washington Law Review*, LVII (1981), 119; M. Truman Woodward, "What the Morial Decision Means," *Judicature*, LXI (April, 1978), 422.

the judges in partisan selection states are initially seated by an appointive process.[30] Since a sitting judge has an inherent advantage in the next election, the electorate's role has, in effect, been vitiated.

Truly, voters confronted with the type of election system described above face a dilemma. They are expected to make something of a rational choice in electing judges. But, lest the integrity of the judiciary be impaired, judicial candidates adhere to voluntary and/or mandatory restraints and do not speak to the issues. In modified one-party states and two-party states the voter can at least vote his or her party affiliation, which may lend some rationality and accountability to the system. But in the South there is often no viable two-party system operating in judicial elections at the state and local level.

Would changing to a merit or nonpartisan system be fairer to the voting public across the South? Experience in states with these systems suggests that a new type of political deception is often found which is just as detrimental to public forthrightness and accountability as the hollow partisan plan. The sop often given to the voter in the merit plan in order to win its adoption is that sitting judges chosen on a merit basis must periodically stand in elections to be either approved or disapproved by the voters. A judge must display near felonious tendencies in order to not be approved by the public. A 1980 study found that only 24 judges out of 1,499 had lost in these ratification elections.[31]

Pressure to force that majority of southern states still using the partisan election process to change to the merit system, the most prominent version of which is pushed by the American Judicature Society and American Bar Association, is certain to mount. However, the states ought to see whether their partisan election schemes could be made more workable and also examine other alternatives before rushing to embrace the merit system. Again, research and scholarly analysis of the situation would be helpful.

CONCLUSIONS

In regard to judicial structure, bureaucratization, and the standardization of procedural rules the South emulates the rest of the nation. A hier-

---

30. James Herndon, "Appointment as a Means of Accession to Elective Courts of Last Resort," *North Dakota Law Review*, XXXVIII (1962), 60; Atkins and Glick, "Formal Judicial Recruitment and State Supreme Court Decisions," 445; Arlen Coyle, "Judicial Selection and Tenure in Mississippi," *Mississippi Law Journal*, XLIII (1972), 90.

31. Susan B. Carbon, "Judicial Retention Elections: Are They Serving Their Intended Purpose?" *Judicature*, LXIV (November, 1980), 223.

archical court structure is in place, replete with the required bureaucratic outrigging to help cases flow up the appellate ladder. With the exception of the lack of appellate courts in Mississippi and Virginia and a continued reliance upon nonlawyer justices of the peace to resolve minor disputes, differences between the South and the rest of the nation in the formal attributes of judicial politics are slight.

Unlike the rest of the nation, however, a typical characteristic of the state judiciary in the South is the heavy reliance on partisan elections to select judges. And this, consequently, is the aspect of southern judicial politics most vulnerable to substantive change—partly because of the "paradox of the partisan judicial election." The paradox is, of course, that the closer a judicial election moves toward a real, competitive partisan situation, with substantial campaigning and political debate, the greater the demand by the legal-judicial elites for an appointive system based on merit. If the two-party system ever becomes so pervasive in the South that it reaches the lower ranks of state office seekers, then, given this paradox, the partisan election system might become extinct. Another force for change might simply be the hypocrisy of the present partisan election process. At best it is misleading, and at worst it effectively disfranchises (in closed primary states) a segment of the voting public.

A factor that may help force the southern states to remodel their judicial selection procedure is that economic and population growth have expanded the legal sphere of influence. Mississippi had 2,265 lawyers in 1970 and 4,325 in 1983.[32] Virginia had a larger increase in civil cases filed in 1981–1982 compared with 1977 than any other state in the union, and South Carolina and Louisiana finished second and third respectively in the annual increase in the nation in criminal cases filed in 1981–1982.[33] With such growth in professional ranks and the sheer number of decisions being rendered, the status of the legal-judicial elite will be heightened and their push for merit selection strengthened.

The forces for reform will meet the countervailing powers of southern history and political culture. Thus, any reform of the selection system will be slow and, like Florida's piecemeal change to the merit system, incremental. Perhaps the slow pace of the reform taking place will allow the requisite study to enhance the rationality of the process. Electorates need to be analyzed as do the backgrounds and decision-making patterns of southern state judges. Judicial campaigns and their financing need to

32. Curtis E. Coker, "President's Message," *Mississippi Lawyer*, XXIX (March–April, 1983), 5.
33. "Litigation Explodes Across USA," *USA Today*, February 28, 1983, Sec. A, p. 3.

be studied. It will be most unfortunate if the changes on the horizon are not predicated on solid empirical findings.

Another matter to be looked at carefully is the nature of the merit selection plan, which is often advocated by legal professional groups as the only alternative to the current system. Experiences in other states suggest that retention elections under merit appointment plans are as misleading in regard to viable voter participation as the South's partisan election mode of judicial selection. Also, the merit system may not eliminate politics as such, but merely substitute, to use Watson and Downing's phrase, "the Politics of the Bench and the Bar" for that of the populace.[34] Such politics take place at a subterranean level with no necessary guarantee of better qualified judges. As Flango and Ducat conclude in a useful recent study on judicial selection, the claim that the merit plan produces better judges or decisions should still be "treated as a research hypothesis, not a proven fact."[35] The caveat, then, is that southern states, without better evidence supporting the advantages of the merit plan, should not unnecessarily limit their selection reform efforts. Instead, once the studies recommended by Jewell are completed, creative alternatives should be explored. The path need not be limited to the traditional route from partisan election to the merit system plan.

Until more data are collected, it is difficult to predict a future course for southern judicial politics. Thus far the only surety is that pressure on the courts will intensify in correlation with the expansion of population, industrialization, and the legal profession. Given proper funding, most southern states have the structure and bureaucracy in place to attempt to cope with increased demands. But the greatest pressure for reform will occur in the area of judicial selection, particularly in the partisan election states. Such reform, however, should be to a system that is procedurally fair and honest and one that increases the opportunity for minority participation and selection.

34. Richard Watson and Rondal Downing, *The Politics of the Bench and the Bar: Judicial Selection Under the Missouri Non-Partisan Court Plan* (New York, 1969).

35. Victor Flango and Craig Ducat, "What Differences Does Method of Judicial Selection Make?: Selection Procedures in State Courts of Last Resort," *Justice System Journal*, V (Fall, 1979), 39.

The Bureaucratization of the South: From Traditional Fragmentation to Administrative Incoherence

Traditionalistic political cultures tend to be instinctively antibureaucratic because bureaucracy by its very nature interferes with the fine web of informal interpersonal relationships that lie at the root of the political system.
—Daniel Elazar (1972)

The contemporary bureaucratization of the South is a fine example of modernization. Governmental bureaucracy is, in fact, identified by the German sociologist Max Weber as one of the primary carriers of the faith in material progress and secular scientific humanism which some fear may seduce the South into the obviously dead-end growth mania of the North. Nevertheless, bureaucratization has occurred in the eleven states of the Old Confederacy, and it is important to grasp the implications of this fact for governmental processes in the South and, more generally, for southern political culture.[1]

This bureaucratic phenomenon is part of the ongoing Americanization of Dixie. The South has participated in the nationwide trends in this century toward the establishment of personnel merit systems based on the model of the national government, the reorganization of state government in a more centralized direction, and a series of administrative and fiscal reforms designed to improve the planning and policy control capacities of state government.

It is interesting that the modernization and professionalization of the

1. I mean the term *bureaucracy* to encompass not only large, hierarchical structures characterized by specialization, division of labor, and impersonality but also the rational and the nonrational behaviors and thought systems that accompany the structures.

administrative branch of government in the South have been so little re-marked by students of southern politics and culture. The essays included in William Havard's excellent *The Changing Politics of the South* do not comment on any of the major lines of bureaucratic development beyond brief references to the establishment of state departments of administration in North Carolina and Arkansas and a discussion of government consolidation in Florida. This is also true of other major works on southern politics published since World War II.[2] Like kudzu, the administrative elements of southern state governments have quietly grown and are on the verge of dominating the governmental landscape, while the attention of citizens and scholars has been focused on more spectacular flora such as resistance to desegregation, the civil rights movement, reapportionment controversies, and the revitalization of the national Republican party.

Viewed in a broad historical framework, the bureaucratization of the South can be seen as a response to problems engendered by urbanization, commercialization, the relatively weak economies of the southern states, and racial politics. The first two phenomena have led to the familiar nationwide problems of calls for broadened governmental services, the need for administrative regulation of business, and intense pressure on state finances. In the South, the weak state economies and the historical burden of racial politics have led to further bureaucratization through the interventionist developmental grant and personnel policies of the national government, as is explained below. As a result of all these pressures southern state governments have vastly expanded their activities in the areas of health and social services, education, recreation, and highway construction. They have also created a somewhat overblown, expensive, and incoherent administrative sector to implement policy in these areas. As many have noted, this developmental pattern in the southern states is similar to that experienced in this century by many developing nations in the Third World.[3]

In attempting to control these fiscal and administrative problems, reformers in the South—recently including many "New South" governors

2. William C. Havard (ed.), *The Changing Politics of the South* (Baton Rouge, 1972). See also Jack Bass and Walter DeVries, *The Transformation of Southern Politics: Social Change and Political Consequence Since 1945* (New York, 1976), Avery Leiserson (ed.), *The American South in the 1960s* (New York, 1964), and Allan P. Sindler (ed.), *Change in the Contemporary South* (Durham, 1963). V. O. Key, Jr., in his *Southern Politics in State and Nation* (New York, 1949), does present some anecdotal material on bureaucratic politics.

3. William H. Nicholls, "The South as a Developing Area," in Leiserson (ed.), *American South*, 22–40; Ira Sharkansky, *The United States as a Developing Country* (New York, 1975). The idea of governmental "incoherence" is developed in Ira Sharkansky, *Wither the State?: Politics and Public Enterprise in Three Countries* (Chatham, N.J., 1979).

and legislators such as Dale Bumpers and David Pryor of Arkansas, Jimmy Carter of Georgia, and State Senator Robert Crook of Mississippi—have mounted a two-pronged assault. The first, "political," prong seeks executive control through strengthening the office of governor, especially in budgetary matters. The second, "administrative," prong involves centralizing, rationalizing, and professionalizing the state administrative apparatus to make it more susceptible to gubernatorial control and to ensure more efficient and effective policy implementation. In what follows I will first discuss the history of administrative reorganization and civil service reform in the South and then argue that in undertaking these reforms the southern states have exchanged a traditional form of governmental chaos for another, more bureaucratic—but still incoherent—form. This development carries significant implications for the contemporary conditions and future prospects of southern government and politics.

TRADITIONAL FRAGMENTATION

By the 1950s, several historical and political trends had operated in the southern states to produce a great proliferation of independent plural-headed agencies and boards, the fragmentation of governmental functions and services, and the decentralization and diffusion of executive responsibility. Alabama provides an example of this development, which is roughly paralleled by events in the other states. Elton Smith and Henry Byrum have divided the history of administration in Alabama into three phases.[4] The first phase, legislative administration, lasted roughly from Alabama statehood in 1819 to the Civil War and was characterized by direct legislative control of executive branch agencies. The governorship during this period was largely a symbolic office. The second phase, that of elected executives, lasted roughly from the Civil War to the turn of the century. During this period control over administrative agencies flowed increasingly from the legislative to the executive branch, but power was divided between a number of executive officials elected independently of the governor.

The third phase, administration by boards, extends from the turn of the century to the present. During this period the independently elected executive officials continue to play a central role. In addition, the number of plural-headed agencies and boards increases substantially. Smith and Byrum report that there were 18 such boards in Alabama in 1875, and 98 in 1974. The creation of new agencies and boards on an ad hoc basis was an accelerating trend in Alabama. Four new agencies were created in the pe-

4. Elton C. Smith and Henry C. Byrum, *Alabama Reorganization* (Auburn, Ala., 1978), 4, 11–12.

riod 1900–1929, 21 were created in the 1930s, about 8 during the 1940s, and then from 1950 to 1977 there were 149 new agencies established. In the 1970s, Alabama was creating new administrative agencies and boards at the rate of 10 per year. Most of these agencies are engaged in regulation of business or the protection of persons and property.[5] The new agencies are mainly quasi-independent or plural-headed bodies.

This proliferation of agencies was not confined to the South. Morris Levitt and Eleanor Feldbaum have identified four main causes for a similar nationwide pattern.[6] First, state constitutional revisions during the late nineteenth and early twentieth centuries were premised in a distrust of strong central government and were therefore decentralist in tone. Second, there was an established tradition, dating from the Jacksonian period, of a "long ballot" that elected numerous state-level officials independent of the governor. Third, from the latter half of the nineteenth to the early twentieth century a reform movement aimed at divorcing administration from politics resulted in the promotion of the council-manager form of government at the local level, civil service reform, and the creation of state-level agencies independent of executive or legislative control. Finally, the accretion of new state-level responsibilities due to the problems following upon urbanization, suburbanization, and commercialization reinforced the pattern of fragmentation.

In addition to the reasons mentioned by Levitt and Feldbaum, the situation in the South was exacerbated by the weak position of governors and the strength of traditional local elites. In South Carolina, for example, in the late 1940s the governor was "little more than a ceremonial chief of state," presiding over a massively fragmented political and governmental system. Members of the South Carolina Senate and House all had their bases of power in various state agencies; they either controlled the agencies through appointment or actually sat on the boards and commissions through election by their fellow legislators. Each county was controlled by the county legislative delegation, with the state senator from the county usually acting as a political boss and running the county as a personal fiefdom. The county legislative delegations appropriated county funds, controlled appointments to county agencies, and fixed the county tax levy.[7]

Each of the southern states thus emerged into the latter half of the

5. *Ibid.*, 21, 37.
6. Morris J. Levitt and Eleanor G. Feldbaum, *State and Local Government and Politics* (Hinsdale, Ill., 1973), 18.
7. Key, *Southern Politics*, 150–52, 155.

twentieth century with dispersed and uncoordinated administrative structures often numbering two hundred or more agencies. Before Governor Jimmy Carter's Executive Reorganization Plan of 1972 was implemented, Georgia had more than three hundred state agencies. The problems of confused lines of political accountability, lack of fiscal control, and general chaos became so obvious and pressing that the stage was set for reorganization and reform.

STATE GOVERNMENT REORGANIZATION

There have been two waves of state government reorganization in this century. The first, dated roughly 1910–1940, focused mainly on the problems of fragmented structure, the proliferation of plural-headed boards and commissions, and the use of the long ballot.[8] This wave of reorganization was given impetus by President Taft's Economy and Efficiency Commission, which issued its report in 1912. No action was taken on the report at the national level, but many states established their own economy and efficiency commissions, and by 1940 over half of the states had undertaken substantial reorganizations.[9]

The results of these efforts in the South during this first wave are shown in Table 1. Tennessee, Arkansas, Louisiana, Mississippi, and North Carolina attempted substantial reorganizations on a bureaucratic "cabinet" model, whereas Alabama, Georgia, and Virginia attempted more "traditional" reorganizations of state-level agencies.[10] The degree of adoption of the reorganizations varied from low to high, but all the reorganizations in the first wave were doomed to failure because they took place before the great spurt in state governmental growth following

8. Neal R. Peirce, "Structural Reform of Bureaucracy Grows Rapidly," *National Journal*, VII (April, 1975), 502–508. See also Daniel R. Grant and H. C. Nixon, *State and Local Government in America* (Boston, 1982), 278–88.

9. Grant and Nixon, *State and Local Government*, 281.

10. The typology of reorganizations used in Table 1 was developed by James L. Garnett as a modification of previous work by George Bell. Garnett divides reorganization plans into three types: traditional, cabinet, and secretary-coordinator. A traditional reorganization is a half-hearted attempt that leaves more than 50 percent of department heads elected or appointed by the legislature, and more than 25 percent of post-reorganization agencies remain plural-headed boards. A cabinet reorganization is a more bureaucratic model that results in fewer peak agencies than the traditional, and from 50 percent to 66 percent of post-reorganization agency heads are appointed directly by the governor. Also, in a cabinet reorganization only 10 percent to 24 percent of post-reorganization agencies remain plural-headed boards. The secretary-coordinator reorganization results in very few peak agencies, almost no plural-headed boards, and more than 67 percent of the agency heads are appointed by the governor. For more detail on the typology, see James L. Garnett, *Reorganizing State Government: The Executive Branch* (Boulder, 1980), 47–48.

TABLE 1
First Wave of Reorganization in the South, 1923–1940

	Year of Adoption	Type of Reorganization	Adoption Mechanism	Degree of Adoption
Alabama	1932	Traditional	M.D.	Low
	1939	Traditional	Statute	M.D.
Arkansas	1929	Cabinet	Statute	Low
Florida				
Georgia	1931	Traditional	Statute	High
Louisiana	1940	Cabinet	Statute	M.D.
Mississippi	1932	Cabinet	M.D.	Low
North Carolina	1931	Cabinet	Statute	M.D.
South Carolina				
Tennessee	1923	Cabinet	Statute	High
	1937	Cabinet	Statute	M.D.
Texas				
Virginia	1927	Traditional	Statute	High

M.D. = Missing Data

SOURCE: Adapted from James L. Garnett, *Reorganizing State Government: The Executive Branch* (Boulder, 1980), Table A.1, pp. 176–92.

World War II. Agencies created in the 1940s and in the following decades were usually made independent of the reorganized structure, causing new incoherence.

The real importance of the first wave of reorganization is the set of ideas that informed the reorganization plans. In retrospect, a "reorganization orthodoxy" may be discerned which continues to guide the plans of reformers to the present day. The major assumptions of reorganization advocates are as follows:

1. Unity of Command: All plural-headed boards and commissions should be abolished, transferred to other departments, or headed by single administrators.

2. Executive Centralization: Administrative responsibility and authority should be concentrated in the governor by strengthening his appointment and removal power, increasing central staff services, removing limitations on gubernatorial terms, and placing ultimate budgetary power in the governor's office.

3. Functional Departmentalization: All agencies should be grouped in departments with broad functional responsibilities.

4. Narrow Span of Control: There should be as few departments as possible in order to enhance the governor's control and pinpoint responsibility.

5. Centralized Overhead Agencies: Short of full-scale reorganization, centralized departments of administration and/or finance should be established to oversee the personnel and/or fiscal processes of all state agencies and boards.

These five ideas are found—either explicitly or implicitly—in the Taft commission report, in the many state reorganization studies prepared by the Brookings Institution in the 1930s, in the report of Franklin D. Roosevelt's Committee on Administrative Management in 1937, and in the reports of the "Little Hoover Commissions" of the late 1940s and early 1950s. They provide the ideational substance of the two-pronged attack on administrative incoherence mentioned earlier. The central aims of the reorganization orthodoxy are political control by the governor combined with enhanced efficiency and effectiveness in the agencies. As Smith and Byrum wryly put it: "Salvation was to be achieved by structure."[11]

During the second wave of reorganization, which started in the early 1960s and continues into the 1980s, several new pressures and reasons for reorganization came into play. Many states were faced with an urban crisis demanding action. Some faced a fiscal crisis of tremendous proportions, since state expenditures nationwide tripled in the decade 1964 to 1974.[12] Also, implementation of the Supreme Court's decision in *Reynolds* v. *Sims* (1964), establishing population as the basis of representation in both houses of a state legislature, gradually produced a new breed of more professional state legislators (as documented in the essay by Bernick, Freeman, and Olson in this volume), and gave urban, suburban, and fiscal problems more salience. A new middle class grew in size and power in the metropolitan areas and began pressuring government for more and better services. New South governors such as James E. Holshouser, Jr., of North Carolina and Winfield Dunn of Tennessee began to appear on the scene and press for budgetary and policy power. Finally, the national government—in pursuit of a native son's Great Society programs in the 1960s—pressured the South through conditional grants-in-

11. Smith and Byrum, *Alabama Reorganization*, 46.
12. Peirce, "Structural Reform," 502.

aid and, after the passage of the 1972 State and Local Fiscal Assistance Act, through revenue-sharing requirements as well, to upgrade health, welfare, educational, and social services programs. Many of the grant-in-aid programs required state governments to comply with specified civil service, equal opportunity, and planning requirements which forced the state governments in the South to "modernize" their public employee systems and administrative structures in order to receive the federal largesse. These sorts of pressures began as early as 1939 with amendments to the Social Security Act which imposed merit system requirements for state workers involved with many grant-in-aid programs, notably those now overseen by the U.S. Department of Health and Human Services. In 1970 the Intergovernmental Personnel Act was passed, which provides state grants for improvement of personnel agencies and services.[13]

The second wave of reorganization brought a tremendous increase in the sheer size of government in the South. Tables 2 and 3 give some indication of this growth at both the state and local levels. The first point to make about the data in Table 2 is that "Sunbelt growth" was unevenly distributed through the southern states, with unusual growth only in Texas and Florida, as Timothy O'Rourke's fine essay in Part One makes clear. Sunbelt growth in the public sector certainly affected all the southern states, however. The greatest increases come in state-level employment, with only Florida and Louisiana registering percentage increases in state employees per 10,000 population less than in the United States as a whole, and the other states registering significantly higher increases. Much of the increase in state employment in the South was in education. Another significant factor was the disproportionate amount of federal grant money that went to the South during the period. In complying with federal grant requirements, additional employees were hired and new categories of employment, such as substate regional planning units, were created.

Table 3 shows further that the South was not playing "catch-up" in state employment, though they were in local employment. At the beginning of the period covered by the data in Table 3, the numbers of state employees per 10,000 population in the United States and in seven of the southern states were roughly comparable. By 1982, all but Florida and Texas had substantially more employees per 10,000 population at the state level than did the United States as a whole. At the local level, all but Florida and Texas had fewer employees per 10,000 population than did the United States, and by the end of the period covered by the table,

13. Grant and Nixon, *State and Local Government*, 290.

TABLE 2
Percentage Increase in State and Local Employment (FTE)
per 10,000 Population, 1957–1982

	Percentage Increase in Population	Percentage Increase in State Employment per 10,000 Population	Percentage Increase in Local Employment per 10,000 Population	Percentage Increase in Total Employment per 10,000 Population*
United States	35	100	61	71
Alabama	27	145	62	82
Arkansas	32	113	67	81
Florida	139	62	68	67
Georgia	50	152	87	102
Louisiana	41	78	74	75
Mississippi	23	123	78	89
North Carolina	38	109	92	97
South Carolina	42	148	64	88
Tennessee	36	136	65	81
Texas	69	148	82	94
Virginia	43	112	94	99

*Does not include state residents employed by the national government

SOURCE: Percentages determined from data in U.S. Department of Commerce, Bureau of the Census, *1982 Census of Governments*, Vol. 6, No. 4, *Historical Statistics on Governmental Finances and Employment* (January, 1985), Table 9, pp. 8–25.

seven southern states had achieved essential parity or surpassed the United States in the number of local government employees per 10,000 population.

The results, so far, of the second wave of reorganization are summarized in Table 4. Arkansas, Florida, Georgia, Louisiana, North Carolina, Tennessee, and Virginia undertook reorganizations, with four of these states opting for a traditional form and two for the cabinet model. Virginia attempted the most extensive reorganization yet seen in the South with its secretary-coordinator plan. By the early 1980s only South Carolina and Texas resisted reorganization pressures in both the first and second wave.

During this period, though full-scale reorganizations were rare, several other bureaucratic reforms were accomplished in the South. By 1980

TABLE 3
Absolute Increase in State and Local Employment (FTE)
per 10,000 Population, 1957–1982

	Number of State Employees per 10,000 Population		Number of Local Employees per 10,000 Population		Number of State and Local Employees per 10,000 Population*	
	1957	1982	1957	1982	1957	1982
United States	68	136	214	344	281	480
Alabama	64	157	198	321	262	478
Arkansas	73	156	180	301	253	457
Florida	71	115	219	367	289	482
Georgia	60	151	213	399	273	551
Louisiana	113	201	202	351	315	552
Mississippi	70	156	202	360	272	515
North Carolina	70	146	179	344	249	490
South Carolina	75	186	192	314	266	500
Tennessee	61	144	206	339	266	482
Texas	50	124	216	392	266	515
Virginia	83	176	168	325	252	501

*All numbers in table are rounded off; totals from first four columns may not add precisely.
SOURCE: U.S. Department of Commerce, Bureau of the Census, *1982 Census of Governments*, Vol. 6, No. 4, *Historical Statistics on Governmental Finances and Employment* (January, 1985), Table 9, pp. 8–25.

only Alabama, Arkansas, Mississippi, and Texas lacked a state department of administration. The creation of these departments has been a nationwide trend since the late 1940s. As Larry Sabato details in his essay, the office of governor in most of the South was greatly strengthened in monetary and budgetary matters, and five states rewrote their constitutions as part of their reorganization activities. Southern legislatures, as well, increased and improved their staff services.

CIVIL SERVICE REFORM

The replacement of "spoils" by merit hiring procedures in the personnel systems of the American states is an older and more familiar story than that of governmental reorganization. The merit system established by the 1883 Pendleton Civil Service Act at the national level became the model

TABLE 4
Second Wave of Reorganization in the South, 1959–1980

	Year of Adoption	Type of Reorganization	Adoption Mechanism	Degree of Adoption
Alabama	—			
Arkansas	1968	Cabinet	M.D.	M.D.
	1971	Cabinet	Statute	M.D.
Florida	1969	Traditional	Statute following constitutional amendment	Moderate
Georgia	1972	Traditional	Statute	High
Louisiana	1975	Traditional	Statute following new constitution	High
Mississippi	—			
North Carolina	1971–75	Traditional	Statutes following constitutional amendment	M.D.
South Carolina	—			
Tennessee	1959	Cabinet	Statute	M.D.
Texas	—			
Virginia	1972	Secretary-coordinator	Statute	High

*M.D. = Missing Data

SOURCE: Adapted from James L. Garnett, *Reorganizing State Government: The Executive Branch* (Boulder, 1980), Table A.1, pp. 176–92.

for those who wanted to reform the system of public employment at the state and local levels. The state of New York immediately set up a civil service commission and merit system based on the national model, and Massachusetts quickly followed in 1884. By 1900, eighty-five cities in the United States had set up civil service commissions, but it was not until 1905 that other states followed the lead of New York and Massachusetts. In that year Wisconsin and Illinois passed legislation creating merit systems overseen by civil service commissions. Serious and widespread reform efforts at the state level began in the 1930s, and by 1980 nearly all the states had reformed their personnel systems and had "general coverage" merit systems based on the Pendleton Act model.[14]

14. *The Book of the States, 1980–81* (Lexington, 1980), 248–49. "General coverage," of course, varies widely in each state.

Civil service reform in the South has followed the national trend. By the early 1980s, only Texas had not reformed its personnel system, though it did have a Merit System Council that covered employees engaged in activities funded by grants-in-aid from the U.S. Department of Health and Human Services. With the exceptions of Virginia and Arkansas, the rest of the states in the South have established merit personnel systems overseen by multimember independent or semi-independent boards appointed by the governor and/or by the legislature.[15] Arkansas and Virginia have personnel agencies headed by single administrators.

The basic purpose of civil service reform remains the creation of a neutral, open public service with appointment based on competitive examinations and offering guaranteed job security for officeholders. With the exception of Texas, the southern states have adopted these goals and have moved in an even more positive direction—away from the negative emphasis on simply protecting employees from political harassment, toward a more positive and active emphasis on attracting the best-qualified people to government employment. The aim, in other words, is the creation of a professional career service. State government employees in the South are no longer severely underpaid relative to employees in the private sphere. Southern state personnel systems now provide for medical insurance, life insurance, paid vacation time, sick leave, and retirement benefits comparable with those offered by non–southern states and many private corporations.

Mississippi is the most recent convert to a full-fledged merit system in the South, and its 1980 reform legislation, passed overwhelmingly by the Mississippi Senate and by a vote of 109 to 11 in the Mississippi House, fully expresses the modern aims of civil service advocates. The Mississippi law establishes a centralized State Personnel Board to administer the system, provides for equal opportunity in recruiting employees, mandates the use of competitive examinations, creates regularized pay scales, and sets up an Employee Appeals Board to hear the cases of employees who feel they were unfairly sanctioned or dismissed from their positions. The law also provides that no state employee can be obliged to contribute to any political fund or be removed or sanctioned for their refusal. Beyond these more traditional merit system functions the law directs the State Personnel Board to institute in-service training programs for state employees, to administer a state government internship program for uni-

15. *Ibid.*

versity graduate students in public administration, and to administer promotion and pay increases on the basis of actual performance.[16]

With regard to the sensitive issues of state employee unionization, collective bargaining, and strikes, state governments in the South are much more restrictive, but even here cracks have appeared in the southern dike. By the end of the 1970s some state employees were unionized in Arkansas, Florida, Louisiana, and Tennessee. Collective bargaining was allowed in Arkansas and Florida, but strikes were prohibited throughout the South.[17] Pressure to allow unionization and collective bargaining can be expected to increase over the next several years.

POLITICAL OUTCOMES OF REORGANIZATION AND CIVIL SERVICE REFORM

Two early post-reorganization experiences are instructive. Austin Peay won the governorship of Tennessee in 1927 on businesslike promises to "repeal laws and reduce government in Tennessee." He immediately developed and implemented the first major cabinet-model reorganization in the South by regrouping sixty-four disparate independent agencies under eight commissioners directly responsible to the governor. He claimed that the resulting efficiency saved the taxpayers over half a million dollars a year. Peay followed reorganization with tax reforms which actually increased the tax revenues of the state and then, using his new relationship with the agencies, "directed an expansion of the road system and public schools that cost far more than the savings from his reorganization."[18]

A second post-reorganization outcome which prompts reflection is the aftermath of the reorganization carried out in 1927 by Governor Harry Flood Byrd of Virginia. Byrd was a self-made businessman and heir to the old family political machine. He ran on a platform of efficiency, limited government, and opposition to state bond issues for highway construction. Once elected, he carried through a traditional reorganization that merged over a hundred agencies, boards, and commissions into fourteen departments. He also reduced the number of elected administrative officials. Byrd, like Peay, quickly increased taxes to build five thousand miles of highways by 1929. He also reduced taxes on capital investments, spearheaded a program to attract industry to the state, and championed state

16. Mississippi Senate Bill No. 2200, Regular Session, 1980, pp. 1, 2, 5, 8, 14.

17. *Book of the States*, 252–54.

18. George Brown Tindall, *The Emergence of the New South, 1913–1945* (Baton Rouge, 1967), 228–29.

regulation of insurance companies. The primary result of Byrd's reorganization was succinctly stated by historian George B. Tindall: "Ironically,
but not incidentally, the resultant centralization served to strengthen an
oligarchy headed by Byrd."[19]

These early reorganization episodes illustrate, first, that though reorganization is sold to the electorate as a means to reduce the size and scope
of government and increase efficiency and effectiveness, the actual results
are quite different. Herbert Kaufman has persuasively argued, in fact,
that administrative reorganization is never undertaken for its publicly
stated goals but is always primarily for political or policy purposes.[20]
During both Peay's and Byrd's administrations taxes were raised, the size
of government increased, and state intervention into the economy increased. It is clear that the administrative reorganization orthodoxy has
always been part of a larger movement toward executive leadership supported by progressives who emphasize the need for strong executives to
address the complex problems of modern society. Many of the studies
that led to restructuring during the second wave of reorganizations were
funded by planning grants from the U.S. Department of Housing and Urban Development.[21]

The more recent Georgia experience also illustrates the gap between
stated and actual reorganization outcomes. The Georgia reorganization
was widely believed to have resulted in the reduction of some 300 agencies to only 22, and its reputed success was an important part of Governor Jimmy Carter's successful bid for the presidency. Actually, of the 178
agencies supposedly terminated by the reorganization plan, only 65
agencies were funded and in operation in 1973 when the plan was implemented. According to one researcher, only 1 agency, the Georgia Educational Improvement Council, was actually terminated. The other opera-
tive agencies all still exist within the 22 "umbrella" departments created
by the reorganization.[22]

19. *Ibid.*, 229–30.
20. Herbert Kaufman, "Reflections on Administrative Reorganization," in Joseph A.
Pechman (ed.), *Setting National Priorities: The 1978 Budget* (Washington, D.C., 1986).
21. Larry Sabato, *Goodbye to Good-Time Charlie: The American Governor Transformed, 1950–1975* (Lexington, 1978), 68. For an excellent succinct analysis of the ideological underpinnings of administrative reorganization see Hugh L. LeBlanc and D. Tru-
deau Allensworth, *The Politics of States and Urban Communities* (New York, 1971),
107–11. See also Charles S. Hyneman, "Administrative Reorganization: An Adventure into
Science and Theology," *Journal of Politics*, I (February, 1939), 62–75, for a timeless discussion.
22. Thomas P. Lauth, "Zero-Base Budgeting in Georgia State Government: Myth and
Reality," *Public Administration Review*, XXXVIII (September–October, 1978), 426. See

Second, though the Byrd and Peay examples might seem to affirm the hopes of the state government reformers who have taken the two-pronged approach of strengthening the governorship and giving him streamlined administrative tools to work with, these hopes are false. The problem with the reorganizationist orthodoxy and the two-pronged approach to reform is that they are based on a fallacious "instrumental" view of bureaucracy which sees bureaucratic agencies as neutral tools of the political leaders of a government.[23] This is a convenient fiction when one is running for elective office, but it is a fiction nonetheless.

Peay and Byrd benefited from holding office in the immediate aftermath of reorganizations they themselves had spearheaded. But what of the next governor, and the next? Once a reorganization is effected, several factors militate against gubernatorial control of the state bureaucracy, the most obvious being the bureaucracy's sheer size and scope. Governors have a limited time in office and come in with a myriad of political commitments. They simply don't have time or opportunity to "master" an entrenched bureaucracy with its long-established practices. Many bureaucratic programs are mandated and protected by state or federal law and are beyond a governor's control.[24] The bureaucrats themselves are likely to enjoy the protection of tenure and appeals processes which insulate them from executive domination. Most importantly, the governor is dependent on the skill and expertise of the agencies due to the complexity of the problems facing modern state government, and this gives the bureaucrats an independent power base. The agencies also develop close ties with their clientele and other powerful groups and elites and often mobilize these allies against budgetary or programmatic attacks from the governor or the state legislature. Finally, as Levitt and Feldbaum have suggested, the expansion of the governor's own staff, a sort of "swelling of the governorship," further di-

---

also Herbert Kaufman, *Are Government Organizations Immortal?* (Washington, D.C., 1976).

23. Excellent discussions of the "instrumental" theory of bureaucracy and other competing theories may be found in Michael J. Hill, *The Sociology of Public Administration* (New York, 1972), and Charles Perrow, *Complex Organizations: A Critical Essay* (Glenview, Ill., 1979). The widespread acceptance of the instrumental theory of bureaucracy is one reason why historians and political scientists have dealt so cursorily with these developments. They do not see bureaucracy as having any historical or political "meaning."

24. These would include those agencies with "quasi-judicial" functions such as railroad and public service commissions which are made independent of the governor to achieve a degree of impartiality, and those agencies of a "quasi-commercial" nature such as insurance and retirement systems, packaged liquor monopolies, and toll road authorities which are made independent to achieve operating flexibility. See LeBlanc and Allensworth, *Politics of States*, 115.

lutes his or her control and power by creating yet another administrative layer between the governor and the line agencies.[25]

A contemporary example sheds further light on the real outcomes of reorganization. In 1971 Governor Jimmy Carter announced that zero-base budgeting (ZBB) would be implemented throughout Georgia state government as part of an overall administrative reform and reorganization. In 1973 ZBB was used for the first time in preparing the Georgia state budget. First developed in the private sphere and later adapted for application to public budgeting, the purpose of ZBB is twofold. First, it promises to overcome traditional "incremental" agency budgeting practices and lead to greater cost effectiveness by requiring all programs to be justified from a zero-base each year instead of assuming their previous year's budget as a given on which to pile incremental requests. Second, it is aimed at centralizing budgetary decision-making in the chief executive, or in centralized budget officials directly responsible to the chief executive, by requiring that more complete information on old, new, and alternative programs be sent up the hierarchy along with budget requests.[26]

Governor Carter's espousal of the two aims of ZBB is shown by statements in his 1971 budget message to the Georgia General Assembly: "No longer can we take for granted the existing budget base. . . . I will insist that the entire range of State services be re-examined and will cut back or eliminate established programs if they are judged to be ineffective or of low priority."[27] Thomas P. Lauth studied the implementation of ZBB in Georgia in detail and concluded that "ZBB has failed to fundamentally change the decision rules used by those who prepare budgets in the state of Georgia." He attributes this outcome to the political environment in which the agency budget makers operate. Only 8.6 percent of budgetary outcomes during the period Lauth studied were nonincremental reductions in department appropriations and no redirection of finances was discernible at the department level.[28]

Lauth cited several political constraints on the budget process which

25. Levitt and Feldbaum, *State and Local Government*, 330. For the presidential analogy see Thomas E. Cronin, *The State of the Presidency* (Boston, 1980).

26. Graeme M. Taylor, "Introduction to Zero-Base Budgeting," in Fred A. Kramer (ed.), *Contemporary Approaches to Public Budgeting* (Cambridge, 1979), 151, 157–58. See also Peter A. Pyhrr, "Zero-Base Budgeting," *Harvard Business Review* (November–December, 1970), 111–21, and Peter A. Pyhrr, *Zero-Base Budgeting: A Practical Management Tool for Evaluating Expense* (New York, 1973).

27. Lauth, "Zero-Base Budgeting," 420.

28. *Ibid.*, 424–27.

led to the relative failure of ZBB in Georgia, including constitutional and statutory requirements, public expectations of stable or increasing services, the impact of the legislative budget process, and regulations on state programs funded wholly or in part by federal grants-in-aid. Two additional bureaucratic constraints noted by Lauth deserve closer attention. Agency budget officers in Georgia cited perceived interest-group pressure as one reason for not fully complying with ZBB procedures. Interest-group support was seen as crucial to the maintenance of agency programs and power, and agency officials were therefore not likely to cut program budgets that enjoyed strong interest-group attention regardless of commands from above.

A second important bureaucratic constraint is found in the differing roles of agency budget officers and the central budget analysts in the Georgia Office of Planning and Budget (OPB). The OPB analysts were looking to cut agency requests and control overall spending in line with Governor Carter's wishes. The agency budget officers, predictably, were more loyal to their agency than to the Carter administration and were open advocates for their agency's programs regardless of gubernatorial preferences.[29]

To put the general point baldly, state government bureaucracy constitutes a "fourth branch" of government with its own interests, politics, policies, and power. Governors are hard pressed to exert competent control over administrative agencies in any case, and reorganization and civil service reform have actually strengthened the agencies against the executive. Because of time and political limitations, the governor must rely on the agency experts and often finds issues placed on the gubernatorial agenda by forces beyond his or her control. As Martha Weinberg points out, governors do not manage in the sense of continuous direction and control, they engage in "sporadic interventions" and "crisis management."[30]

The current emphasis on professionalism and credentialism in state administration in the South brings additional problems for executive control. Committed professionals develop strong ties outside of their agencies to regionally and nationally organized professional associations. They have an interest in implementing the most advanced level of service available — as defined by their professional associations — and in staying current with the latest techniques and concepts in their fields through

29. *Ibid.*, 426–27.
30. Martha Wagner Weinberg, *Managing the State* (Cambridge, 1977), 209.

continuous training.[31] These professional prerogatives may conflict drastically with a governor's program commitments.

CONCLUSION: ADMINISTRATIVE INCOHERENCE

Despite the hopes of reformers, reorganization and civil service reform merely substitute one type of incoherence for another. The key to understanding this is to see that bureaucracy is not just a set of organizational structures and processes; it is also a state of mind. "Believing that what his agency is doing for the public is vitally important, feeling that some programs are worth fighting for, or wanting to expand the prestige, scope and power of his agency, each administrator strives to insure that he is a successful combatant in the conflict between departments."[32] State-level bureaucratic agencies are in a perpetual war of all against all for funding, personnel, perquisites, and programs. We in the South have traded the crude fiscal irresponsibility, latent racism, and traditional elite control of the earlier system of fragmented government agencies for the professionalization, specialization, turf-guarding, and inflationary push of an incoherent bureaucratic structure.

It should be stated, if only briefly, that accompanying the transition have been some significant benefits to the South. At the material level there has been a deepening and broadening of government services. Better schools, improved social services, and paved roads are undoubted pluses. Other claimed material benefits, such as cost efficiency and balanced budgets, are not likely to materialize, for obvious reasons. Beyond this, civil service reform and federal pressure have institutionalized a commitment to equal opportunity. State government employment in many southern states is one of the most racially integrated sectors of the economy, although not at the decision-making levels, where blacks are still grossly underrepresented.

It is interesting to speculate on the broader impact of bureaucratization on the political culture of the South. As Daniel Elazar has noted, traditionalistic political cultures, such as those he identified in nine of the states of the Old Confederacy (Florida and Texas are the exceptions), tend to be "instinctively anti-bureaucratic." Bureaucracy is viewed negatively in traditionalistic cultures because it depersonalizes government; a spoils system under the control of traditional elites is seen, by political leaders at least, as superior to a merit system of public employment.[33]

31. Ira Sharkansky, *Public Administration: Agencies, Policies, and Politics* (San Francisco, 1982), 264.
32. Levitt and Feldbaum, *State and Local Government*, 235.
33. Daniel J. Elazar, *American Federalism: A View from the States* (New York, 1972), 100–102.

A certain folk wisdom persists in these traditionalistic views, of course, and it is especially fruitful to consider in this context the work of those who have been interested in the similarities between the less-developed states in the United States and the less-developed nations of the Third World. Sharkansky has noted that in less-developed nations and American states there is a politically significant gap between modern elites—who are young, urban oriented, well educated, and committed to economic, social, and political change—and traditional elites, who are opposed to change, committed to rural values, local customs, and indigenous religion.[34] This is obviously true, and the tension between the elite class of bureaucratic and corporate professionals and the more traditional legislative, executive, and business elites in the South will be a significant aspect of state politics for the foreseeable future, though the major battles of the war may be hidden from public view.

There is also an antidemocratic consequence that seems inescapable. Under the traditionalistic regime of the South the citizenry, black and white, was locked out of power by entrenched economic and political elites committed to the maintenance of a racially segregated and economically stratified society. In the past twenty-five years much has changed, as demonstrated by the other essays in this book. But a tragic continuity exists as well; the people are still locked out of power. Precisely at the point when the civil rights movement began the enfranchisement of blacks, effective political and governmental power began shifting from the elected officials in the South to the new professional bureaucratic elites. As a result, the recent liberalization of the suffrage in the South is, to some degree, rendered symbolic.[35]

We could continue and discuss the bureaucratic horrors of goal displacement, the Peter Principle, trained incapacity, and Parkinson's Law, but enough has been said to demonstrate the importance of the bureaucratization of the South in understanding politics in the region. A quiet bureaucratic revolution has occurred, and it will take decades before its full impact can be assessed. In the meantime one thing is certain: like kudzu, it will always be with us.

34. Sharkansky, *Public Administration*, 276.
35. For a different perspective, see Marcus E. Ethridge, "Regulatory Policy Administration and Agency-Citizen Linkages in Southern States: Some Hypotheses and an Exploratory Analysis," in Laurence W. Moreland, Tod A. Baker, and Robert P. Steed, (eds.), *Contemporary Southern Political Attitudes and Behavior: Studies and Essays* (New York, 1982), 268–85.

Continuity and Change PART FOUR

Truly much is new in southern politics. Yet we must never forget that much remains as well from the old politics. Just a brief list of persisting patterns drawn from the essays in the volume would include at least the following:

The South still suffers the lowest per capita incomes, only 85 percent of the national average in 1980.

It remains the least-industrialized region; many plants only recently moved from the Frostbelt are skipping over the South to relocate in the Third World.

Growth remains keyed to federal spending for infrastructure improvements and defense.

A larger percentage of the South's citizens than those of other regions still live below the poverty level, including some one-quarter of all Mississippians, with their fate tied to federal social programs.

The philosophy of the limited state implemented by the Bourbons in the late nineteenth century in reaction to the spending of Reconstruction governments holds strong, with the region making less effort to raise revenue than elsewhere; only Louisiana ranks in the top one-half of the fifty states in terms of taxes per thousand dollars of personal income.

The South continues to do less for its poor, devoting only 9 percent of its revenues to social programs versus 14 percent in the Frostbelt.

Southern workers are still far less unionized than those of any other region.

Racist symbols remain, from "Dixie" to the Confederate flag to the statues of the small black boy holding a fishing pole that one finds occasionally on lawns when driving the back roads.

The KKK still lives, as do segregation academies, and segregated clubs such as the famed one in Augusta which President Reagan visited in late October, 1983.

Blacks and whites still split over social welfare programs.

The Old South effort at vote denial has given way to the New South practice of vote dilution by rampant racial gerrymandering, selective annexation, the runoff primary requirement found in nine states of the Old Confederacy, the dual registration system only recently dismantled in Mississippi, inconvenient registration hours and locations, at-large elections, and appointive offices.

Political behavior is polarized along racial lines, with blacks holding no more than 3 percent of the South's political offices, though constituting some 20 percent of the population.

The Bourbon South's tradition of nonparticipation and the legacy of a constricted electorate means southern turnout continues to lag behind national levels.

State Democratic parties remain factionalized, disproving at least one of Key's predictions.

Socialization of the Solid South generation of whites to local Democratic politics persists.

Republicans remain very much a minority, a party built from the top down with a narrow base in the electorate.

Campaigns, much as in Solid South days, are still often more entertainment than instruction, with the thirty-second television spot serving the same purpose as the political huckstering at the "forks of the creek" in the old days.

Manipulation of symbols and a lack of substance in campaigns continue.

Judges, governors, bureaucrats, and—to a lesser degree—congressmen, senators, and state legislators tend still to be overwhelmingly white Anglo-Saxon Protestant males—Democrats with business or law backgrounds.

These officials are conservative on fiscal and social welfare issues (and southern state legislatures were the burial ground for the ERA).

The "Boll Weevil" faction in the U.S. Congress remains the swing bloc which often gives conservative Republicans their winning vote totals.

As noted in the Preface, the intertwining of these traditions with the new politics is often baffling. This uneasy mix of past and present in contemporary southern politics was well illustrated in the October, 1983, congressional decision to honor that most important of twentieth-century southerners, Dr. Martin Luther King, Jr., with a national holiday.

Senator Jesse Helms, a North Carolina Republican, led the opposition, invoking the time-honored southern strategies of first the possibility of a filibuster and then, failing to gain support, the submission of several amendments, five in all. These ranged from one to recommit the bill to the Judiciary Committee to one that would ban the King holiday until a holiday was also declared in honor of Thomas Jefferson. Unsuccessful on these, Helms attacked King's reputation, charging him with links to the Communist party and with "action-oriented Marxism." Helms also proposed an amendment to obtain Senate access to all federal records on King. His lawyers along with those of the New Right (which has deep southern roots formed in the Wallace and Goldwater campaigns) filed suit in U.S. district court in Washington, D.C., to get the papers released. Judge John Lewis Smith, Jr., refused their requests and declared that the records will remain sealed until 2027.

Exercising leadership on the other side of this issue was another southerner, a New South type, Senate Majority Leader Howard Baker (R-Tenn.). Baker ensured quick consideration of the bill, helped defeat the amendments, and intervened between Helms and Senator Edward Kennedy (D-Mass.) when the two tangled. He also spoke movingly for the legislation, declaring, "I have seldom approached a moment in this chamber when I thought the action we are about to take has greater potential for good." And, "We intend to acknowledge and to celebrate the nobility of all of our citizens in the opportunity which they must have to participate in the fullness of America's future."

This debate and political struggle thus reveal both the old style and the new orientation present in contemporary southern politics. In the final analysis even "Ole Strom" Thurmond voted for the legislation, being, like Wallace, a bridge from the old to the new politics. In a wonderfully appropriate historical coincidence, the new holiday honoring King falls on the same day on which Alabama—"The Heart of Dixie," as it likes to bill itself—customarily honors the great General Robert E. Lee!

How to dispense with the bad old traditions, those elements of our historical nightmare, as a Marx would call it, yet retain that which is valuable and meritorious—Egerton's "sense of history, grace and space, of soul," that "talent for defining the commonweal" Percy refers to—is the task before the South at this moment. It is a large task indeed, and there are no certain guides. Yet the appropriate questions must be posed and seriously pondered, for it is the unique ability of mankind to query the future. And it is therefore fitting for this study to close with a fine and provocative essay by Cecil L. Eubanks on these very matters.

Eubanks begins by reviewing and summarizing the dramatic changes characterizing contemporary southern politics which the contributors to this work have explored so well. He then turns to the task of placing these transformations within a theoretical and explanatory perspective which illuminates their collective meaning and significance. For that, Eubanks draws on Daniel Elazar's analysis of the three competing subcultures undergirding American politics, finding that the South's changes turn on a crucial transition in its "traditionalistic" political culture. Eubanks then evaluates the turn to modernity in southern politics, echoing some of the cautions raised as far back as the 1920s and 1930s by the Agrarians, and also by Flannery O'Connor and Percy. He closes with a thoughtful, hopeful plea for the future.

Contemporary Southern Politics: Present State and Future Possibilities

CECIL L. EUBANKS

> Why do they come? What do they seek?
> Who build but never read their Greek?
> —Donald Davidson
> "On a Replica of the Parthenon"
>
> The happiness of the South drove him wild with despair.
> —Walker Percy
> The Last Gentleman

A remarkable paradox of modern American politics is that in the past two decades, the region of the country least sympathetic to change, the South, appears to have changed the most. Documenting that change is not difficult. It begins, no doubt, in the postwar migrations of thousands of non-natives to the South, immigrants who brought with them, as we shall see, political experiences and cultural beliefs decidedly different from those of the Old Confederacy. The removal of the stigma of racism following the passage of numerous civil rights acts, accompanied by the growing realization that the North had significant racial problems of its own, obviously encouraged migration to the South. Important as well were the federal projects in defense, water navigation, electrification, and highway construction. More significant factors, however, were the combined attractions of climate, lower taxes (both personal and corporate), and growing local markets. The result of this has been the reentry of the Old South into the political and economic mainstream of the nation.

This growth and accompanying migration led, of course, to greater economic diversification and growing urbanization. Atlanta, Houston, and Miami became important centers of commerce, and the South became, for the first time, a region in which the majority of its population lived in metropolitan areas. As competing economic interests invaded the

South and its newly created cities, the political climate was characterized by two significant developments: greater political competition and an increased demand for public services. Thus, the role and nature of government in the lives of southern citizens changed dramatically.

But, the changes wrought in the politics of the South are more immediately and fundamentally built upon the presidency of a native son, Lyndon Johnson, and the passage, during his administration, of one of the most far reaching pieces of legislation in modern history, the Voting Rights Act of 1965. It is from this act and this presidency that a veritable pyramid of political reform has emerged, much of it documented in the preceding essays of this collection.

Electoral rules in general have changed more dramatically in the South than anywhere else in the nation. Gone are poll taxes, literacy tests, and white primaries, as well as less subtle methods of voter discrimination. The impact of the Voting Rights Act and of the reapportionment revolution has dramatically altered the character of southern elections. Most obvious of these changes is the enfranchisement of the black voter and the subsequent election of black public officials for the first time since Reconstruction. An equally important change has been the greater degree of party competitiveness in presidential and statewide elections. (The election of Jimmy Carter in 1976, signifying the return of the South to the Democratic party—with the exception of Virginia—was quickly reversed in 1980. Then only Georgia remained in the Democratic presidential column.) As the opportunity for political expression increased for blacks as well as whites, the predicted growth of the Republican party at the state and local level has not materialized as rapidly as expected. Political attitudes change slowly and are more dependent upon environmental agents of socialization.

Although two-party competition is coming to the South slowly, the image-producing media campaign has entered southern politics very quickly. The new metropolitan, commercial centers of the South have also become communications centers. From their midst comes the new campaign expert, as well as the technology necessary to use that expertise. The professional campaign consultant has permeated southern elections at all levels, taking advantage of weak local party organizations and equally weak factions that exist in the dominant, Democratic party. Candidate style and image have become considerably more important, as has the ability to pay for the expenses of media campaigning. The millionaire governor, for example, is not uncommon in the New South.

Nonetheless, the impact of the Voting Rights Act, a broader-based electorate, and court-ordered redistricting has created conditions for the emergence of new and sometimes more progressive faces in southern politics. The new governors, for example, are likely to be younger, better educated and, in general, better equipped for the task of being governor. Moreover, the institution of the governorship has made significant gains in the last two decades. One-term limitations have given way to two-term limitations. As mentioned earlier, statewide gubernatorial elections are becoming increasingly competitive in terms of two-party democracy. Five southern states have completely abandoned their archaic constitutional structures, creating stronger, more responsible chief executives. The result has been a new breed of governor with increased racial moderation, fiscal conservatism, and some concern for tax reform, environmental protection, and education.

Accompanying the new governorships has been a correspondent reform of state legislatures and bureaucracies. The demands of increasing industrialization and urbanization in the South have been sufficient to generate appeals for more and better-quality public services. The typical state legislature of the Old South, poorly staffed and consisting of part-time, low-salaried legislators, was not very well equipped to meet these newly created demands. Electoral reforms have resulted in a broader political recruitment base for state legislators. Better pay and full-time legislators, increased professionalism in staff, and improvement of resources available to legislatures, such as computerization, have been common institutional reforms of the past two decades. These new tools of professionalism have given the state legislatures the resources to attempt more effective legislative oversight of state governmental programs. Ironically, legislative reform has also created a more competitive advantage for state legislatures as they confront the increasingly strong chief executives of the states and demand a correspondingly greater role in state decision-making. This transformation of state legislatures and governors has, finally, given the states a more effective base from which to compete for power and authority within the federal system and with the national government.

As Max Weber made abundantly clear at the beginning of the twentieth century, modernization, industrialization, and urbanization cannot occur without the development of public administration. The states of the South have followed this pattern of development by expanding their bureaucracies and reforming them. Personnel merit systems, centralized government authority, administrative and budgetary reforms designed to enhance the states' ability to plan and control policy efficiently: all are present in the political development of the southern states. It was, of course, inevitable. As the activities of state governments increased, in health, education, social services, and a host of other fields, an administrative sector was necessary to implement these policies.

Finally, the expansive programs of Lyndon Johnson's Great Society, designed in part to upgrade the services of state governments, also required that the states "modernize" their administrative structures. The South has indeed come of age in this final layer of the pyramid of contemporary governmental reform. On the base of increased citizen participation and expectation have been built more competitive party systems, stronger and more professional state legislatures and chief executives, large metropolitan areas of commerce and politics, and ever-expanding public bureaucracies. Change in the South, to repeat, has been dramatic. That change, however, needs to be placed in a broader theoretical and explanatory framework, and it needs to be subjected to at least a cursory evaluative analysis.

POLITICAL CULTURE AND CHANGE IN THE SOUTH

The broader theoretical framework which seems best suited to an analysis of change in the New South is a very provocative analysis of political culture by Daniel Elazar in *American Federalism: A View from the States*.[1] Political culture is a composite of the beliefs, behavior patterns, and perspectives of a people. It is rooted in their historical experiences and transmitted from generation to generation through the process of socialization and acculturation. In identifying those facets of a political culture that are important to an understanding of American states, Elazar focuses on three ingredients: the beliefs and expectations of a people, both the general public and politicians, about the nature of politics and government; the question of who are the legitimate activists in the political system, from officeholders to bureaucrats; and how the activities of governance are practiced by citizens and politicians in the context of their perceptions about politics and legitimacy.

Using these criteria, Elazar argues convincingly that the national culture of the United States is a synthesis of three major subcultures, which he calls *individualistic, moralistic,* and *traditionalistic.* Each subculture is a Weberian ideal type and not a full description of reality. Nonetheless, each political subculture can be found in the political systems of the United States, often with a very specific regional orientation.

The individualistic political culture views human existence as essen-

1. Daniel J. Elazar, *American Federalism: A View from the States* (New York, 1972), 84–126.

tially a collection of private concerns. Government is given the task of encouraging private initiative and access to the marketplace. Indeed, the political order itself is seen as a marketplace where systems of negotiation and bargaining are built on mutually obligatory relationships. More often than not, these take place in the context of a strong party system built upon loyalty. The party is the mechanism for restraining and regulating the system of mutual obligations. Essentially nonideological, the individualistic model is not particularly concerned with abstract notions of the common good. Politics is a business, where professionals distribute the rewards of political power. Not surprisingly, among the general public, politics is likely to be viewed as corrupt, perhaps necessarily so.

The moralistic political culture regards politics as the common, public search for the good life. Questions about the content of that public good are the proper concern of politicians and the general public. Therefore, widespread public participation is encouraged; indeed, citizens have a duty to participate in the public realm. This concern for the common good takes precedence over party and personal loyalties. In fact, the positive image of politics common to this culture often leads citizens and politicians alike to support nonpartisan political activity, thereby opening the political system to "amateurs." As might be expected, the citizens of this culture show considerably less toleration for corruption in political life. Because of the positive image of politics taken by the moralistic political culture, governmental intervention in economics and social existence is encouraged, although usually on a very local level.

The traditionalistic political culture is suspicious of the marketplace mentality of the individualistic political culture and much more elitist in its conception of the common good than the moralistic culture. As its name implies, the traditionalistic political culture looks to the past, a preindustrial past, of strong social and family bonds. Government has an important role in this culture, the maintenance of traditional order; but citizen participation is limited to a paternalistic elite. Political competition takes place not on a party level but on the level of factional alignments which are extensions of the traditional social ties that are so common to this culture. Political leaders are the guardians of the traditionalistic culture.

Elazar is quick to warn against regarding any one of these three cultures as superior to the other. Each has its strengths and weaknesses. Whereas the moralistic culture brings with it a continuing concern for the good society, that concern has often taken fanatical and narrow-minded expression. The individualistic model has contributed greatly toward the toleration and acceptance of divergent groups into its pluralistic culture, but often at the expense of an equally tolerant attitude toward political corruption. Finally, the traditional culture is frequently not very tolerant of major groups of citizens and has a legacy of denying rights to significant portions of its citizens. Yet, that same culture searches diligently for stability and continuity and, in the process, often produces a unique collection of political leaders.

Elazar maintains, again in very thorough and convincing fashion, that the political cultures summarized above are reflections of three distinct migrations in American history and exist, consequently, in three distinct regions of the country. The Puritans of New England, with their visions of establishing "the city on the hill," brought their moralistic political culture with them as they moved westward from New England across New York into northern Pennsylvania, Ohio, and most of Michigan, Wisconsin, Minnesota, and Iowa, establishing, along with their Scandinavian counterparts, a greater New England.

Non-Puritan English and German settlers occupied the middle states in the colonies and migrated into southern Pennsylvania and central Ohio, as well as Indiana, Illinois, and Missouri, reinforced by immigrants from western Europe. Their political culture was highly individualistic.

The southern colonies were settled by an Old World landed gentry, intent on perpetuation of a plantation slave system at the exclusion not only of slaves but of individual small property holders. These inhabitants of Virginia, the Carolinas, and Georgia moved westward into Alabama and Mississippi, taking their traditional culture with them. Louisiana, which was settled by the French, shared this same political culture. Our concern here is primarily with this third cultural model, the traditionalistic, with its presence in the Old South and with what is happening to that culture as the New South emerges.[2]

The Old South was, to a large extent, based upon an aristocratic agrarian myth. Its common historical experience of slavery and war made it, for decades, the most distinctive region of the United States. Its aversion to change, partly attributable to its traditionalistic culture, partly to its forgotten status, as the rest of the nation hastened into industrialization after the Civil War, kept it isolated. As a result, the South retained its identity to a greater degree and for a far longer period of time than any of the other regional manifestations of political culture. Ironi-

2. Elazar's discussion of cultural migrations takes into account the exceptions to the major patterns that dominate American westward migration, for example the settlement of the moralistic Scotch-Irish in the mountains of Virginia, the Carolinas, and Georgia. See *ibid.* 104–14.

cally, its strong regional coherence kept its influence alive nationally. The adoption, after the Civil War, of the Thirteenth, Fourteenth, and Fifteenth amendments to the United States Constitution represented an attempt to replace the traditionalistic culture of the South with the individualistic and moralistic cultures of the North. As Reconstruction ended, however, the Solid South emerged in the United States Congress and was able, with the willing assistance of northern politicians, to thwart congressional implementation of those amendments for almost a century.[3] This intransigent defense of a culture that had been defeated on the battlefield contributed even more to the regional identity of the Old South, some would say to a siege mentality.

The region maintained its traditionalistic culture at home as well. The states of the South were characterized, as are all traditionalistic cultures, by low voter turnout, even among those who were allowed to participate. Elite participation in politics was the norm, with a high degree of personalism attached. This is amply demonstrated in the close association of traditional southern state politics with family ties: the Byrds in Virginia, the Longs in Louisiana, and the Talmadges of Georgia. Further evidence of this personalism was the political competition that took place along factional lines within the dominant Democratic party. Executive power was viewed with suspicion; the southern governors were notoriously weak, even in contradistinction to southern legislatures that could hardly be characterized as strong, but were relatively so. Power was centralized in the Old South but largely inactive, at least so far as policy innovation was concerned. Local governments had neither the desire nor the resources to assume responsibility for expansion of educational and social services. The policy direction of the traditionalistic system was primarily designed to maintain the existing status quo. Tragically, this was most evident in the bitter stand taken by the region on matters of racial equality.

As we have seen, much if not all of this has changed, dramatically changed, in the last two decades. It is not difficult to see why and how, given Elazar's cultural framework of analysis. Whereas the migrations of southerners to northern cities immediately before and after World War II would take a traditionalistic culture into an individualistic and moralistic environment, it was not until the 1960s and 1970s that the reverse became true. The Sunbelt migration, hinged as it was to economic development, brought to the Old South an individualistic culture, with a few moralistic overtones, and created a South in cultural crisis. This transformation of

3. *Ibid.*, 172–73.

the South from a traditionalistic culture to an individualistic culture, or some combination of the two, presents a fascinating political scenario, as well as some considerable cultural misgivings on the part of southerners.

The Voting Rights Act, especially with the accompanying civil rights movement, had a strong moralistic character to it, as did the judicial drive for electoral redistricting, but the pyramid of reform based on those actions is distinctly individualistic in character. Participation among the southern electorate has increased, but campaigns have taken on the character of public relations enterprises conducted by professionals. The political recruitment base has been expanded, at least for state legislative posts, but a professional elite seems to be replacing the personal oligarchies. Political parties, though stronger at the state level, are still highly factional at local levels. More important, the newly emerging parties of the South are not issue-oriented organizations that look to officeholding as a means of implementing programs. They are typically individualistic in their orientation as they look to political power as a means of distributing rewards.

The New South legislatures and governors are characterized by a greater sense of professionalism and responsible location of power, which is often associated with a moralistic culture; but they are more characteristic of pluralistic individualism, with strong interest-group involvement in policy formulation and review. Their "progressivism" is often limited to race and governmental reform and does not extend to economic and social welfare issues. Indeed, one particularly astute observer of the New South noted that listening to the pronouncements of politicians from "both parties who are attempting to translate business issue-orientations into public policy" (a typical feature of the individualistic culture) was like being "transmigrated into the McKinley era."[4] It would appear that at least on some social welfare issues, the populist predecessors of the New South governors were more "progressive."

It could be argued that the New South bureaucracies constitute a moralistic concern for the proper and professional implementation of public policy, yet the Old South, traditionalistic distrust of bureaucracies remains strong. The reform bureaucracies of the New South have loosely constituted merit systems designed to continue awarding some small advantage to favor and patronage, and they are laden with interest-group involvement (a common characteristic of an individualistic cultural orientation).

These observations that the modern South has come into close contact

4. William C. Havard (ed.), *The Changing Politics of the South* (Baton Rouge, 1972), 25.

with and been deeply affected by an individualistic culture should come as no surprise. Much of the impetus for reform, much of the migration into the new urban areas of the Sunbelt was and is economic. That is the *modus operandi* of the individualistic culture. In this sense, southern isolation has ended, and the South has finally become a part of the nation, for the individualistic cultural model has come to dominate national political life as well.

These reforms and the subsequent incorporation of the South into the Union have given some southerners, native and immigrant, reason for critical reflection. Whereas there is nearly universal joy over the demise of racist public policy, considerable doubt remains about the wisdom of replacing a traditionalistic culture with an individualistic one. The first musings about the dangers of modernity in the politics and social life of the South came from a group of unashamed southern traditionalists writing in the 1920s, the Agrarians. It is to them and to their modern counterparts that we turn for an evaluation of the changes that have occurred in the New South.

THE AGRARIANS AND THE SEARCH FOR CONTINUITY

In 1930 a group of southern intellectuals issued a manifesto in the form of a collection of essays entitled, *I'll Take My Stand: The South and the Agrarian Tradition.*[5] The collection was a vigorous defense of the traditionalistic culture of the South, although its authors did not use Elazar's phrase. Instead, they argued against the dominant culture of American society, the industrial, and for their own culture, the agrarian. Their opening statement of principles put the matter succinctly: "All [of the authors] tend to support a Southern way of life against what may be called the American or prevailing way; all as much as agree that the best terms in which to represent the distinction are contained in the phrase, Agrarian versus Industrial."[6]

What were those characteristics of the agrarian (traditionalistic) culture that they wished to preserve? Conversely, what were those characteristics of the industrial (individualistic) culture they warned against? Again, their joint statement of principles clearly delineated their hope and their warning. The admonition consisted of an observation that the South showed signs of wanting to join the rest of industrial America under the euphemism "the new South." That temptation ought to be re-

5. Twelve Southerners, *I'll Take My Stand: The South and the Agrarian Tradition*, introduction by Louis D. Rubin, Jr. (Baton Rouge, 1977).

6. *Ibid.*, xxxvii.

sisted. Industrialism needed to be examined more carefully and critically. The hope consisted of an invitation to all sympathetic communities to become members of a national agrarian movement.

Industrialism, for the Agrarians, signified a society that had chosen to invest its economic resources in applied sciences to an extravagant and uncritical degree. The purpose of a technology was to render labor more effective and enjoyable. Yet industrialism had achieved neither end. In its frenetic search for more and more laborsaving devices it had only managed to increase the tempo of labor and to make it more insecure. The cure-all of applied science, more and bigger machines, was self-defeating! In a fashion reminiscent of the early Marx, the Agrarians argued that industrialism had brutalized the labor process. (It should be noted that they were unaware of the early Marx and were very critical of the excessive optimism and collectivism of the socialists.) The inevitable consequences of industrialism in American life were overproduction and the attendant drive toward the ever-increasing consumption of those products. Accompanying this transformation of the public into steadfast consumers would necessarily be the rise of modern advertising, designed to persuade the consumers to want and need the products applied science could furnish them.

More fundamentally, industrial, urban societies, the Agrarians contended, present a highly simplified form of nature, a form in which humans are deluded into thinking that nature can be conquered. Lost in the industrial mind is any sense of the mysterious and contingent in nature. Lost, essentially, are both the religious and the artistic perspectives. Gone as well are the simple amenities of life, such as hospitality, conversation, family life, romantic love, and manners. Religion, the arts, and sociality are all dependent upon the "right relations of man-to-nature" and on "right relations of man-to-man." Industrialism perverts those relations.

The Agrarians believed simply that the ethos of industrial life was too debilitating to the human spirit to be desired. They called their agrarian ideal a "genuine humanism" rooted in the soil and appreciative of the culture of work and leisure surrounding the soil; and they argued that if we did not summon the political resources necessary to recall this ideal, we would be doomed to an existence of impotent aimlessness.[7]

The statement of principles in *I'll Take My Stand* said little more than what is summarized above. The essays that followed were very disparate. Some, like Robert Penn Warren's defense of segregation in "The Briar

7. This discussion of the Agrarian philosophy is based on their collective statement of principles at the beginning of *I'll Take My Stand*, entitled "Introduction: A Statement of Principles," *ibid.*, xxxvii–xlviii.

Patch," though consistent with the traditional plantation agrarianism of the Old South, were contradictory to the very spirit of a call for renewed human dignity. Warren later repudiated this stance, as did John Crowe Ransom and Allen Tate. Others appeared to be longing for a restoration of plantation aristocracy and have been dismissed as excessively atavistic. Nonetheless, stripped of its racism, devoid of its romantic, agrarian economic simplicities, and removed from its legitimate protest against the treatment of the South as a conquered province to be colonized, *I'll Take My Stand* is an impressive declaration of cultural war on the North and on industrial, individualistic modernism. The essays that still evoke interest are those that recall the romantic dream of the good life, the traditional life, the life of leisure, of religion, of customs and good manners.

In a conference on *I'll Take My Stand*, held in 1980 to commemorate the fiftieth anniversary of its publication, the three surviving members of the Agrarians reflected upon their product. They were in agreement that, if anything, they had underestimated the dehumanizing power of industrial society and its destructive capacity. Robert Penn Warren summarized his feelings with the following statement: "You can't discuss the economic man without the philosophical man, or the philosophical man without the artistic man. They all imply value-creating processes that man inevitably is stuck with. So as far as man is not all of these he is not human. He has merely the shape of man but he is not human, he's not a complete man."[8]

The Agrarians were men of letters and were largely ignored or scorned in national publications that reviewed their work. But social analysts of the 1950s echoed their complaints about industrial society with diagnostic phrases like "the organization man," "the other-directed man," "the authoritarian personality," "the lonely crowd," and "mass-man."[9] All are, to one degree or another, lamentations over the passing of what Warren was referring to as the complete man. The lament is still alive in some of the literary utterances of the modern South. Expressions of it are found in the writings of two southerners, Flannery O'Connor and Walker Percy.

8. Robert Penn Warren, "Discussion: The Agrarian-Industrial Metaphor: Culture, Economics, and Society in a Technological Age," in William C. Havard and Walter Sullivan (eds.), *A Band of Prophets: The Vanderbilt Agrarians After Fifty Years* (Baton Rouge, 1982), 187–88.

9. The mass society critics referred to include the following: Theodore Adorno *et al.*, *The Authoritarian Personality* (New York, 1950); Erich Fromm, *Escape from Freedom* (New York, 1941); Herbert Muller, *The Uses of the Past* (New York, 1952); David Riesman, *The Lonely Crowd* (Garden City, 1950); William H. Whyte, *The Organization Man* (Garden City, 1956).

In a letter to a friend, O'Connor captured the spirit of the Agrarian attack on the lack of moral sensibilities in modern individualistic society. She wrote: "It is easy to see that the moral sense has been bred out of certain sections of the population, like the wings have been bred off certain chickens to produce more white meat on them. This is a generation of wingless chickens, which I suppose is what Nietzsche meant when he said God was dead."[10] In similar fashion, Walker Percy's aptly titled novel, *The Last Gentleman*, relates the comment of an engineer to a playwright: "I have recently returned to the South from New York, where I felt quite dislocated as a consequence of a nervous condition. . . . Only to find upon my return that I was no less dislocated here."[11] The two heroes of *The Last Gentleman*, Will Barrett and Sutter Vaught, search for authenticity in a world of wingless chickens, southern and modern, where ambiguity reigns and the only possible human stance seems to be waiting, watching, and listening.

O'Connor and Percy are concerned primarily with the religious question of grace, from a Catholic perspective. Both are distressed with the contemporary devaluation of the divine presence and its transforming capabilities.[12] Both believe that devaluation has penetrated the life of modern "civilization," including its southern manifestation. In O'Connor's opinion, the loss of mysterious presence in modern life is so profound, new methods of communicating it must be found. Thus, her stories abound in grotesque and bizarre imagery, necessary, she believes, to awaken the "wingless chickens." Percy, influenced more by the existentialist tradition, creates heroes in various stages of the search for authenticity. They are castaways who often announce the bad news: "Something is wrong here; I don't feel good."

Percy, O'Connor, the mass-society theorists, and, of course, the Agrarians are expressing strong second thoughts about the triumph of progress and the economic confinement of the human soul. Modern culture has not measured the human being in a manner sufficiently high or deep to do justice to our capacity for good and evil. The fact that it is able to retain such a good opinion of itself is the final ironic condemnation of the culture's false optimism.

These are harsh pronouncements with which to conclude a book on

10. Flannery O'Connor, *The Habit of Being: Letters,* ed. Sally Fitzgerald (New York, 1979), 90.

11. Walker Percy, *The Last Gentleman* (New York, 1966), 320.

12. For an interesting discussion of the religious dimensions of O'Connor's and Percy's writings, see Peter S. Hawkins, *The Language of Grace* (Cambridge, Mass., 1983).

the New South. Surely much of the progress of the South in the last two decades is worth celebrating. It is clear that a return to the Old South is an impossibility. No one, not even the Agrarians, wishes to make that journey; as one of their number, Stark Young, put it, "even if that were possible; dead days are gone, and if by some chance they should return, we should find them intolerable."[13] Indeed, much of the traditionalistic cultural model is intolerable — its racism, its elitism, its glorification of an agrarian ideal that never existed. Equally clear, however, is the fact that the changes occurring in the New South, so-called progressive changes, are not so forward-looking when viewed from the traditionalistic point of view. From that perspective, the suburbs of Memphis and Nashville are no different from the suburbs of Buffalo or Cleveland. The city of Houston is well on the way to being the Detroit of the future. The Madison Avenue techniques of campaign managers are simply another means of manipulating human beings. The professionalism of state legislatures and gubernatorial offices has not yet managed to control the pollutants of modern industry. Nor have these legislatures and their local government counterparts managed to create or maintain educational systems of quality. Bureaucracies, local, state, and national, have never lived up to their Weberian promise. Political parties are still havens of irresponsible egoism and corruption, and behind the facade of professionalism at all levels of governance is the illusion that the fundamental issues of human existence are amenable to political solutions. The South's coming of age, then, is merely a sign of its entrance into the modern era, and that may not be cause for celebration.

What the Agrarian and modern critics tell us is that change too is a mystery; to again quote Stark Young, "In the shifting relation between ourselves and the new order lies the profoundest source for our living, I mean change in that almost mystical sense by which, so long as we are alive, we are not the same and yet remain ourselves."[14] If there is any progress or advance in southern culture and politics, it must be mindful of its own nature, the center, the romantic core of its traditionalistic self and of the need for continuity with that self.

13. "Not in Memoriam, But in Defense," in Twelve Southerners, *I'll Take My Stand*, 328.
14. *Ibid.*, 359.

The Contributors

E. LEE BERNICK, associate professor of political science and director of the Center for Social Research and Human Services at the University of North Carolina at Greensboro, is the author of articles on state legislatures and governors. His most recent research is on the impact of Jesse Jackson's presidential campaign on the Democratic party in the South.

CHARLES S. BULLOCK III is Richard Russell Professor of Political Science at the University of Georgia. He is past president of the Southern Political Science Association and has served as chair of the Legislative Studies Group of the American Political Science Association. Among his recent books are *Public Policy and Politics in America*, *Implementation of Civil Rights Policy*, and *Public Policy in the Eighties*.

MARY DELORSE COLEMAN, assistant professor of political science at Jackson State University, has written several articles on black politics, including "Reapportionment and the Race Factor," with Leslie Burl McLemore, in the *Western Journal of Black Studies*.

RICHARD L. ENGSTROM is research professor of political science at the University of New Orleans. He has written several articles on black politics, including "The Election of Blacks to City Councils: Clarifying the Impact of Electoral Arrangements on the Seats/Population Relationship," with Michael D. McDonald, in the *American Political Science Review*, and is at work on a study of the Supreme Court's response to the issue of racial vote dilution.

CECIL L. EUBANKS, associate professor of political science at Louisiana State University, is the author of *Karl Marx and Friedrich Engels: An Analytical Bibliography*, a second edition of which appeared in 1984. His other writings have appeared in *Southern Quarterly*, *Political Science Reviewer*, and the *American Journal of Political Science*.

PATRICIA K. FREEMAN is associate professor of political science at the University of Tennessee at Knoxville. She has published articles in *Legis-*

lative Studies Quarterly, the *Journal of Politics*, and the *Western Political Quarterly*. Recently she completed a study of interest-group activity in Tennessee.

EARL W. HAWKEY is administrative programming manager at the Seattle University site of SCT Corporation. Previously he served as assistant director of facilities management at the University of Missouri—Central Administration. Among his recent publications is "Southern Conservatism, 1956–1976," in Laurence W. Moreland, Robert B. Steed, and Todd A. Baker (eds.), *Contemporary Political Attitudes and Behavior*.

JAMES F. LEA is professor of political science at the University of Southern Mississippi. He is the author of *Kazantzakis: The Politics of Salvation* and *Political Consciousness and American Democracy*.

ALLY MACK is associate professor and chair of the Department of Political Science at Jackson State University. She recently published *Black Electoral Participation*, which she co-authored with Fred Banks and Mary DeLorse Coleman.

LESLIE BURL MCLEMORE is dean of the Graduate School, director of research administration, and founding chair of the Department of Political Science at Jackson State University. An authority on southern politics and the civil rights movement, he is the author of numerous articles, the most recent being "Strategic Choices," in Thomas E. Cavanaugh (ed.), *Race and Political Strategy: A JCPS Roundtable*, and, with Mary DeLorse Coleman, "Traditionalism in Biracial Politics in Mississippi's Second Congressional District," in Michael Preston, Lenneal J. Henderson, Jr., and Paul L. Puryear (eds.), *The New Black Politics: A Search for Political Power*.

RONALD G. MARQUARDT is professor of political science at the University of Southern Mississippi. A member of the bar of the state and federal courts in Mississippi, he has published several articles in political science, legal research, and law-related journals. He presently is serving as editor of the *Journal of Paralegal Education*.

DAVID M. OLSON, professor of political science at the University of North Carolina at Greensboro, is author of *The Legislative Process: A Comparative Approach* and co-author of *American State Political Parties and Elections.* He is currently coordinating a multinational study of parliaments and economic policy formation.

TIMOTHY G. O'ROURKE is associate professor in the Institute of Government at the University of Virginia. He is the author of *The Impact of Reapportionment* and co-author, with Richard H. Leach, of *State and Local Government: The Third Century of Federalism.* His articles on voting rights and federalism have appeared in the *Virginia Law Review*, the *Journal of Law and Politics*, the *Alabama Law Review*, and the *Southern Review of Public Administration.*

JOSEPH B. PARKER is professor of political science at the University of Southern Mississippi. He is author of *The Morrison Era: Reform Politics in New Orleans* and "Ronald Reagan's 'New Federalism,' " in *USA Today*, and co-editor of *Mississippi Government and Politics in Transition.*

LARRY SABATO, associate professor of government and foreign affairs at the University of Virginia, has written extensively on American political campaigns and elections and on gubernatorial politics. His recent books include *The Party's Just Begun: Shaping Political Parties for America's Future*; *PAC POWER: Inside the World of Political Action Committees*; *The Rise of Political Consultants: New Ways of Winning Elections*; and *Goodbye to Good-Time Charlie: The American Governorship Transformed.*

T. McN. SIMPSON III is associate professor of political science at the University of Tennessee in Knoxville. Jimmy Carter's governorship has been the focus of most of his writings, including "One Appraisal of the Carter Administration, 1971–74," in *Georgia Political Science Association Journal.* He is also the editor, with Dorothy F. Olshfski, of *The Volunteer State: Readings in Tennessee Politics.*

DAVID VALENTINE is a senior member of the research staff for the Missouri Senate. He has collaborated with John Van Wingen in writing several papers on partisan identification and on the role of realignment in the American political system, including "Partisanship, Independence, and the Partisan Identification Question" in *American Politics Quarterly.*

JOHN VAN WINGEN is a systems project analyst for the Florida Department of Education and has collaborated with David Valentine on several publications (see above).

EDWARD M. WHEAT is associate professor of political science at the University of Southern Mississippi. His primary area of research is administrative law, and recently he has written "Publication of the Orders of Federal Administrative Law Judges," published in *Law Library Journal.*

Index